BILINGUAL EDUCATION AND BILI
Series Editors: Nancy H. Hornbe

M000291504

Language and Identity in a Dual Immersion School

Kim Potowski

MULTILINGUAL MATTERS LTD
Clevedon • Buffalo • Toronto

Library of Congress Cataloging in Publication Data
Potowski, Kim
Language and Identity in a Dual Immersion School/Kim Potowski
Bilingual Education and Bilingualism: 63
Includes bibliographical references and index.
1. Language and languages–Study and teaching (Elementary. 2. Immersion method
(Language teaching). 3. Anthropological linguistics. I. Title.
P53.44.P68 2007
418.0071–dc22   2006031789

British Library Cataloguing in Publication Data
A catalogue entry for this book is available from the British Library.

ISBN-13: 978-1-85359-944-6 (hbk)
ISBN-13: 978-1-85359-943-9 (pbk)

Multilingual Matters Ltd
UK: Frankfurt Lodge, Clevedon Hall, Victoria Road, Clevedon BS21 7HH.
USA: UTP, 2250 Military Road, Tonawanda, NY 14150, USA.
Canada: UTP, 5201 Dufferin Street, North York, Ontario M3H 5T8, Canada.

The policy of Multilingual Matters/Channel View Publications is to use papers that
are natural, renewable and recyclable products, made from wood grown in
sustainable forests. In the manufacturing process of our books, and to further support
our policy, preference is given to printers that have FSC and PEFC Chain of Custody
accreditation. The FSC and/or PEFC logos will appear on those books where full
accreditation has been granted to the printer concerned.

Typeset by TechBooks Ltd.
Printed and bound in Great Britain by the Cromwell Press Ltd.

Contents

Acknowledgements viii

1 Introduction 1
  Purpose of the Book 4
  Organization 5
  Notes 6

2 Immersion Classroom Research and Methodology
  of this Study 7
  Language Immersion: Program Descriptions 7
  Research Findings 11
  Research on Two-Way Immersion in the United States 17
  Research Questions and Methodology of the
  Current Study 26
  The Role of the Researcher in Ethnographic Studies 30
  Notes 31

3 Inter-American Magnet School 33
  History 34
  IAMS Today 39
  Language Policy 42
  Curriculum 47
  Student Outcomes 49
  Parental Involvement 51
  Conclusions 52
  Notes 53

4 Fifth-Grade Language Use and Proficiency 54
  Ms. Torres' Classroom 54
  The Four Focal Students 56
  Source of Language Data 59
  Spanish Use: Quantity 60
  Spanish Use: Functions 67

Conclusions 86
Appendix 4.A Transcription Conventions 88
Appendix 4.B Variables 89
Appendix 4.C Functions and Topics of Students' English . . . 90
Functions 91
Notes 92

5 Identity Investments in Fifth Grade 93
   Classroom Expectations for Spanish Use 94
   The Four Students 100
   Conclusions 113
   Notes 115

6 Language Use in Eighth Grade 116
   Official Eighth-Grade Language Policy 116
   Language Use during Spanish Language Arts and
   Social Studies: General Observations 123
   Language Use during a Typical Social Studies
   Current Events Class 126
   Findings 129
   Conclusions 136
   Notes 137

7 Spanish Proficiency in Eighth Grade 138
   Measures 139
   Results 144
   Conclusions and Pedagogical Implications 161
   Appendix 7.A Oral Story Text, "La jardinera," with
   Verbs Identified for Inherent Lexical Aspect 165
   Appendix 7.B Multiple-Choice Instructions
   and Test Items 166
   Appendix 7.C Oral Narrative Texts of Six Students 168
   Appendix 7.D Written Story Narratives 170
   Notes 171

8 Identity Investments in Eighth Grade 173
   The Four Focal Students 174
   Other Students 196
   Conclusions 198
   Note 199

9   Conclusions 200
    School-Level Practices 202
    Classroom Activity Types 206
    The Important Role of Dual Immersion in Heritage Language
    Maintenance and Foreign Language Learning 210

    Epilogue 214

References 217

Acknowledgements

A multiyear project such as this would not have been possible without a great deal of support, encouragement, and caffeine. First and foremost, I am deeply indebted to the Inter-American Magnet School community. "Ms. Torres" and "Ms. Maas" in particular, as well as numerous other teachers, parents, administrators (notably Maria Cabrera), and students, gave generously of their time, experience, and knowledge. They were rightly very proud of the school they created, and I thank them for inviting me to learn about it.

Special thanks to "Carolina," "Melissa," "Matt," and "Otto," the four focal students, and their parents, for agreeing to be part of this study. I have very fond memories of our interactions, from your first days of fifth grade up through your eighth-grade graduation. It was a pleasure to work with such great kids.

Anna Maria Escobar and Shelley Roberts mentored me as I designed and carried out the first year of this study. Their complimentary approaches – Anna Maria as the consummate variationist, Shelley as the ethnographer extraordinaire – pushed me to develop muscle in both areas. Erica McClure, Georgia "Joey" Garcia, and Giuli Dussias also provided valuable feedback during the early stages of this project. Tara Fortune was an inspirational dissertation buddy.

Several colleagues read later versions of this research, including Carol Klee, Dee Tedick, Donna Christian, and Ofelia Garcia. The Series Editors at Multilingual Matters, Nancy Hornberger and Colin Baker, provided excellent suggestions for the final manuscript. Rebecca Freeman Field also gave a close, insightful reading. Tommi and Marjukka Grover kept everything on schedule. My heartfelt thanks to all of you.

People who assisted me with data entry and analysis include Renata Garcia, Janine Matts, Silvina Montrul, and the talented and patient statisticians Stacie Hudgens and Kevin Li. Un montón de gracias también a Alejandra Brito.

My move to Chicago would not have been possible without the offer of a teaching position by Lucía Elías-Olivares, who in 1999 was the Interim Head of the Department of Spanish, French, Italian & Portuguese at the University of Illinois at Chicago. A fellowship from the Diffenbaugh Foundation also supported data collection during 1999–2000.

Other Chicago institutions, especially Wicker Park's Filter Café and Bucktown's Café de Lucca, kept me going with coffee, a laptop connection, and a blissfully noisy, anonymous writing environment.

Finally, my husband, Cliff Meece, and my in-laws, Gayle and Tom Meece, have been unconditionally supportive of my work, for which I love and thank them. I hope that my sons, Nicolás and Samuel, will be lucky enough to attend a school as wonderful as the Inter-American that I came to know.

Chapter 1
Introduction

Language immersion is thought to be the most successful of several programs types that teach languages other than English at the elementary school level. Immersion delivers a substantial portion of the school curriculum in the second language (L2) rather than treating it as a separate subject. This approach is based on the premise that people learn a second language much as they learned their first: by being exposed to natural language use, and by being socially motivated, indeed required, to communicate. Learning the language is therefore a by-product of learning new content material, although a focus on linguistic form often does enter the curriculum in later years.

Canadian immersion programs were established in the 1960s under middle- and upper-middle-class parental pressure for more effective French language education. At that time, Quebec was experiencing ethnolinguistic tensions as Francophones began making demands for linguistic and cultural equality (Genesee, 1987: 8), and French immersion sought to promote "a more fair and a more interesting society . . . for all ethnolinguistic groups in the Canadian mosaic" (Lambert, 1984: 9). These were soon followed in the 1970s by similar programs in the United States. Research in both the United States and Canada over the last three decades has indicated that immersion results in the highest levels of L2 competence of all elementary foreign language programs, at little cost to children's first language (L1) development. Additionally, immersion students often develop more positive sociocultural attitudes toward native speakers of the L2 (Lambert, 1984: 15).

In the late 1960s and early 1970s, United States educators began developing a program type called *dual* or *two-way* immersion. These programs integrate into the same classrooms native-speaking language minority children (those who already speak the non-English language) along with English-speaking children learning the minority language. Instruction in the minority language can range from 50% to 90% of the school day. The presence of approximately equal numbers of native speakers of both languages in the classroom theoretically provides opportunities for students to communicate with native-speaker peers (Christian, 1996b), creating benefits

1

for both groups. Three of these advantages will be mentioned briefly. First, unlike typical U.S. "bilingual education" programs for language minority students – which in reality do not promote bilingualism, but rather seek to transition students to all-English classrooms as soon as possible – dual immersion encourages students' native language development, thus making an important contribution to heritage language maintenance in the country. Second, while many bilingual education programs utilize pull-out classes that separate students from their English-speaking peers, dual immersion allows language minority students to remain in classrooms with their native English-speaking peers, resulting in linguistic and sociocultural advantages (Christian, 1996b). Third, native English-speaking students who are learning the non-English language benefit from having native-speaking peers in the classroom instead of relying on the teacher as the sole source of input (Genesee, 1987: 131). As of May 2005, there were 317 dual immersion programs operating in elementary schools in the United States in 10 different languages, with 96% of them (298) operating in Spanish (Center for Applied Linguistics, 2005).

Research examining standardized test scores suggests that both one-way and two-way immersion results in above-average levels of academic proficiency (Cohen, 1975; Lambert, 1984; Lindholm-Leary, 2001; Swain & Lapkin, 1982). Notably, in a comparison of the different educational models available to language minority students in the United States, including pullout ESL and transitional native language support, dual immersion resulted in the highest levels of academic achievement (Thomas & Collier, 1997). Dual immersion also results in high levels of proficiency in both English and the non-English language for both groups of students (Christian *et al.*, 1997; Lindholm-Leary, 2001).

Despite the encouraging findings of standardized tests, we know very little about actual language use in one-way or in dual immersion classrooms. According to Genesee, there has been "little systematic documentation of how language is used in immersion classrooms by either students or teachers," leaving us with "an insufficient empirical basis on which to draw firm conclusions about the discourse characteristics of immersion classrooms and, therefore, about the impact of classroom interaction styles on language learning" (1991: 190). This remains the case in 2005, with less than half a dozen published studies documenting quantified observations of immersion classroom language use.[1] Tarone and Swain called this lack of classroom research striking, given the "ample evidence that social context can cause the speech of second-language learners to vary substantially in its grammatical and phonological structure" (1995: 176). On the basis of their observations, Tarone and Swain (1995) proposed that one-way immersion classrooms become diglossic over time, with students preferring to use English with one another and reserving the L2 almost exclusively for academic purposes. Recent research has supported this claim (Broner, 2000; Fortune, 2001).

We know even less about students' language use in dual immersion classrooms, which are arguably more complex than one-way immersion because of the presence of students who are native speakers of the non-English language. Studies of language use in dual immersion classrooms are necessary because combining students from different language backgrounds does not ensure that they will interact (Genesee, 1985: 554), nor that they will do so in Spanish when it is the "official" language of the instructional period. We need answers to some very basic questions about dual immersion language use, answers that may vary from school to school and even from classroom to classroom: How much Spanish do students use? With whom do they speak Spanish, under what circumstances, and for what purposes? Does the presence of L1 Spanish speakers in dual immersion classrooms increase the amount of overall Spanish use by students, from what has been found in one-way immersion classrooms? Given that most theories of second language acquisition (SLA) recognize the need to actually produce the language, and since it is reasonable to assume a similar requirement for heritage language development and maintenance, it is crucial to examine students' Spanish output in dual immersion classrooms.

Research in any type of immersion classroom becomes more complex when we acknowledge that classroom opportunities to use Spanish can be given by teachers and by peers, can be created by the students themselves, and can also be resisted by students. Whereas traditional SLA research has utilized the concept of motivation to explain learners' desires to practice their L2, recent qualitative work in the field of English as a Second Language has shown that people's identity investments play an important role in their language use (McKay & Wong, 1995; Norton, 2000; Willett, 1995). Researchers argue that it is necessary to examine learners' reasons for creating and resisting opportunities to use a particular language, since "a learner's motivation to speak is mediated by other investments that may conflict with the desire to speak – investments that are intimately connected to the ongoing production of the learners' identities and their desires for the future" (Norton, 2000: 120). McKay and Wong (1996) claim that in order to understand success and failure in language learning, one must move beyond a "language-as-code" approach and instead view the L2 learner as a complex social being. Norton (2000) argues that SLA theory needs to develop a conception of language learners as having complex social identities[2] that must be understood with reference to larger and often in-equitable social structures, which are reflected in day-to-day interactions.

Although there have been several in-depth ethnographic studies of dual immersion schools that illustrate the complex sociocultural nature of these environments (Carranza, 1995; Freeman, 1998; McCollum, 1994), to date, investment has not been employed in regular or dual immersion research. The present study combines a quantification of dual immersion students' classroom language production with a qualitative investigation of the identity investments that may have promoted or hindered their Spanish use.

Purpose of the Book

The purpose of this book is to describe and explain the patterns of Spanish and English use by four dual immersion students (two Spanish L1 and two Spanish L2) in fifth grade and again in eighth grade. It also seeks to describe their Spanish proficiency in eighth grade, their final year at the school, along with the Spanish proficiency of the rest of their classmates. Unlike previous dual immersion research, this study used systematic observations, audio and video recordings of naturally occurring classroom speech, and a combination of standardized and specially designed language proficiency measures.

In addition, this study utilized qualitative research methods, including interviews and long-term participant observation, to explore the relationship between students' identity investments and their classroom language use. It was found that students who had strong investments in using Spanish, because it enriched their sense of self or their status within their families and communities, used Spanish more often. It was also found that one student with problematic participation habits was not granted the floor as often during Spanish lessons, which limited his opportunities to practice the language. As noted by Gal (1979) in research on sociolinguistic communities, macrosocial factors can influence the language choices of speakers through their effects on the shape of social networks and on the statuses speakers want to claim (1979: 17). My study therefore takes a sociolinguistic perspective on language use in this dual immersion classroom, using qualitative research methods to explore relevant factors that were both internal and external to the classroom. Qualitative data were also useful when attempting to explain the apparent gender-based differences in language use.

As noted by Elías-Olivares *et al.* in research on sociolinguistic communities, only after we understand the linguistic habits of the speakers of

Spanish can we begin to formulate a program of language planning that can be implemented (1985: 4), and dual immersion is arguably a form of linguistic planning (Freeman, 1998). This study suggests that although dual immersion can be a successful model for linguistic and cultural education for both language minority and language majority students, both L1 and L2 students may not be using as much Spanish as educators believe. Nor are they using Spanish for a wide variety of communicative purposes. It suggests that the prevalence of English in the wider society affects students' language use within the classroom, even when Spanish use is fostered by teachers and the curriculum. It also calls for an examination of the role of peer groupwork, which is believed by some educators to foster collabora- tive knowledge construction, but which resulted in high levels of English use in this classroom.

Having summarized what this book will attempt to achieve, it may be useful to briefly mention what it does not. Given that it is a case study of one school, it does not address the overall effectiveness of dual immersion schools across the country. Lindholm-Leary (2000) is a better resource for a national picture of dual immersion. Nor does it analyze the curriculum or lesson types or their effectiveness. In this sense, it is principally not a pedagogically oriented book. To give another example, this book points out specific areas in Spanish in which the students had difficulties and suggests that teachers implement lessons with a greater focus on language form, yet no specific lesson plans are offered. Readers interested in best practices in dual immersion might consult Soltero (2004), which devotes lengthy attention to common instructional approaches in dual immersion programs, as well as Tedick and Fortune (2005). A very noticeable trait of Inter-American School is its commitment to social justice, another topic that I describe briefly but that was not the object of in-depth study. Finally, educators seeking advice about how to structure a dual immersion pro- gram will probably find Soltero's (2004) treatment of program models and other administrative concerns more useful.

Organization

Chapter 2 reviews relevant research in one-way and two-way immersion contexts. It also explains the methodology of the study. In Chapter 3, I de- scribe the setting, Inter-American Magnet School, one of the oldest dual immersion schools in the United States. In Chapter 4, I present the quan- titative findings of the four focal students' classroom language use in fifth grade. Chapter 5 describes the fifth grade students' investments in speak- ing Spanish, in an attempt to explain the language use patterns reported in Chapter 4. In Chapter 6, I present findings on classroom language use in eighth grade, while Chapter 7 describes the Spanish proficiency of the entire graduating class. Chapter 8 revisits the question of students' identity investments in learning and speaking Spanish, this time during their eighth-grade year. Chapter 9 offers conclusions about the role of this dual immersion school in heritage language maintenance and foreign language learning, as well as suggestions for future research studies.

Notes

1. Some studies of language use in one-way immersion contexts have used very small corpora or have lacked systematic quantification, which do not provide sufficient detail about their classroom language production.
2. Defined by Norton as "how a person understands his or her relationship to the world, how that relationship is constructed across time and space, and how the person understands possibilities for the future" (2000: 5).

Chapter 2
Immersion Classroom Research and Methodology of this Study

Dual immersion education seeks to accomplish multiple goals. For language minority students, dual immersion promotes the learning of English as a Second Language (ESL) in addition to maintaining the students' first language. For monolingual English speakers, dual immersion seeks to provide a rich foreign language acquisition environment. In this way, dual immersion programs are a combination of what Hornberger (1991) calls *maintenance* and *enrichment* bilingual education. Dual immersion also promotes high levels of academic achievement for all students. In addition, many programs have strong social justice themes and "alternative" curricula. Given that both one-way and two-way immersions are complex learning environments, research has approached them from many different angles. This chapter will present a brief history of language immersion and describe salient research on both one-way and two-way immersion classrooms. Then, it will describe the particular research methodology that I used during the two years of my study at Inter-American Magnet School.

Language Immersion: Program Descriptions

One-way immersion

In typical one-way immersion programs, all children are native speakers of the country's dominant language, and they are taught the regular school curriculum totally or partially in a foreign language. Canadian one-way immersion programs were established in the 1960s under middle-class and upper-middle-class parental pressure for more effective French language education for their children. At that time, Quebec was experiencing ethnolinguistic tensions as Francophones began making demands for linguistic and cultural equality (Genesee, 1987: 8). In 1965, parents of an Anglophone Montreal suburb convinced the school district to set up an experimental kindergarten French immersion class. An important goal of the program was functional competence in French through its use as a natural means of communication and instruction, but the primary goal was improved relationships between English and French Quebecois (Genesee, 1987: 11). The parents cited their own low French proficiency as evidence of the failure of foreign language teaching in Canada, which typically consisted of an hour of instruction per day.

The goals of French immersion today are the same as when such programs were first developed. Teachers seek to develop students' "functional competence in the L2" in addition to normal levels of L1 competence, grade-level academic achievement, and appreciation for the target language group's language and culture (Genesee, 1983: 3). Immersion was designed to create the same kind of communicatively-rich conditions that characterize first language acquisition, particularly creating desire in the students to learn the L2 in order to engage in meaningful communication. Language learning is content based, which means that French is learned *through* math, science, and social studies. That is, Anglophone children are taught the regular school curriculum in French by teachers that present themselves as monolingual. The teacher is usually the only native speaker model with whom the students interact.

Since students' comprehension of the L2 generally precedes their production of it, they are permitted to use English, which all teachers understand, during the early stages of the program. According to Genesee (1983: 7), it is common in kindergarten and the early part of first grade to hear students using English while the teacher uses French. However, as children progress through the grades, they are encouraged to use more French with teachers and peers. Initial literacy instruction is in French, and English literacy skills are typically introduced in second grade. Subjects taught in English are added in later grades, so that by sixth grade about half the curriculum is in English and half in French (Swain & Johnson, 1997: 2).[1]

Soon after the introduction of the first immersion programs in Canada, United States educators began to show interest in immersion programs. After visiting the St. Lambert program in 1971, Campbell (1984: 116) helped establish the first early total Spanish immersion program in the United States for English L1 speakers in Culver City, California. It was similar to Canadian models in that all curriculum in kindergarten and first grade was delivered in Spanish, and teachers presented themselves as monolingual in Spanish until English was introduced for the first time in second grade. At that time, teachers also taught in English, but did not mix languages in an instructional period. According to Genesee (1987: 116) the goals of immersion programs for majority language children in the United States were to produce linguistic and cultural enrichment contexts within the school system, to create magnet schools[2] with a balanced ratio of ethnolinguistic groups of the area, and for English L1 children living in communities with non-English-speaking populations to become bilingual.

According to the last update of the Center of Applied Linguistics, in 2003 there were 151 schools in the United States that offered total or partial one-way immersion (Center for Applied Linguistics, 2003). Several languages were offered, including French, Hawaiian (Slaughter (1997) describes one of many immersion programs in Hawaii seeking to maintain local indigenous languages), Japanese, German, Arabic, Cantonese, Inupiaq, Russian, and Yup'ik. According to Met and Lorenz (1997: 243), approximately 60% of U.S. immersion programs are *partial* and 40% are *total* immersion, and all are of the *early* type.

Two-way (dual) immersion

Dual immersion classrooms contain a mixture of English-speaking and native-speaking children of the non-English language. In other words, at all times, part the class is immersed in its L2 and the other half receives instruction in its L1, giving rise to the program descriptor term "two-way" or "dual" immersion. The presence of native speakers of both languages theoretically provides opportunities for all students to communicate with native-speaker peers (Christian, 1996b).

Christian (1996b: 74) cites the Coral Way Elementary School in Dade County, Florida, as the first two-way bilingual school in the United States. The program was established in 1963 by members of the Cuban community fleeing the Castro regime, who believed their children would soon be returning to Cuban schools. During the 1960s, another 14 such schools were set up in Dade County. The James F. Oyster Bilingual Elementary School in Washington DC is another famous dual immersion program, established in 1971 through an initiative by local parents and politicians to produce a school that crossed language, cultural, ethnic, and social class lines (Freeman, 1998). In 1975, San Diego and Chicago saw the creation of dual immersion programs, Chicago's school being the Inter-American Magnet School, the focus of this book.

United States dual immersion programs grew at an astounding rate in the late 1980s and early 1990s. In 1987, only 30 dual immersion programs had been identified in the United States (Lindholm 1987). But just eight years later, Christian and Whitcher (1995) reported 182 dual immersion programs operating in 19 states, with 92% of them teaching in Spanish. This represents a stunning 507% increase in the number of dual immersion programs in the country since 1987. And as of May 2005, the Center of Applied Linguistics documented a total of 315 dual immersion programs[3]

Table 2.1 Growth of dual immersion programs in the United States

Year	Number of programs	Percent increase
1987	30	n/a
1995	182	507%
2005	315	18%

operating in elementary schools in 28 different states in 10 different languages, with 95% of these (298 schools) teaching in Spanish. This represents slightly greater than a 10-fold increase in dual immersion programs in the 18 years since 1987. These data are represented in Table 2.1.

Other languages taught in United States dual immersion programs include Korean, Cantonese, Navajo, French, Arabic, Hawaiian, Japanese, Russian, and Portuguese. Instruction in the non-English language can range from 50% to 90% of the school day, giving rise to the common program descriptor terms "50–50" and "90–10". Christian (1996b: 80) reported that three fourths of all dual immersion programs followed either the 50–50 or the 90–10 model, and that most 90–10 models were found in the western United States (especially California) and the 50–50 programs were found in the eastern, Midwestern, and southern parts of the country. In March 2000, U.S. Secretary of Education Richard Riley lauded the achievements of dual immersion programs, calling them "the great wave of the future" and challenging the nation to increase the number of dual immersion schools to at least 1000 over the next five years (United States Department of Education, 2000).

The theoretical rationale behind dual immersion programs combines those of bilingual education programs and one-way foreign language immersion programs. Spanish and English native speakers study together in both languages, so there is considerable L2 input for each group (Krashen, 1981) as well as opportunities to negotiate meaning in order to make input comprehensible (Long, 1981) and to produce L2 output (Swain, 1985). The presence of native speakers of each language is said to constitute an improvement over traditional bilingual programs and over one-way immersion programs. They are thought to be superior to regular bilingual education programs both because L1 development is encouraged and because English learners are not isolated from native English-speaking peers. Their advantage over one-way immersion is that the students have native Spanish-speaking peers, whereas in one-way immersion their only native-speaker model is the teacher (Genesee, 1987: 131). Dual immersion is a form of maintenance bilingual education for language minority students, because it encourages Spanish maintenance even after English proficiency has been developed. It is also the only bilingual education model that targets native English speakers. This challenges the dominant pattern of language education in the country that focuses on rapid transition to English and ignores the Spanish development of native and nonnative speakers.

According to Christian (1996b: 67–68), the three goals for dual immersion students are as follows: (1) to develop high levels of proficiency in the L1 and in the L2; (2) to achieve academic performance at or above grade level; and (3) to demonstrate positive cross-cultural attitudes and behaviors and high levels of self-esteem. The methods through which these goals are realized depend largely on local conditions, demographics, and community attitudes. Each program makes a selection from a variety of characteristics. For example, a program may allocate the two languages by content, such as teaching social studies and math in Spanish, and science, arts, and music in English. The two languages may be allocated by person, with each teacher using only one language. There are also dual immersion programs that separate languages by day, such as Monday is English and Tuesday is Spanish, and students are exposed to all content lessons in both languages.

Research Findings

Much research has been conducted in both one-way and two-way immersion contexts. In the sections that follow, I will first describe briefly several research projects that have been carried out in one-way immersion programs around the world. Then I will turn my focus to dual immersion programs, briefly describing research on such programs around the world and then focusing on the United States, including the academic achievement, linguistic development, and classroom language use of dual immersion students.

One-way immersion

Academic proficiency has generally received the bulk of research attention, most likely because program evaluators have been primarily concerned with demonstrating to concerned parents and educators that immersion students are neither disadvantaged in general academic achievement nor in their L1 development (Swain & Johnson, 1997: 3). Canadian one-way immersion studies have indicated that children suffer no loss in academic achievement compared with control group peers in traditional all-English programs (Genesee, 1987; Lambert & Tucker, 1972).

As for their English language development, only during the primary grades of early total immersion (prior to the introduction of English language arts instruction) did immersion students score significantly lower than Anglophone control group students (Genesee, 1983; Swain & Lapkin, 1982). However, this lag was recuperated within a year of having begun English language instruction.[4]

Regarding target language proficiency, Genesee (1987) reported that early immersion students scored significantly higher on all measures of French language proficiency (speaking, listening, writing, reading, and linguistic competence) than their peers in mainstream schools who received French as a Second Language instruction. Since the control group received only 20 to 30 minutes of French instruction per day, this may not come as a surprise. More impressive, yet more complex, were the comparisons to native French-speaking children attending French schools in Quebec. Immersion students scored as well as native French-speaking peers on listening and reading comprehension measures (Genesee, 1978; Harley & Swain, 1977; Lambert & Tucker, 1972). However, their French production was found to be less nativelike. Specifically, immersion students tended to produce simple French constructions and lexical simplifications and evidenced reduced verb systems (Adiv, 1980; Harley & Swain, 1977, 1984; Lapkin, 1984). Swain (1981) argued that this difference between native speaker and immersion students' spoken French was due to the relatively low exposure to French and little opportunity to produce French in immersion classrooms. Other studies have been done on immersion students' language (Lapkin, 1984), specific linguistic structures (Adiv, 1980; Harley & Swain, 1984; Wright, 1996), and sociolinguistic proficiency (Swain & Lapkin, 1990), which will be reviewed in greater detail in Chapter 7.

Met and Lorenz (1997: 263) wrote that, unlike in Canada, few U.S. one-way immersion programs formally assess students' foreign language learning. This is because many teachers feel their primary responsibility is for students to demonstrate achievement in the local school district curriculum at a level comparable to their nonimmersion peers. These programs often rely on informal teacher judgment of student progress in the L2. Some U.S. immersion programs, however, have begun to examine students' oral Spanish language proficiency more formally.[5] Studies of Spanish reading comprehension and writing, for example, have found that native Spanish-speaking controls performed significantly better than nonnative immersion students, especially in the earlier grades (Barfield & Rhodes, 1993; Campbell, 1984; Cazabon et al., 1998), a finding similar to those in Canadian French immersion settings. According to Campbell, even after seven years, immersion students "do not sound like native speakers of Spanish . . . they make grammatical and pronunciation errors, and they misuse or are ignorant of vocabulary that would be common knowledge to native speakers of their own age groups" (1984: 131), although he emphasized that the grammaticality of most students' output far exceeded its ungrammaticality. In general, similar to their French-learning counterparts in Canada, the Spanish of one-way immersion students in the United States has been found to be nonnative-like in several aspects, especially number and gender agreement, the expression of present and past tense, object pronoun omission, the subjunctive, and definite articles (Boyd, 1975; Cohen, 1975, 1976; Plann, 1979). Despite these shortcomings, immersion produces higher levels of L2 proficiency than any other elementary school foreign language program type (Genesee, 1991: 186).

Studies abound of one-way immersion programs outside North America. In Europe, researchers have studied cultural practices in schools in Hungary (Duff, 1995, 1997), Ireland (Ó Riagáin, 1988), Finland (Björklund, 1997), and Spain, including Catalonia (Artigal, 1997) and the Basque Country (Arzamendi & Genesee, 1997). In Australia, one-way immersion students' language learning processes, involving both French and Chinese as second languages, have been documented (de Courcy, 2002). In Asia, specifically Singapore (Lim Swee English *et al.*, 1997) and Hong Kong (Johnson, 1997), students immersed in English have not been found to achieve the levels expected by authorities. In South Africa, Nuttall and Langhan (1997) describe the problems associated with using English as a medium of instruction, including the importance of native-language literacy as a foundation. South America has seen a good deal of research on immersion education, involving international languages such as Spanish and English as well as involving indigenous languages such as Quechua and Guaraní (Mejía, 2005). In particular, Spezzini's (2005) analysis of Paraguayan students' English proficiency and motivations for learning resembles the goals set forth in the current study.

In spite of this impressive recent collection of published research reports in one-way immersion contexts, Genesee (1991) claimed that there was little systematic documentation of how students and teachers actually use language in immersion classrooms, leaving us with "an insufficient empirical basis on which to draw firm conclusions about the discourse characteristics of immersion classrooms and, therefore, about the impact of classroom interaction styles on language learning" (1991: 190). This remains the case in 2005, with less than half a dozen published studies documenting immersion classroom language use. Such studies are particularly necessary in dual immersion contexts, given that combining students from different language backgrounds does not insure that they will interact (Genesee,

1985: 554), or that they will do so in the target language when it is the "official" language of the instructional period. Tarone and Swain found the lack of in-depth observation of language use and interaction in immersion classrooms striking, given the "ample evidence that social context can cause the speech of second-language learners to vary substantially in its grammatical and phonological structure" (1995: 176). I will now briefly review studies in one-way immersion classrooms that use natural language use as their data source. A later section will review classroom language use studies in dual immersion programs.

Cohen and Lebach's (1974) early study of the Culver City Spanish immersion program in California reported that second graders used English about half of the time in the classroom. In a study in third- and sixth-grade French immersion classes, Swain and Carroll (1987) found that during the French portion of the day, student turns were less than two thirds as frequent as during the English portion of the day. The most frequent source of student talk was during teacher-initiated turns, where the students' responses were "linguistically controlled," but extended talk of a clause or longer was more likely to occur when students initiated interactions. Overall, less than 15% of student turns in French were more than a clause in length. The authors suggested that greater opportunities for sustained talk could be accomplished through more groupwork, more opportunities for student-initiated talk, and the use of more open-ended questions by teachers. However, they found that during groupwork, students tended to revert to their shared L1. They concluded that simply providing opportunities to speak French was not sufficient: "Students need to be motivated to use language accurately, appropriately, and coherently" (Swain & Carroll, 1987: 77).[6]

Parker *et al.* (1995) found a clear preference among students for Spanish during teacher-fronted activities and for English during groupwork. In groups, students only used Spanish to perform a limited number of task-related purposes: reading text, rereading or reinstating information drawn from target-language materials, and producing answer-oriented output (Parker *et al.*, 1995: 245). They used English, however, for a wider range of speech acts, including performing calculations, managing group interaction, explaining things to each other, and expressing difficulties with a task. In addition to using more English in class, students used English during lunch, recess, and with their friends in general. In another study Blanco-Iglesias *et al.* (1995) found that from kindergarten through third grade, immersion students used Spanish almost exclusively when talking with the teacher, but patterns of language use changed in fourth and fifth grades. In these grades students began using more English when addressing the teacher and one another, especially during groupwork. When they did use Spanish with one another, it was only for academic topics, never to socialize with one another. The authors suggested that the children's increased use of English was due to the emerging development of a preadolescent speech style, which allowed peers to mark themselves as in-group members. Much of the English used by the students included vernacular slang like "You messed up," "You jerk!" and "That's cool."

In their review of such research on language use in immersion classrooms, Tarone and Swain (1995) sought to answer a question that had not yet been posed: *Why* do one-way immersion students increasingly avoid using their L2 in peer interactions as they move into higher grade levels? They proposed that if one takes a sociolinguistic perspective on immersion classrooms, viewing them as speech communities, they can be considered to obey the constraints already established by sociolinguists for other speech communities. Specifically, a variety of speech styles and registers are available to most speakers and are used for different purposes, appropriate to different social contexts and role relationships. The authors argued that in immersion classrooms, children learn the second language for purely academic purposes. Since they do not receive input in nonacademic language styles that serve children's essential discourse needs for play, competition, positioning in the peer group, arguing, and insulting, they use the L1 instead. These discourse needs, according to Tarone and Swain, are essential to children's interactions with one another, because through these functions, speakers locate themselves in a complex social hierarchy by forming alliances and asserting superiority (1995: 169).

These functions take place in students' L1, the vernacular of the classroom, because "the need to perform the social functions is far greater to the children's *social identity* than the need to stay in the L2 . . . when they have and share the L1 style they need" (1995: 169, emphasis added). According to the authors, since preadolescents and adolescents signal their identities and identification with one another through dress, hairstyles, music preferences, and vernacular language, the increased use of the L1 beginning in fifth- and sixth-grade immersion classrooms becomes more understandable. Indeed, use of a superordinate speech style (in this case, the non-English language) in peer interactions may mark the speaker as a nonmember or "lame" (Tarone & Swain, 1995: 169, based on Labov, 1972).

Tarone and Swain (1995) concluded that immersion classrooms can be seen as becoming increasingly diglossic over time. *Diglossia,* a term usually associated with Ferguson (1972), refers to a situation in which one language is used for formal functions and another language for informal functions. In this case, the authors proposed, the immersion language (Spanish, French, etc.) serves academic/official functions and the native language (English) serves social functions. They also suggest that educators may need to accept this fact rather than struggle to get students to use the L2 more often and in informal contexts.

Broner (2000) and Fortune (2001) sought to address these proposals put forth by Tarone and Swain (1995). They each examined language use among children in fifth grade one-way immersion classrooms in the Minneapolis–St. Paul area of Minnesota. Broner (2000) found that 63% Spanish use and 35% English use overall,[7] and that when the interlocutor included an adult, the children used Spanish between 95% and 100% of the time, which conformed to the "expected public linguistic behavior" of the classroom. However, when the interlocutor was a peer, Spanish use dropped to 58%. When on task, all three students used Spanish 75% or more, but when off-task, their Spanish use dropped to 34%. The author contended that the hypothesis put forth by Tarone and Swain (1995) that upper-grade immersion classrooms are diglossic was supported by two of the three students.

Similarly, Fortune (2000) examined a one-way immersion school[8] in St. Paul, Minnesota. The author found that students used Spanish during Spanish lessons 33% of the time. In addition, while the Spanish L1 students did not use more Spanish than their L2 peers, they did trigger greater Spanish use from their peers, which is an important area for future study. Regarding the relationship between students' language choice and whether they were working or socializing, Fortune found that students' Spanish turns were for academic purposes 42% of the time and for social purposes 58% of the time, which does not appear to support the diglossia hypothesis put forth by Tarone and Swain (1995).

Two-way immersion

This section will focus on research conducted in United States dual immersion contexts, but there are several dual immersion programs in other parts of the world that have published research on various themes. For example, Bekerman (2005) describes the contextual challenges facing a Hebrew-Arabic program in Israel. He found greater use of and proficiency in Hebrew among students, which reflects the higher status of Hebrew and its speakers – the 80% Jewish majority in the nation-state of Israel. Although Jewish and Palestinian parents alike sought cross-cultural understanding and bilingual proficiency for their children, and school personnel were attempting to "tilt the balance in favor of Arabic" (9) during the third year of school operations, the author concludes that the "attempt to sustain full symmetry in the use of both the Arabic and Hebrew languages failed" (15) and was further complicated by the introduction of English language lessons. However, the details offered about language use practices in the school, although relatively scarce, might help explain these results. We learn that teachers sought "to prevent language segregation or compartmentalization into specific disciplines or time slots" and that "all aspects of the curriculum were taught in both languages, with two teachers present at all times" (8). If no classroom time or lessons were consistently protected as Arabic-only domains, and if students were always spoken to in the language they understood best, then it stands to reason that the Hebrew children were not pushed to develop their Arabic proficiency. They could simply tune out Arabic and attend to the repetition in Hebrew.

Another Israeli dual immersion context, the "Oasis of dreams" or Neve Shalom/Wahat Al-Salam elementary school, is the subject of an analysis by Feuerverger (2001). The goal of the school is to "create national identities informed by moral vision and social ethics in order to . . . become active and critical citizens in a diverse, pluralistic Israeli society" (Feuerverger, 2001: 54). The author documents how children learning their second language (Hebrew or Arabic) interacted more with classmates who spoke the language natively, which profoundly altered their attitudes towards the other group. Although this study does not report on students' classroom language use or their L1/L2 proficiency, it is a rich ethnographic portrait of the social benefits of dual immersion in, notably, an ethnically troubled region.

Research on Two-Way Immersion in the United States

Academic achievement

In dual immersion contexts, several studies indicate that students' academic achievement reaches levels higher than local norms. Thomas and Collier (1997) found that dual immersion resulted in the highest academic achievement for language minority children over all other bilingual program types. On writing measures, Lindholm and Aclan (1991) found that two groups of first through fourth graders in two dual immersion programs, half Spanish-speaking and half English-speaking, exhibited the following trends: (1) by third grade, both groups were scoring average to very high in Spanish reading and math achievement (interestingly, the English L1 students outperformed the Spanish L1 students when tested in both Spanish and English); (2) by fourth grade, native English speakers showed average performance on English math tests, although they had not yet had math instruction in English; (3) the English reading performance of native English speakers approached average by second and third grades, while native Spanish speakers approached average by fourth grade. Lindholm-Leary (2001) presents an extensive evaluation of academic achievement data from over 6000 students in 21 dual immersion schools across the United States.

In spite of these successes, Valdés (1997) offered a cautionary note against dual immersion programs in the United States. She was particulary concerned with the education of language minority students, who have traditionally experienced high dropout rates, grade retention, and low test scores. She rightfully reminds us that "simply introducing native-language programs will not automatically solve all [their] educational problems," which are rooted in societal, institutional, interpersonal, and interpsychic realities. She suggested that societal-level power imbalances filter into these schools in several ways. On a linguistic level, she suspected that teachers may modify their Spanish somewhat (i.e. water it down) in order that the nonnative children can understand it, and wondered if such conditions would limit Hispanophone children's acquisition of nativelike Spanish competence. She conceded that there may not be such modifications, and if there were, they may be so slight as to have no effect on L1 Spanish development.

Valdés (1997) also called attention to the fact that research reports on dual immersion often concentrate on how well mainstream children speak Spanish, while ignoring the English acquisition of Spanish-speaking children, reflecting mainstream assumptions that Hispanophone children are expected to learn English. She warned that the main beneficiaries of the language resources offered in dual immersion may in fact be the members of the English-speaking majority, who after learning Spanish in dual immersion would be equipped to take bilingual jobs traditionally held by bilingual language minorities. But according to Valdés (1997) this concern is probably unjustified, because in spite of the disturbing finding that English L1 children scored higher on standardized tests of Spanish math and reading than did native Spanish speakers (Lindholm & Aclan, 1991), other research (Edelsky & Hudelson, 1982) suggests that Anglophone children in dual immersion contexts do not really acquire lasting competence in Spanish and therefore do not threaten the economic advantages of bilingualism traditionally held by Spanish L1 speakers.

In conclusion, Valdés (1997) wrote that conversations about dual immersion programs must not ignore the deep racial and linguistic divisions in the communities surrounding the schools, particularly since "we know little about what impact mainstream children's original attitudes have on minority children with whom they interact" and "we are experimenting in potentially dangerous ways with children's lives" (1997: 417). Far from arguing for the discontinuation of dual immersion, she suggested that these programs deserve further cautious study.

Several points should be considered when analyzing Valdés' (1997) arguments. Dual immersion is likely no more harmful to language minority children than traditional transitional bilingual programs, particularly since they have been shown to result in higher test scores than any other option available to limited English proficient (LEP) students (Thomas & Collier, 1997). Additionally, the dual immersion school studied by Edelsky and Hudelson (1982) that Valdes cites was not representative of all dual immersion contexts. The authors stated explicitly that the school's goals "did not include explicit attention to mutual second-language learning on the part of both Anglos and Chicanos" (1982: 203) and there were "no expectations that the marked language [Spanish] would be used by unmarked [monolingual English] language speakers" (1982: 225). The children in that study, three Anglo first graders, had a maximum of two years' exposure to Spanish during preschool and kindergarten. It is unfair to assume that their Spanish production during their first-grade year was indicative of what they could learn in subsequent years, or what they would learn in a program that expected and supported their Spanish language development. In fact, Snow *et al.* (1987) found that K-6 Spanish immersion program graduates who were not studying Spanish in high school scored 58% on speaking and 65% on listening measures, indicating some degree of lasting competence in Spanish. Finally, Valdés criticisms of dual immersion ignored the ways in which it can contribute to Hispanic students' Spanish maintenance. This was one of the focuses of my research.

Classroom language use

Aside from the findings of Potowski (2004), which will be presented in Chapter 4, no classroom-based research in a dual immersion setting has quantified how much each language was used during instructional time. Christian *et al.* (1997) offered general observations about dual immersion students' classroom language use. Before discussing them, I would like to briefly describe findings of other important aspects of dual immersion classrooms that, although not rigorous quantifications of language use, are important for understanding the complexities of students' language use in dual immersion contexts. For example, Delgado-Larocco (1998) identified how two specific classroom instructional practices affected students' level of language production and ultimate academic achievement.

First, she found that the Initiation-Response-Evaluation (IRE) sequence[9] dominated lessons. Since students' performance demonstrates what they have learned, the author suggested that instructional practices that better enhance student participation in classroom discourse may have a positive effect on their academic performance. Second, although there were no differences between Spanish- and English-speaking students' participation during lessons, the native English-speaking students dominated the initiations during playtime. The author noted that this early use of English as the language of peer social communication may set a pattern that is automatized by the time native English speakers reach higher levels of Spanish proficiency, and may be too strong to overcome in the higher grades. She concluded that the increase in the status of Spanish in dual immersion classrooms "by itself may not override the effects of interacting sociopolitical factors and the existing power relationships outside the classroom" (Delgado-Larocco, 1998: 50).

McCollum (1994) conducted a three-year ethnographic study of a dual immersion school in the Southwest United States in order to identify factors that influenced students' language use. She found that the 21 Hispanic focal students "almost exclusively use[d] English for academic purposes at school" (1994: 10). She attributed this "refusal" to speak Spanish to the fact that the Spanish language arts teacher corrected students' Spanish varieties, which included nonprestige forms and vocabulary such as "truje" for "traje" and "asina" for "asi." The teacher also focused on formal analysis of Spanish rather than its use for communication. According to the author, such practices were questioned by the students through "students' body language and asides to each other," which "showed they did not understand why their variety of Spanish was not good enough for the classrooms" and that they "switched to English in order to avoid being corrected" (1994: 10). Additionally, McCollum identified two practices in the school that marked it as an English domain: the standardized national achievement test in English received much more attention and preparation than did the Spanish standardized test, and daily announcements included a new English vocabulary word but never a Spanish word. Such factors led students to choose to use "mainstream linguistic capital [English] to match the school's hidden curriculum that stipulated [that] learning in English took precedence over all else" (McCollum 1994: 11).

Carranza (1995) analyzed interactions between dual immersion teachers and students in three different schools in an attempt to "specify the various levels of social interaction at which language use should be interpreted, and . . . describe the forces at play in the students' language choices"

(1995: 170). She found that utterances produced aloud for the whole class to hear during classroom tasks were "most often" made in Spanish, while talk that either managed the performance of a task or was off-task tended to be in English. Students with high Spanish proficiency used Spanish even during unsupervised talk, while students with low Spanish proficiency used English even when talking to teachers. In addition to the speaker's own Spanish proficiency, the interlocutor's Spanish proficiency (actual or perceived) proved to be relevant: students used English with an Anglo-looking visitor, suggesting that this was due to "a feeling of 'pretense' when two people communicate in one language, knowing that both can be more effective in another" (1995: 174). She noted that "in general," students used Spanish with adult native Spanish speakers in the schools.

However, when language proficiency could not account for a student's language choice with another student, the peer relationship between them determined the choice of English, even when the children were both native Spanish speakers. This finding that English was preferred by even Spanish L1 students, despite efforts to promote both languages equally, echoes the findings of McCollum (1994). Carranza (1995) also found that the more strictly the "Spanish time" rule was enforced by a teacher, the more Spanish was used by students. However, no further details were provided on language rule enforcement, a potentially fruitful area of future immersion classroom research.

Freeman (1998) worked in the Oyster dual immersion school in Washington DC. This school promoted Spanish and English as equal languages by rejecting mainstream U.S. expectations of a homogenous, monolingual society. However, Freeman (1998) found cases of "leakage" of the dominant discourse from outside the school. Although students who knew Spanish were positioned as resources of cultural capital for those who were learning it as an L2, Freeman's (1998) analysis of microlevel language episodes revealed that higher-level English skills were required in the school than Spanish skills. For example, the "opening" activity in kindergarten required more complex structures in English than it did in Spanish. Additionally, the majority of unofficial talk was in English (1998: 195). As noted by Delgado-Larocco (1998), it is essential to recognize the real extent of English domination in daily classroom exchanges, or English hegemony can become part of the school's hidden curriculum (1998: 78). Although Freeman (1998) did not systematically analyze or quantify language use, this ethnography provides a very comprehensive and useful account of many levels of one dual immersion school.

Finally, Hadi-Tabassum's (2006) critical ethnography explored how race, ethnicity, and gender were relevant to student learning in a dual immersion school. One particularly notable finding in that study was that the students themselves contested the enroachment of English into officially Spanish-speaking domains of the classroom. This stands in stark contrast to most dual immersion contexts (including the school that is the focus of this book), where students are happy to use English as much as possible.

As mentioned at the beginning of this section, Christian *et al.* (1997) offered general observations of dual immersion language use after visiting three schools in different parts of the United States. They indicated that "in general," dual immersion students were observed using Spanish during Spanish lessons while talking to the teacher and while engaged in academic activities, particularly younger children. In the lower grades, when anglophone children had just begun acquiring Spanish, students were "sometimes" observed addressing the teacher in English during Spanish time. This was less common in the upper grades. The use of Spanish during English time was very rare, occurring most frequently among Spanish-dominant children. In contrast, English was often used during Spanish time for social interactions among peers of both language backgrounds, especially when the teacher was not within earshot:

> English was used frequently in all grades whenever the teacher was not present or was not the direct addressee. English was the predominant language among students in classrooms where they did not fear being punished for using English during Spanish time. (Christian *et al.*, 1997: 30)

The authors noted a marked student preference to use English as much as possible, particularly among older students, and noted that "the Spanish-speaking students had acquired English and even preferred to use English in interactions with other English and Spanish speakers (Christian *et al.*, 1997: 69). Additionally,

> in the lower grades, students code-switched when they did not have the appropriate vocabulary or grammar in their second language. In the upper grades, however, the use of English during Spanish time did not reflect students' inability to express themselves fully in Spanish; using English was clearly a deliberate choice. (Christian *et al.*, 1997: 58)

Despite their preference for English, the students were "able to comprehend spoken and written Spanish and English and were able to produce meaningful, fluent speech in both languages" (1997: 60).

Very fortuitously for my research, one of the schools profiled by Christian *et al.* (1997) – namely, Inter-American Magnet School (IAMS) – was located in Chicago, and was the same school in which I began collecting my data a few years later. The authors noted:

> As at the other two sites, English was clearly the preferred language for social purposes for those students who had achieved a certain level of fluency in it. At IAMS there appeared to be an even greater use of English by students when speaking among themselves than at the other two sites. (Christian *et al.*, 1997: 85–86)

At IAMS, students used more English and the teachers tended to tolerate more English during Spanish time in the classroom than teachers in the other two programs observed. Some became less tolerant when the students directed their utterance to the teachers in English rather than Spanish. The authors suggested that this might have been because teachers themselves "were not as exclusive in their use of that language during the instructional period as were teachers at the other two schools profiled" (1997: 83). The authors also noted that the level of English proficiency was rather high among the native Spanish speakers at the Inter-American. About 45% of the Hispanic students entered the program bilingual, while "some" knew only English or only Spanish. And although 71% of the students were Hispanic, only 35% were LEP (compared with 40% and 54% at the other two sites). It may be that students at IAMS used more English than students at the other two sites because they knew more.

Other factors may have also influenced the greater English use at the Inter-American. Christian *et al.* (1997) noted that IAMS had a larger percentage of African-American students (13% compared with 5% and 2% at the other two sites). The experiences of African-American students in immersion classrooms were considered by the Cincinnati Immersion Project, which contains some of the nation's most extensive immersion programs, "because many of them speak a nonstandard dialect" and are thus "functioning in a second language during half the school day and a second dialect during the other half" (Holobow *et al.*, 1991). In other words, faced with the double task of acquiring standard English and the immersion language, African-American immersion students may experience larger cognitive loads and differential academic and linguistic achievement. The 1987 study examined only the English test scores of pilot kindergarten students and found that African-American students scored just as well as their white counterparts in mastering English literacy, but since no examination of students' L2 use or proficiency was done, the question of their L2 use remains unanswered. During my observations at IAMS, I learned

Wow!

that 90% of the students receiving pullout Spanish as a Second Language services were African-American, lending support to the idea that African-American students may experience greater challenges in learning the L2 in immersion contexts.

In their conclusions, Christian *et al.* (1997) wrote that at the Inter-American,

> getting the Spanish proficiency of both language groups to meet [their] English proficiency levels has been a challenge. While some English-dominant students excelled in Spanish, many did not see the need to learn Spanish (at least in the earlier grades) and were *not motivated to learn it.* The Spanish-dominant students, too, were so drawn by the dominance of English in society that they were *not motivated* to improve their Spanish language skills beyond oral proficiency. (1997: 86, emphasis added)

Motivation was also mentioned by immersion researchers Swain and Carroll (1987). But, to date, no one has formally studied this construct in an immersion context. Chapters 5 and 8 of this book explore the students' reasons for using or not using Spanish in class, but goes beyond the traditional concept of motivation – which has limitations because of its static and binary nature – through Norton's (2000) construct of investment, which allows for situation-specific interpretations of individual behavior.

The studies discussed here provide important insights into language use in immersion settings. However, we still lack thorough documentation on the quantity of L1 and L2 use in dual immersion classrooms, as well as an understanding of students' reasons for that language use. My study sought to quantify dual immersion students' classroom language use and, like Tarone and Swain (1995), to understand students' own perspectives on those uses. It is important to document students' language use in order to understand the linguistic environment of dual immersion classrooms and evaluate whether such schools' goals are being met. Indeed, Carranza (1995: 176) suggested that students' participation in dual immersion classrooms is highly significant because it not only affects the learning of content but also constitutes opportunities to use, practice, and learn the L2.

Language proficiency

Next, let us consider findings of students' language development in dual immersion contexts. In general, Spanish-speaking children learn English better than the English-speaking children learn Spanish. Christian *et al.*

(1997), presenting observations of three dual immersion contexts across the United States, found that Spanish L1 students scored "fluent" on oral Language Assessment Scales (LAS-O) in English by third or fourth grade. At the California school, 95% of the English L1 students' oral Spanish was "fluent" by fourth grade (as measured by the SOLOM/SOPR), but only 65% of the English L1 students in Virginia had reached that mark by fourth grade. English L1 students were "able to express themselves with ease in Spanish," although their syntax and vocabulary were more limited than those of the Spanish L1 students. It is worth mentioning that in first grade, only 88% of Spanish L1 first graders had tested as "fluent" in Spanish (which calls into question the researchers' definition of "fluent" and/or the validity of the test), but the number rose to 100% in fifth grade, suggesting that the program contributed to the Spanish development of Spanish-speaking children.

Pérez (2004) studied the literacy practices at two dual immersion schools in San Antonio, Texas. Younger children interacted with whole texts in addition to receiving skill instruction in phonemic awareness, phonics, and other areas. They also engaged in writing as a cultural activity. According to the author, "all students made connections between the two languages and multiple literacies" and did not speak of separate skills used for reading or writing in Spanish or English. In the upper grades, students engaged in guided reading, literature, and spelling practice in both languages. Although the content was more challenging, teachers maintained a strict separation between languages during instructional time; but yet students were allowed to communicate in either language. The author states that by third grade, "all the children in this study were biliterate" and that as they advanced through the grade levels, their literacy skills in both languages became more sophisticated, exhibiting "bidirectional influences," defined by Hornberger (1989) as the use of knowledge of one language in helping communicate or solve linguistic difficulties in another language.

Curiously, only two studies to date have examined in detail the Spanish grammatical performance of dual immersion students. Potowski (2005) found similar distributions of preterite and imperfect by aspectual category among Spanish L1 and L2 students in a dual immersion classroom. However, the students were differentiated by accuracy – higher levels of Spanish proficiency resulted in more accurate production of preterite and imperfect. That is, the tense/aspect system, although fairly advanced, was not completely acquired by L2 Spanish students by the time they graduated from this dual immersion program. Félix-Brasdefer (in progress) found that although Spanish L1 students regularly produced and recognized both the subjunctive and the conditional in oral and written tasks, the Spanish L2 students rarely produced or recognized these forms, even in a written multiple-choice format. Chapter 7 will summarize the grammatical and pragmatic findings of eighth graders upon graduating from Inter-American Magnet School.

Research Questions and Methodology of the Current Study

This study took place over two years at Inter-American Magnet School in Chicago, Illinois. In 1999–2000 I studied a fifth-grade classroom, and in 2002–2003 I returned to study the same students during their eighth-grade year. In order to better understand general language use patterns at the school, I sought to learn about the classrooms and teachers, about the individual students and their families, and about the school's values, goals, and struggles. Thus, I needed to observe frequently and widely. This required my being accepted throughout the building and at different events. I presented myself at the August 1999 and 2002 faculty meetings and asked for permission to visit all classrooms as well as the cafeteria, gymnasium, playground, and assemblies. I also received permission to attend monthly meetings of both the Local School Council and the Parent Advisory Committee during the first year of the study. Teachers, staff, parents, and students were all very accepting of my presence and accommodating of my requests. They allowed me access to many aspects of school life such as Open House nights and student dances; they granted me multiple interviews and informal chats in the hallways; they invited me to their homes; they allowed me valuable class time to administer tests and questionnaires and provided me with written records. A study of this nature would not have been possible without such cooperation by all the members involved, for which I am very grateful.

Year 1: Fifth grade (1999–2000)

I focused on a fifth-grade classroom based on several studies reporting that language use in one-way immersion classrooms begins to shift to English around fourth and fifth grade (Blanco-Iglesias et al., 1995; Met & Lorenz, 1997; Tarone & Swain, 1995). In addition, one study found that by the fifth grade, Spanish language learners in dual immersion scored as fully proficient in Spanish (Christian, 1996). Finally, unlike younger children, 11-year-old students seemed more likely to be able to talk about their social identities and their investments in the Spanish language.

Between January and October 1999, I made 20 day-long classroom observations, visiting a total of 15 different classrooms ranging from preschool to eighth grade. In October 1999, I selected one fifth-grade class and began conducting participant observations there several mornings a week during classes taught in Spanish. Next, I selected four focal students. The decision to focus on a small group of students permitted me to examine their language use in greater depth. I chose two girls and two boys, one of each who had English as their only home language and one of each who spoke Spanish at home. I took field notes about their language use and about behaviors that seemed to reflect the students' attitudes toward Spanish, toward the teacher, and toward one another. The students sat in clusters of four to five desks, which were rearranged approximately every month. I sat with a different cluster of desks every two or three visits. I also observed students in gym, lunch, recess, computers, music, and academic classes taught in English.

In order to quantify the amount of Spanish and English being used during Spanish lessons, I placed a stereo cassette recorder on the desk of one of the four focal students, supplemented by a video camera on a tripod in a corner of the room that was focused on the group that was being audio recorded. A total of 53 hours over 22 lessons were recorded between December 1999 and May 2000. For the corpus I analyzed for this book, I selected a total of 12 hours and 35 minutes recorded during 16 lessons (11 in Spanish language arts and 5 in Spanish social studies) over a five-month period, resulting in $6\frac{1}{2}$ to $8\frac{1}{2}$ hours of recorded classroom data per student. On the recordings, students routinely went off-task, spoke English during Spanish time, and sometimes used swear words, lending confidence to my belief that they did not see me as an authority figure who would discipline their linguistic or other behaviours. The corpus was selected on the basis of the criteria that sought to represent a balance between teacher-fronted lessons (7 hours, 38 minutes) and groupwork lessons (4 hours, 58 minutes) and fairly equal amounts of data for each student. Field notes taken during those sessions supplemented the audio/video recordings, allowing further analysis of the interactions.

The main unit of language use analysis was the *turn*, defined as when an interlocutor stops talking or is interrupted by another interlocutor's turn (Ellis, 1994; Levinson, 1983). The $12\frac{1}{2}$ hours of data from Spanish language arts and Spanish social studies lessons contained 2203 student turns. Percentages of Spanish and English use were calculated for each of eight variables: (1) class type, (2) participant structure, (3) interlocutor, (4) topic, (5) selectedness, (6) mean length of turn, (7) student gender, and (8) student L1. These variables are explained in greater detail in Appendix B of Chapter 4.

In addition to quantifying Spanish and English use, I sought to explore students' reasons for their language use. According to Tarone and Swain (1995: 170), "The sort of evidence we need ... is best provided qualitatively, either by ethnographic discourse analyses of individual children in the classroom, by verbal reports from these learners, or both." I employed an ethnographic case study approach in order to understand individual students' language use as a product of their investments (Norton, 2000) in the identities they wanted to present. The concept of investment, which encompasses the multiple facets of students' identities and positionings, is described more fully in Chapters 5 and 8.

In order to understand these students' investment in Spanish, I first gave them a written questionnaire to explore their attitudes toward Spanish, including their perceptions of the importance of Spanish in their personal lives, in Chicago, and in the school. I also read several pieces of students' journal writing about their Spanish use. I also recorded interviews with students, their parents, and the teacher. They were semistructured, in that I used a set of questions as a guide, but the participants were allowed to respond freely. I interviewed the students in English because I wanted them to be able to express themselves well, and English was the dominant language for all four students. The interview was not intended to rate the students' Spanish proficiency, but to probe issues of investment in learning and speaking Spanish. Had I interviewed them in Spanish, I am certain that the responses would not have been as natural and rich.

I also recorded one-parent interviews with each child's mother. Because one child did not have a father living in his home, talking with mothers provided more uniformity across the four interviews. I used English with the two mothers of the Spanish L2 students. With the two Spanish L1 mothers, I used the language that the mothers had used with me when I met them during a class field trip, Spanish with one and English with the other. Parent interviews were used to provide information on the child's language background as well as on the parents' language attitudes, given that children's language attitudes have been shown to reflect those of their parents (cf. Feenstra, 1969). The mothers also provided important insights on how they perceived their children's investments in Spanish.

In addition to our frequent informal conversations, I conducted two recorded interviews with the fifth-grade teacher, Ms. Torres, about issues that interested me during ongoing data analysis. I attempted to understand her decisions as she sought to promote the students' Spanish use; her ratings of the students' Spanish proficiency, participation, and attitudes; and her attitudes toward the focal students themselves. A teacher's attitudes toward learners can influence the question frequency and feedback patterns directed to them (Jackson & Costa, 1974). Tucker and Lambert (1973) considered teacher attitudes more important than even parental or community attitudes in influencing students' classroom second language acquisition.

The use of various qualitative methods (such as observations, interviews, journals, and questionnaires) translates into different lenses through which to examine the issue being studied. I triangulated my analysis in an attempt to present the most reliable interpretation of the setting by comparing student, parent, and teacher interview data, my observations, and students' comments within the corpus. I also had the parents, teacher, students, and school administrators read my written reports, which were approved with minor revisions.

Year 2: Eighth grade (2002–2003)

In the second year of the study, I observed the same four focal students during their eighth grade and final year at the school. I observed a total of 48 lessons conducted in Spanish, 20 of which were recorded using a digital voice recorder. I noticed very early that students used little Spanish with the teacher and practically none with one another, making a detailed turn-by-turn analysis unnecessary. Therefore, instead of focusing on four students and transcribing, coding, and analyzing all of their turns, as I had done during the first year of the study, what I did instead was analyze a typical class in current events, calculating the percentage of teacher turns and student responses in each language. That is, I recorded and observed the four focal students as well as their 48 classmates and analyzed their language use patterns, which I supplemented with field notes taken during all 48 of my classroom visits.

In order to better understand the eighth graders' language choices, I interviewed not only the four focal students, but also eight of their classmates, for a total of 12 students. This constituted 30% of the eighth-grade class. I also returned to the four focal students' homes to interview their mothers about language use issues. Finally, I interviewed several teachers and administrators to broaden my understanding of language use in the school. Finally, in order to objectively gage students' abilities in Spanish upon graduating from Inter-American, I administered a series of measures that are described in Chapter 7. These included tasks in speaking, listening, reading, and writing, as well as assessments of grammatical accuracy and sociolinguistic appropriateness.

In summary, the research questions that guided this study of Inter-American Magnet School were as follows:

(1) What were the *language use patterns* of a group of four focal students during fifth grade, and again in eighth grade, during Spanish-language lessons?

(2) What were the relevant *investments* of the four focal students that con-
    tributed to or hindered their Spanish use?
(3) What was the *Spanish proficiency* (oral fluency, writing, reading, gram-
    matical, and sociolinguistic appropriateness) of the 53 students in the
    graduating class of 2003?

The Role of the Researcher in Ethnographic Studies

Qualitative research places a high premium on researcher disclosure.
Issues of researcher subjectivity, the role of the researcher in the setting,
the "observer's paradox," and reciprocity with group members are all important to explore and disclose in ethical ethnographic research. I shall
now briefly discuss each of these points.

One of my principal subjectivities was my interest in the children using
and being exposed to Spanish, which caused me to view the use of English
during Spanish lessons as negative and unfortunate. This viewpoint may
have blinded me to other important aspects of the classroom and of students' interactions and learning. Additionally, being a female English L1
Anglo-American may have influenced my perceptions, the ways in which
people interacted with me and in my presence, and the details they dis-
closed in interviews[10] (cf. McCollum, 1994).

I did not present myself as Spanish monolingual to the students, and
I used both languages when talking with them. While observing lessons
taught in Spanish, I used Spanish with them almost exclusively. During
these times, some students would address me in English, but my Spanish
response would sometimes (but not always) cause them to shift to Spanish. At other times, including in the cafeteria, on the playground, and in
the hallway, I used English with students. It is undeniable that my presence and my language use with the children may have affected the language they used when I was within earshot and when they were being
recorded. This is often referred to as the "observer's paradox": we want to
find out how people behave when they are not being systematically observed, yet we can only obtain these data through systematic observation
(Labov, 1972: 209). With the fifth-grade teacher I used only Spanish, both
publicly and privately. With the eighth-grade teacher, I used Spanish in
front of the students and English in all other contexts.

I was conscientious about maintaining an appropriate yet friendly role
in the classroom. Approximately one third of the time I spent in the classroom, I circulated to help students finish tasks. At other times, I attempted
as much as possible to remain a nonparticipant observer. The students,
who called me "Ms. Potosí," became accustomed to having me in class,
in the gym, in the cafeteria, and on the playground. Some of them asked

me for help with their classwork and occasionally chatted with me about their families and other events that were important to them. I also compared taped classes with field notes written during nontaped classes and found similar patterns of language use, except for occasional humorous comments directed to the tape recorder (such as "Calling all aliens!" and "Houston, we have a problem"). This suggests that students behaved similarly whether or not they were being recorded.

I attempted to establish an ethical and reciprocal working relationship with the school and with the teachers. I did a portion of Ms. Torres' photocopying each week, gave Ms. Maas teaching ideas and occasionally taught sample lessons for her, staffed donation tables at school functions, designed Valentine's Day Dance tickets, and joined a letter writing campaign in support of the school's request for a new building. Perhaps most appreciated by the principal was the zip code map I created on the basis of where students lived, which proved useful in the school's requests for busing and for a new building. After data collection was completed, I gave Ms. Torres a 10-volume Spanish encyclopedia set for her classroom. I did not make a similar gift to Ms. Maas' classroom because she was leaving the school. I also made a modest donation to the Parent Advisory Committee fund.

Many members of the Inter-American community read drafts of articles and manuscripts and invited me to present to the faculty about my findings. They showed great attention to detail in correcting factual errors and requesting clarifications. In addition to making a contribution to our understandings of dual immersion education, it is my hope that this book is of particular use to the Inter-American community – its founders, the dedicated professionals who work there, the parents who choose this school from among many other options, and the children who study there – as the school continues into its fourth decade of teaching children Spanish, English, and about the world around them.

Notes

1. Several alternatives to early total immersion were developed in Canada, including early *partial* (half of the school day in each language), *delayed* (immersion begins in 4th or 5th grade), and *late* immersion (which begins in 6th or 7th grade). Usually French was taught as a subject prior to participation in a delayed or late immersion program (Swain & Johnson, 1997: 3).
2. Magnet schools are public schools that typically offer an "enriched" curriculum. They enroll students from an area wider than the local school district. Parents usually participate in a lottery for their children's admission.
3. Although survey numbers likely do not count every dual immersion program in the country, they indicate that there are twice as many dual immersion (315) than one-way immersion programs (151) in the United States.

4. Canadian immersion educators have been careful to remind their U.S. counter-parts that the success of immersion programs does not constitute support for the *submersion* of language minority children in all-English classrooms in the United States. Submersion is the policy of placing LEP children in all-English classrooms without any ESL or L1 support, leaving them to "sink or swim." Submersion is technically an illegal practice ever since the 1974 Supreme Court case *Lau vs. Nichols* mandated language support for LEP students. Three important features distinguish immersion from submersion. First, in immersion, all students have zero L2 competence upon beginning the program. In submersion, LEP students must compete with native English-speaking children in the classroom, with whom they can rarely catch up. Second, immersion teachers are proficient in the children's L1 and permit them to use it during the first few years of the program. In submersion, communication between LEP children and teachers who do not understand the children's L1 is very difficult. Third, immersion constitutes an *additive* environment in which a second language is added at no cost to the L1. Submersion is *subtractive*, in that the L1 is usually replaced by English. Submersion of LEP children is thought to produce "a disproportionate number of children who fall behind in class, question their ethnic identity, and drop out of school" (Crawford, 1995: 144).

5. Such programs use measures such as the Student Oral Language Observation Matrix (SOLOM), the Student Oral Proficiency Rating (SOPR), the Language Assessment Scales – Oral (LAS-O), or the Center for Applied Linguistics' *CAL Oral Proficiency Exam* (or COPE) in Spanish.

6. Other authors who have used natural classroom data (but did not systematically document it for quantification purposes) include Lyster (1998), who examined error analysis in the form of teacher recasts; Tardiff (1994), who looked at the role of teacher talk; and Swain and Lapkin (1998), who focused on negotiations between immersion students during classroom lessons.

7. Since Broner (2000), Fortune (2001), and Potowski (2004) used different procedures to code their language data, the percentages they report are not entirely comparable.

8. Although the school that Fortune (2001) studied utilized a one-way immersion curricular approach, there were heritage Spanish-speaking students in attendance. The author, calling this a "hybrid program," notes that it raises interesting questions for dual immersion researchers (Fortune, 2005).

9. In this sequence, teachers ask questions to which they already know the answers, one or more students respond, and the teacher evaluates their response. These exchanges provide fewer opportunities for students to nominate topics and take turns speaking, yet is the most common type of interaction found in traditional classrooms (Cazden, 1988).

10. Ms. Torres (the 5th-grade teacher profiled in Chapter 5) claims she did not know that I was not Hispanic until I told her so, and she suspected that other teachers might not have known, either.

Chapter 3
Inter-American Magnet School

Proposition 227 was passed last year. If Anglo-American fails,
California fails. If California fails, the United States fails.
Adela Coronado-Greeley, cofounder of Inter-American
Magnet School, addressing the teachers in August 1999

Inter-American Magnet School (IAMS) is one of over 500 elementary schools in Chicago and is one of 28 elementary magnet schools in the city. The magnet school model, begun in the city in the 1970s in response to court ordered desegregation, was designed to promote racially mixed school populations. Unlike the majority of U.S. elementary schools, which are open only to students living within defined neighborhood boundaries, magnet schools are usually open to all students within the school district. Such schools usually offer an enriched curriculum, such as a science, arts, or languages. Although magnet schools are free and open to the public, they often have admission requirements, such as test scores or a lottery system. IAMS utilizes a lottery system that selects students solely on the basis of racial-ethnic categories and gender. In order to achieve the desired balance, all applicants are separated into categories based on race (Latino, white, black, etc.), and then separate, random computer lotteries are held on the basis of gender: a lottery for Latino girls, one for Latino boys, one for white girls, one for white boys, and so on. In this way, approximately 16 students are chosen for enrollment in each preschool class. There are no tests or other requirements for admission to IAMS.

The success of IAMS is reflected in the number of parents seeking to enroll their children there. An average of 1100 applications are received for 65 preschool spots each year, creating a substantial waiting list. Magnet school principals are permitted to assign 5% of the available spots at their discretion, and at IAMS these openings usually are given to children of IAMS teachers. Siblings of current IAMS students are accepted without participating in the lottery[1] and account for approximately 45% of the student population. The school's innovative and successful model is regularly profiled in local and national newspapers and even international publications such as the *London Times Educational Supplement* (May 21, 2003).

History

IAMS has a rich history as one of a few public schools in Chicago founded by parents. It grew from a humble preschool program that struggled to keep its doors open. The school's cofounders Adela Coronado Greeley, a community organizer, and Janet Nolan, an early childhood specialist, were both new mothers nurturing visions of an inclusive bilingual school. Adela's parents had emigrated from Mexico in 1926. As a child in East Los Angeles, she was punished for speaking Spanish in school. But her father emphasized that their family had "descended from kings" (hence their surname Coronado, which means "crowned") and that Spanish was to be their only home language. When she married an Irish-American man, she believed it was important for her children to be comfortable with both families and cultures. Feeling that the local schools did not appreciate difference, she feared that her children, instead of being proud of being Mexican, would feel ashamed. She also wanted her children to be able to speak Spanish and "know their family stories." Her work as a community organizer and at a school begun by parents on the south side of Chicago led to her conviction that a school could be started where she lived on the north side as well.

Janet Nolan, an Irish-American woman, had received a scholarship to study Spanish in Puerto Rico for 10 weeks. There, she was impacted by the program director and his wife, who used English, Spanish, and German with their children. She also observed children in Mexico City who studied half of the day in English and half in Spanish, marveling at how fluent they became in both languages. She later taught English as a Second Language and directed an early childhood center in the Yucatan region of Mexico. There, she saw that young children could easily learn more than one language: her students spoke Spanish, English, and a Mayan language which they learned from their servants. Claiming that she "didn't want my daughters to go through what I went through to learn Spanish," she spoke to them only in Spanish. Yet when her three-year-old daughter requested that she not speak Spanish with her in public, she began thinking about founding a preschool that supported her personal convictions and used each language 50% of the time, thereby strengthening children's pride in the language.

Adela and Janet were introduced to each other at a bilingual education event in Guatemala by a woman who had heard them talk separately about their ideas for a school. They began meeting in Janet's living room to discuss their options and worked to gather support from Head Start, Hispanic parents, and teachers. When they finally landed a meeting with an official from the Board of Education, their immediate goal was a preschool program, but they made it clear that their vision was one of friendships developing between children of different backgrounds that would be passed on to the parents and influence the entire city. When the official responded enthusiastically that they should write a proposal, Janet and Adela continued with visits to the Urban Progress Center, churches, and schools. They put up flyers and asked bilingual coordinators for permission to speak to parents. Eventually they decided that the area encompassed by Chicago streets Howard, Montrose, Lake Shore Drive, and Kedzie would be the boundaries for their preschool.

The next step was to submit a proposal to the Illinois State Office of Bilingual Education. Over the course of a few months, each member of the group assembled by Adela and Janet researched a different part of the proposal, and Janet crafted the master document. In 1975, the Superintendent of District 2 accepted the preschool proposal, but Adela laughs when she admits, "I don't think she even looked at it! I mean the proposal specified that we parents would hire the teachers and work with them to write the school's curriculum, goals, and philosophy. We were so naïve, it is miraculous that we succeeded." The proposal was submitted to the State and eventually funded at half of the amount requested, which was barely enough to pay for two teachers. Since bilingual funds would be used, the school could admit Spanish-speaking children only. A teacher from Cuba named Mrs. Addy Tellez was to be the Spanish-dominant teacher, and Janet was to be the English-dominant teacher. The founders continued to go door to door to enlist children for the school.

However, the school could not be established without teacher aides, a bus, or materials. One of Adela's friendships helped the fledgling program take an important step forward. The woman, a member of the Chicago School Board, accompanied Adela to a meeting with an official from Title VII, a federal program that funded bilingual initiatives. The board member told the official that Adela's preschool program needed a bus, teacher aides, and $5000 for materials. The official agreed to grant them what they needed, which Adela credits to her friend's position on the board. Armed with these material necessities, Adela and Janet's group now had twenty members, including parents, teachers, bilingual coordinators, and university professors.

Despite an accepted proposal, a grant from the state, and some funding, the program still had no building. Janet and Adela were given the names of schools whose enrollments had been decreasing. Such schools might welcome the fledgling program as a separate entity within their school, thus increasing enrollments and avoiding having to close their doors. The first school they approached had a very domineering principal who refused the program, so Janet and Adela looked elsewhere. Finally, the Mary Bartelme School in the Rogers Park neighborhood accepted the preschool program in their building as the "Mary Bartelme Early Childhood Bilingual Center." According to Janet, the principal's stance was one of benign negligence: "Do what you want, and do it well, just don't bother me." In 1975, the first classes were scheduled to begin with 40 children in the morning and 40 in the afternoon, but only 60 students were recruited. A single bus provided transportation for all of the students. The children spent 90 minutes with the Spanish teacher before switching to the English teacher, Janet, who recalls, "We had no materials whatsoever. We were photocopying from books and making do as best we could. But the parents believed in us." Janet's daughters, who spoke Spanish, were the only Anglo children at the school, and Adela was head of the parent council.

After two years of directing the preschool, Adela and Janet again went before the superintendent, this time for permission to expand to kindergarten. He responded that they could have a kindergarten, but admonished them not to ask for anything else. Janet and Adela began interviewing potential teachers in Janet's home. They also met with parents, who did not want the program to end after kindergarten. Adela recalls the parents' vision and high expectations for their children, and one parent in particular who excitedly talked about having the program continue through high school and college. In 1977 a kindergarten class was added, and by 1978 a first-grade class had been added as well. It was a parent, Mr. Regalado, who suggested the name "Inter-American" for the program. Up until this time, the school was still functioning without books. When parents complained to the Board of Education, books and other materials were soon on the way. As Adela recalls, "The parents have always been the strong arm in our school."

It did not take long for the school to become popular. State officials liked the proposal and brought visitors to observe, so by its third year, superintendents from all over Illinois were visiting Inter-American. The next major event was what secured the school's future. Janet saw a two-inch notice in the newspaper, sponsored by the Chicago Public Schools, seeking proposals for magnet schools that would integrate the city's schools. Janet and Adela brushed off their original proposal, and in 1978 Inter-American was accepted as a magnet school with a dual language program. But even before the school received magnet status, some English-speaking parents were noticing that Inter-American students were learning two languages, and they wanted to enroll their children. Adela said, "I'll never forget a woman named Mrs. Joan O'Malley, who stood there with her hands on her hips and said to me, 'Why should my daughter Shannon be learning only one language?' Her daughter was the first 'illegal' student, we didn't tell the board." Now an adult, Shannon heads a bilingual program in a Chicago suburb. Janet remembers trying to recruit English-speaking students for the school by attending private school fairs, but "twenty five years ago, parents wanted their kids to learn French. That has all changed now."

By 1979, Inter-American served preschool through third grade and no longer fit at Bartelme. They moved to LeMoyne School, just east of Wrigley Field, and although they lost many good students in the move, they en-rolled approximately 60 children at each grade level, divided into two classrooms. Once again, Adela credits benign neglect on the part of admin-istrators: "The principal was so busy he ignored us, which was good." They added grades at the rate of one per year and soon outgrew their section of the LeMoyne building. Although Inter-American was still just a program within the 'regular' school, other teachers felt that Inter-American staff and students were getting more than their share because they had magnet funds as well as Federal Title VII bilingual funds. The Board of Education was actively trying to find another location for them, but, according to Adela, "no one wanted us because of our active, assertive parents."

In 1983, the Chicago Public Schools decided to invest federal desegre-gation funds into three new dual language schools. The Superintendent of District 2 visited Inter-American to see the work they had done. Janet re-membered her as "very tough, but aware of things that were done right." The superintendent was so impressed that she accepted Inter-American program and moved it to Morris School, which had declining enrollment. It was to be converted from a regular school into a 100% dual immersion school, and its name changed to Inter-American Magnet School (IAMS). The 280 students at Morris could either enter the dual language program or transfer to another school. The majority of the students stayed, as did the former principal of Morris, although she was not in favor of bilingual education and did not allow parents into the building. She approved of just one class of Spanish throughout all grade levels, but not a full-fledged dual immersion program. Some Morris teachers, who were also against dual immersion, told the seventh graders that being taught in two lan-guages was "ruining them." Both Janet and Adela recall this time as one of tremendous conflict.

As has always been the case, IAMS parents came to the school's aid. One parent, who was head of bilingual education at the Board of Education, encouraged other parents to speak at board meetings. He also brought in a consulting team from Texas to work during several Saturdays with a group of 200 parents and teachers in the school cafeteria. There were two main questions they sought to answer. First, when is IAMS at its best? The answer: when the parents and teachers together make the decisions for our school. Second, when is the school at its worst? The answer: when forced into a top-down decision-making structure. A formal statement was prepared and sent to the Board of Education. Within two months, the Morris principal took early retirement in order to assist her ailing father.

Now IAMS faced the task of finding a new principal. An advisory council comprising six parents and four teachers interviewed 17 candidates. The council originally wanted a Latino principal, but a woman named Mrs. Harding stood out above the others. She and her Hungarian family had moved to post–World War II Germany. When she immigrated to the United States at age 13, she was placed into first grade because she did not speak English. The committee felt that Mrs. Harding's background, as well as her trilingualism in Hungarian, German, and English, gave her the necessary sensitivity and understanding of the realities faced by linguistically and culturally diverse students. According to Adela,

> She understood our philosophy. Somehow she understood the philosophy, the two languages bringing about a cultural acceptance and the importance of maintaining the language. She could articulate this very well. She also appreciated the value of active parents and teachers, and would give them the means by which to do what they were doing so well.

After Mrs. Harding was hired, the battles were less intense and the school grew smoothly. IAMS graduated its first class of eighth graders in 1985, and today the vision statement is the same as it was in the original proposal. It emphasizes academic excellence, celebrating the cultures and the languages of the students in the school, a commitment to social justice, and the importance of parents and teachers working together.

Both of the school's founders point to constant self-evaluation and fresh ideas from new teachers as responsible for keeping the school successful. For example, when the dual language program first began in 1978, it taught 50% of the day in each language. This worked well for students' English acquisition, but they were losing their Spanish proficiency. In 1990, Adela attended a conference in California and was influenced by a talk given by Dr. David Dodson, whose manuscript she claims became IAMS's "Bible." But instead of the 90% Spanish–10% English model he espoused, which IAMS thought would hinder students' English development, they decided to adopt a model of 80% English–20% Spanish until fourth grade, supplemented by English as a Second Language (ESL) or Spanish as a Second Language (SSL) pullout when necessary. Other important examples of innovation followed: the practice of tracking children by ability, as was common practice when the program was founded in the 1970s, was eliminated; class size was reduced from 28 to 22 by putting resource teachers in the classrooms; and the length of the school day was extended in order to provide full recess for students and a break for teachers.

IAMS Today

Today, IAMS serves as a model for administrators, teachers, and parents, evidenced by the average of two visitors it receives a week (Urow & Sontag, 2001). Now in its third location at the former Morris School, IAMS occupies the entire three-story building and is educating a second generation of students. Many children of graduates, teachers, and clerical staff attend the school, and all are known on a first-name basis. In 2003 the granddaughter of cofounder Janet Nolan began preschool there. IAMS is now the oldest dual immersion program in the Midwest and the second oldest in the country (Coral Way Bilingual School in Miami, Florida, was founded in 1963). As of late 1998, Chicago's public schools offered 18 dual immersion programs, but only IAMS offers a dual immersion program that spans preschool through eighth grade and enrolls approximately equal numbers of English- and Spanish-speaking children.

There are two classrooms in preschool and three per level in K through eighth grade. At all grade levels, English-dominant and Spanish-dominant students study together in the same classrooms. There are five curricular cycles: early childhood (preschool and kindergarten), primary (first and second grades), middle (third and fourth grades), intermediate (fifth and sixth grades) and upper (seventh and eighth grades). Teachers in the same grade level collaborate on thematic units, fostering curricular articulation. In addition, classroom activities at all grade levels and cycles incorporate cooperative learning strategies that expect students to work in groups and to assist each other with language and academic questions.

The student population at IAMS has remained fairly constant since the 1980s. The following data come from the 2002 Illinois School Report Card. There were approximately 640 students total in preschool through eighth grade. These students were 70.9% Latino, 14.6% European American, 12.7% African-American, and 1.9% Asian/Pacific Islander or Native American. Approximately 40 students per year are identified as learning disabled (LD). These students are included in the mainstream classes but also receive pullout support from special education teachers. In 2002, approximately 50% of the student body qualified for free or reduced lunch, indicating that they came from low-income households. However, this percentage had declined from 60% in 1999, which means that the school lost some federal and state funding. In fact, the socioeconomic profile of the student body has changed steadily since the school's beginnings. Janet Nolan pointed out that IAMS used to be a port of entry for disenfranchised Latino parents who developed a public voice at the school, but these days she does not see as many of these types of parents.

Similarly, the proportion of students labeled limited English proficient (LEP) has declined considerably, from 48.7% in 1990 to a low of 26.1% in 1999–2000 (Kirk Senesac, 2002). During 2002–2003, the final year of this study, it had risen slightly to 31.1%. Since LEP students are Spanish dominant, their presence in the school contributes to the mission of creating a Spanish-speaking environment, a point to which I will return in the subsequent chapters. Although LEP students received ESL pullout classes at IAMS until 2003, they have always been integrated with English-speaking peers during most of the day. In the spring of 2000, 98% of IAMS teachers responded to a questionnaire about their students' home language, which revealed that 33% of the students came from homes where absolutely no Spanish was spoken.

In 1999–2000, of the 30 different zip codes in the city in which Inter-American students lived, the four areas that accounted for fully 48% of the student body – Logan Square/Humboldt Park, Avondale/Saint Ben's, Albany Park/Ravenswood, and Old Irving Park – had large Hispanic populations. However, a change in busing policy has affected the socioeconomic and linguistic composition of the student body. Until 1991, magnet schools were required to draw 10% of their students from the immediate area in which the school was located. The dramatic increase in property values in Lakeview, the neighborhood where IAMS has been located since 1983, meant that at least 10% of the student body was affluent, white, and English monolingual. However, in order to decrease busing costs, in 2001 the Chicago Public Schools raised the neighborhood quota to 30% of the student population, thus increasing the population of wealthier Anglo children at IAMS. In addition, many Hispanic children who graduated from IAMS in the 1980s and 1990s climbed out of their parents' poverty level into the middle class and are now sending their English-dominant children to IAMS.

Adela Coronado-Greeley has emphasized her concern about these socioeconomic changes. Now in her sixties and retired in California, she returned at the beginning of the 1999–2000 school year to talk to the teachers. She calmly but unequivocally stated that the school's raison d'être was not to enrich English-speaking children; it had been founded to empower Spanish-speaking children. She was concerned that there were not enough poor students at the school. In an interview she told me, "IAMS needs more poor children. There's tremendous wealth in economic differences. Middle class kids can learn from kids in poverty." Janet Nolan echoed this concern when she told me, "Our success has been our undoing. We couldn't get middle-class, English-speaking students when we first started out. Now we have very educated people applying for the school."

The lottery system for student enrollment was explained at the beginning of this chapter. When I asked school administrators whether they could implement additional categories within the lottery system, such as socioeconomic level or language dominance, they indicated that district regulations did not permit them to do so. Adela's reaction to this was that IAMS should recruit students more actively in poorer and in Spanish-dominant neighborhoods. When I mentioned the Mexican neighborhoods of Pilsen and La Villita on Chicago's Southwest side, I was reminded that the new regulations limited busing to students who lived within six miles of the school, and these neighborhoods are just beyond that maximum distance. Should the school be relocated to a different neighborhood, a possibility I will discuss at the end of this chapter, the hope is that the local population will be linguistically and socioeconomically more diverse than that in Lakeview, providing the school with more low income students and more Spanish-dominant students to comply with the school's original mission.

As mentioned earlier, IAMS receives over 1000 applications per year for fewer than 100 spots. Parents whose children are accepted must sign a contract demonstrating that they understand and agree with the dual language philosophy and practices of the school. The majority of IAMS students enter in preschool and remain through eighth grade. Some 25 students per year transfer to other schools, usually because their families move to the suburbs or out of state. Several teachers and parents have admitted that some parents pull their children out of IAMS after fifth grade in order to attend middle school elsewhere, because of the pressures of high school selection requirements and the fear that IAMS' upper cycle is not rigorous enough. A handful of students transfer out of IAMS because completing schoolwork in Spanish proves to be too difficult for them. In later sections, I will return to the issue of students who struggle with Spanish.

Teacher development is very strong at IAMS. The school participates in a program called *Futuro* ("Future") with Chicago State University. *Futuro* participants are college students paid to work as teacher aides for the first half of the school year, during which time they become acquainted with school routines and take university coursework required for certification on-site. They then become student teachers in the same classroom during the second half of the year. By allowing for a full year-long experience at the school, the program generates well-qualified dual immersion teachers, some of who eventually accept positions at IAMS (Urow & Sontag, 2001). Since 1991, five IAMS teachers have received the prestigious Golden Apple award for excellence in teaching, and in 1993 the school's cofounder Adela Coronado-Greeley was named Illinois Teacher of the Year by the Illinois State Board of Education. In 2003–2004, 100% of IAMS classroom teachers were bilingual; this number was slightly lower in 1999–2000. Potential teachers are interviewed by a committee of parents, teachers, and administrators.

Language Policy

According to official school policy, in preschool through fourth grade, the curriculum is taught 80% in Spanish and 20% in English. In grades 5 and 6, Spanish is used for 60% of the curriculum, and in seventh and eighth grades, the curriculum is split evenly between Spanish and English. This means that through fourth grade, English is used only in English language arts classes and in resource classes (music, gym, and computers), although students learn to read in their dominant language. Table 3.1 displays the distribution of content areas in the two languages from preschool through eighth grade (Urow & Sontag, 2001).

During Spanish time, teachers give directions, speak, read books, and sing only in Spanish. The same policy is carried out in English during English time. Since most children enter the school monolingual, in the early grades it is expected that they will often respond in their first language instead of their second language. Teachers encourage students to speak their second language by praising their efforts. They may also repeat a student's comment in the target language and invite the student to do the same. By third grade, students are expected to speak, read, write, and understand their second language. Students who enter the program late or who have difficulties with their L2 receive second language pullout classes. Because of the school's language goals, the hands-on math and science programs and the social studies material they adopt must be available in both Spanish and English (Urow & Sontag, 2001).

As is the policy in most United States and Canadian immersion programs, language teaching at IAMS is content based; this means that language is acquired through the learning of content instead of being the principal focus of instruction. For example, when students write math journals in Spanish, the teacher can analyze their comprehension of math concepts as well as their linguistic development. She or he can then hold a mini language lesson based on this information (Urow & Sontag, 2001).

Table 3.1 Inter-American language and subject matter distribution

Grade	%	*Spanish* Subjects	%	*English* Subjects
Preschool	80	Language arts Math Music	20	Language arts Gym
Kindergarten	80	Language arts Math Science Social studie Music	20	Language arts Gym
1	80	Language arts Math Science Social studies	20	Language arts Music Gym
2	80	Language arts Math Science Social studies	20	Language arts Music Gym
3	80	Language arts Math Science Social studies	20	Language arts Music Gym
4	80	Language arts Math Science Social studies	20	Language arts Music Gym
5	60	Language arts Math Science Social Studies	40	Language arts Math Science Social studies Music Gym
6	60	Language arts Math Science Social studies	40	Language arts Math Science Social studies Music Gym

(Continued)

Table 3.1 Inter-American language and subject matter distribution (*Continued*)

Grade	%	*Spanish* Subjects	%	*English* Subjects
7	50	Language arts Math Science Social studies	50	Language arts Math Science Social studies Music Gym Gym
8	50	Language arts Math Science Social studies	50	Language arts Math Science Social studies Music Gym

In first through fifth grades, students spend all day in self-contained classrooms with the same teacher. During the year I observed fifth grade, Spanish language arts, math, and half of the social studies curriculum were taught in Spanish in the mornings. English language arts, science, and the other half of the social studies curriculum were taught in English. All classes were taught by Ms. Torres.[2] In sixth through eighth grades, the structure becomes more like a middle or junior high school. Students alternate between three classrooms each day, and one of these is designated their homeroom. During the eighth grade year of this study, students received math and science instruction from Mrs. Castro, English language arts from Ms. Gingiss, and social studies (half in English and half in Spanish) and Spanish language arts from Ms. Maas. In the following sections and in Chapters 4 and 6, I will give an indication of the degree to which this official policy is followed in actual practice.

Spanish use in the school

In many ways the school was marked as a Spanish-speaking space. The hallways on all three floors exhibited students' work on current topics of study almost entirely in Spanish. I routinely observed school staff directing or disciplining children in the hallways in Spanish. Even more notably, public announcements during the school day were often done in Spanish without an English repetition, including summons for students to report to the main office or requests that visitors move their vehicles from the parking lot. I saw several teachers display a tenacious dedication to Spanish during Open House nights. When one third-grade parent requested that homework be sent home with an English translation so that she could help her son, the teachers replied that such a practice would undermine the need for the children to challenge themselves to comprehend the Spanish instructions. Teachers also described ways in which parents could foster their children's Spanish development. It was evident that many students – both Spanish L1 and L2 – were developing remarkably high levels of oral and written Spanish proficiency. I watched third graders write out answers to math problems and heard sixth graders debate the death penalty entirely in Spanish.

However, despite the school's official goals to value Spanish and English equally, many practices revealed that English was the dominant language. Chapters 4 and 6 provide greater detail on classroom language use, so only general observations will be made here. I routinely observed teachers using English during lessons that, according to the official classroom schedule, were supposed to be in Spanish (the same was found in the dual immersion school studied by Carrigo, 2000). These teachers explained that the corresponding books were in English, or that it was more important for students to know the material in English for standardized tests or for high school. McCollum (1994) also cited the influence of standardized tests in dual immersion school language use. Numerous IAMS teachers pointed out to me that the English-language standardized tests were forced on them by the district and the state. IAMS does administer Spanish standardized tests to all of its students (most recently the *Logramos* tests of reading comprehension, vocabulary, and math) in addition to the required English tests, but the Spanish tests do not affect student promotion and did not produce the same flurry of concern and preparation as the English tests. The nonacademic or "resource" classes of music, gym, and computers were all taught in English. Several teachers complained that this eroded the percentage of Spanish instruction that students were supposed to receive each day.

I also noticed that all schoolwide competitions, such as the science fair, history fair, and story writing competition, were in English only. This is probably because students who win these competitions go on to compete at the district and state levels, where all entries are expected to be in English. Yet there are no schoolwide competitions of any kind in Spanish to promote it as a language of academic achievement. The school's Young Authors competition does allow entries in Spanish, but the understanding is that only Spanish-dominant children will submit entries in Spanish; at no time are all students expected to participate in competitions that take place in Spanish.

One of the three dual immersion schools profiled Christian *et al.* (1997) was IAMS. The researchers noted:

> As at the other two sites, English was clearly the preferred language for social purposes for those students who had achieved a certain level of fluency in it. At IAMS there appeared to be an even greater use of English by students when speaking among themselves. (85–86)

Christian *et al.* (1997) also noted that the level of English proficiency of the native Spanish-speakers at IAMS was higher than that of the Spanish speakers at the other two schools they profiled. During the year of their study, only 35% of IAMS students were judged to be LEP, compared with 40% and 54% at the other two sites. Roughly 45% of the Hispanic students entered IAMS already bilingual (no definition of the term *bilingual* was provided) and "some" of them knew only English or only Spanish.

In their conclusions, Christian *et al.* (1997: 86) wrote that at IAMS,

> getting the Spanish proficiency of both language groups to meet [their] English proficiency levels has been a challenge. While some English-dominant students excelled in Spanish, many did not see the need to learn Spanish (at least in the earlier grades) and were *not motivated to learn it*. The Spanish-dominant students, too, were so drawn by the dominance of English in society that they were *not motivated* to improve their Spanish language skills beyond oral proficiency. (emphases added)

In Chapters 5 and 7, I will explore students' motivation to speak Spanish but using the much broader concept of investment (Norton, 2000). Worth noting here is the fact that various characteristics of the student population affect the enactment of language policy. Although 70% of the students are Latino, only half of these students are Spanish dominant when they enter the school. The other half are either bilingual in English and Spanish or are actually English dominant. English proficiency is particularly common for Latinos with older siblings who have learned English in school, as well as for Latinos whose families have been in the United States for two or more generations. The linguistic balance at IAMS, then, currently does not match the ethnic balance of the student population. In later chapters, I will demonstrate how even those students who enter preschool Spanish dominant eventually graduate dominant in English. Both Janet and Adela were aware of these trends and felt that the school should push for the right to select students using linguistic criteria and therefore enroll more Spanish-dominant children.

The difference in status between Spanish and English was also apparent in practices related to students who needed support in their L2. Until 2003, students who needed support in English received pullout ESL classes, and those who struggled with Spanish received pullout SSL classes. The ESL classes were taught by a knowledgeable second language acquisition (SLA) professional who had published articles and presented at national conferences. However, the SSL teacher during the year I observed fifth grade had no SLA training, claiming that she needed none in order to "just teach them the language." On the six occasions that I made prearranged visits to her class, very little language instruction took place. The students colored items on vocabulary sheets, cleaned the blackboard, or watched children's videos in English. They occasionally conjugated verbs on the board or took vocabulary tests, but I never observed students engaging in authentic communicative activities in Spanish. The teacher spoke to the students in English, but when she did ask them a question in Spanish and they did not know the answer, she would snap, "Why don't you know that?" When this teacher retired the following year, SSL instruction was taken over by experienced language teachers, but in 2003 both the SSL and the ESL positions were eliminated. I will return to the issue of the role of SSL instruction in a dual immersion school in Chapter 9.

In summary, despite the school's goals of equality of Spanish and English proficiency, there was clearly "leakage" (Freeman, 1998) from the outside English-dominant world that gave priority to English, a theme that will be revisited in the subsequent chapters. Several key figures in the school have expressed awareness that the Spanish goals and practices need examination. For example, the Local School Council develops a list of priority recommendations each year called the School Improvement Plan. The number one item on the list in 2002 was to "review the implementation of the dual language model, ensuring that the school maintains the dual language program and satisfies the academic needs of all students."

Curriculum

In 1978, a group of teachers and parents developed the "Curriculum of the Americas." It focuses on the indigenous, Hispanic, and African cultures, the three predominant groups that make up Latin America today. The curriculum also represents the linguistic and cultural diversity of the school's student body (Urow & Sontag, 2001). Students focus on one culture per year through interdisciplinary units. They study Native North Americans in first grade, the pre-Colombian Taínos from Puerto Rico in second grade, the Andean Incas in third grade, the Mesoamerican Mayas in fourth grade, the Aztecs in fifth grade, and the influence of Africa in the Americas in sixth grade. In seventh and eighth grades, the focus shifts to United States, Illinois history, and Latin American literature.

These units are interdisciplinary and often culminate in what one teacher described as "living museums" in which students put on short plays, explain cultural practices, hand-make artifacts, and explain geography to other students entirely in Spanish. For example, in fourth-grade math, students learned the Mayan numbering system. In social studies, they examined various social aspects of the contemporary Maya, including their experiences with the Mexican and Guatemalan governments and their struggles to maintain their languages. In English language arts, students read *The Corn Grows Ripe*, a semicontemporary story about a Mayan boy. In science they studied agriculture, Mayan foods, and astronomy, and gleefully imitated the cacophony of sounds in the rainforest. As a culminating activity, they created Mayan "towns" and carried out a *trueque* (barter or exchange) in the school gym. All IAMS teachers and students were invited to bring an item to trade, while the fourth graders sat at mats with their own items to trade.

Commenting on the Curriculum of the Americas, one teacher admitted, "We end up not covering a lot of the traditional Chicago Public Schools curriculum, such as Chicago history or ancient Rome, Egypt, and Greece. We decided not to worry about this, or about standardized test scores. The kids do just fine on the tests anyway." In order to provide what they felt was a more comprehensive assessment of students' progress, a group of teachers developed an alternative report card. Many IAMS teachers also use portfolios and other alternative assessment techniques. All faculty believe that learning is a constructive process in which students must be actively engaged in order to learn. The use of realia and experiential learning not only provides opportunities for students to discover their own knowledge, it also allows teachers to provide rich, meaningful, grade-level input in both languages and hence promote successful language acquisition. Teachers also hold very high expectations for their students' learning; the combination of priorities on a safe, caring environment and on academic success has been dubbed "caring and daring" (Christian *et al.*, 1997).

In order to understand the significance of IAMS' linguistic and curricular practices, it is instructive to contrast the school's practices with English-only sentiments that are common in other parts of the United States. In 2002, only 30% of elementary schools in the country taught a foreign language, and almost all of these programs utilized a FLES model that teaches the L2 for only half an hour a day (Branaman *et al.*, 1998). Very few FLES students achieve any lasting proficiency in the L2, much less participate in a Curriculum of the Americas in Spanish. When one considers that New Mexico was not permitted statehood until enough English speakers lived there, that for years Nebraska outlawed teaching in any language besides English before ninth grade, that language loyalty oaths were commonly extracted from U.S. schoolchildren (Dillard, 1985; Marckwardt, 1980), and when one considers the 1998 dismantling of bilingual education in California, the practices of IAMS attest to a far more progressive orientation. In fact, each morning students recite the pledge of allegiance first in English, followed by a translation in Spanish, before ending with a "Pledge of Allegiance to the World" in English:

I pledge allegiance to the world
To care for earth and sea and air
To cherish every living thing
With peace and justice everywhere

One demonstration of the effects of the social justice orientation of the school came in March 2003, when a group of 50 sixth-, seventh-, and eighth-grade students at IAMS conducted a walkout in protest against the U.S. attack on Iraq, despite some level of discouragement from the school administration. Students in slightly more than 30 Chicago area schools held similar acts of resistance, although IAMS was the only elementary school to do so. The sixth-grade teachers also organized their students to create an antiwar mural in the school hallway. Several teachers display progressive commitments through their curriculum and their personal activities. For example, many IAMS teachers expressed opposition when the school district began requiring that students pass a standardized test to be promoted to fourth grade. One IAMS teacher served on the Chicago Teachers Union's testing committee, where she began organizing critical forums about the harmful effects of high-stakes testing associated with the federal No Child Left Behind initiative.

Two other school practices that promote social and community responsibility are Senior Buddies and Reading Buddies. In the Senior Buddies program, IAMS students are paired with residents of a senior home. The students visit the residents, share stories, and create craft gifts for them. The Reading Buddies program is internal to IAMS and consists of older students gathering with younger students during language arts time to read to one another. This activity also promotes the familial atmosphere that so many parents and students praise at IAMS.

Student Outcomes

IAMS students regularly score above city and state norms on standardized tests of academic achievement. The state of Illinois requires the Illinois

Table 3.2 Percentage of students who meet and exceed state goals on the ISAT

		IAMS	*Chicago*	*Illinois*
Reading	Grade 3	76	33	63
	Grade 8	81	57	71
Writing	Grade 3	47	32	55
	Grade 8	88	52	70
Math	Grade 3	81	38	69
	Grade 8	61	20	47
Social science	Grade 4	38	28	59
	Grade 7	51	34	58
Science	Grade 4	53	33	64
	Grade 7	67	47	72

Standard Achievement Test (ISAT), which tests reading, writing, and math in grades 3, 5 and 8, and science and social studies in grades 4 and 7. The Chicago Public Schools adopted a second exam, the Iowa Test of Basic Skills (ITBS, or "Iowas"), administered in grades 3 through 8 and covering reading and math. These tests are required of all students, except recent immigrants who have completed fewer than three years of schooling in the United States. Table 3.2 shows IAMS students' achievement on the ISAT and compares them with students in the Chicago school district and in the state of Illinois.

Despite some variability in social sciences and science results, IAMS students consistently outperform their peers in the Chicago Public Schools and often outperform students across the state. Some limited data are available about how IAMS graduates fare in high school. According to the 2003 Consortium on Chicago School Research, they have lower dropout rates than students overall in the Chicago Public Schools.

In addition to the required English tests, IAMS students take standardized tests in Spanish. In all other Chicago Public Schools, these tests are required only of students whose English is considered not strong enough for the required standardized tests in English. IAMS, however, requires the Spanish tests of all students, except those who receive pullout SSL instruction, in an effort to give Spanish equal status and in order to document students' Spanish proficiency. Prior to 2002, students took the *La prueba de ubicación* test, but in 2002–2003 the school switched to *Logramos*. In 2003, the eighth graders scored in the 60th percentile rank in vocabulary and reading comprehension, and in the 91st percentile in mathematics. Since only recent immigrants normally take tests in Spanish, no comparison data are available for the school district or the state. Further exploration of students' Spanish proficiency will be taken up in Chapter 6.

One of the principal goals of IAMS, clearly stated in their philosophy document, is "the development of fluency and literacy skills in both languages." Many students do reach high levels of fluency and literacy in their L2, but their English skills far surpass their Spanish skills. This topic will be the focus of Chapter 6. However, as Freeman (1998) was told by a teacher in Washington DC, dual immersion education is about "much more than language." While it may fall short of its language ideals, IAMS very successfully reaches its other important goals. Reports from IAMS graduates attest to the lasting effects the school had on them. All IAMS students, upon graduating from high school, are eligible to compete for a $500 college scholarship. The scholarship was begun by IAMS cofounder Adela Coronado Greeley in memory of her daughter, Rosalinda. Over 20 students applied per year in the late 1990s and early 2000s, and when asked what they valued most about their experience at IAMS, they claimed that they learned to appreciate different cultures and how to accept others. On one occasion, an African-American girl who resisted Spanish while at IAMS admitted that in high school she began to appreciate how much more Spanish she knew than her peers, and claimed that her interest in studying the language had blossomed.

Parental Involvement

The two most visible parent organizations at IAMS are the Local School Council (LSC) and the Parent Action Committee (PAC). The LSC, mandated by the State for all Illinois public schools, is the school's governing body. It is composed of six parents, two community members, two teachers (all of whom serve two-year terms) and the principal. Parent and community members are selected by parents, and the teacher representatives are selected by faculty and staff. The LSC establishes school policies, hires and evaluates the principal, and controls school funding. I attended all monthly LSC meetings during 1999–2000. One of the biggest issues that year was the District's threat to eliminate busing for IAMS's preschool program, which would disproportionately affect low-income families.

The PAC is a voluntary parent organization that meets monthly to organize fundraisers and parent volunteer activities, and occasionally to examine challenges to school policies. They also help pay part of the children's choir program and the purchase and maintenance of copy machines for teacher and office use. I attended almost all PAC meetings during

1999–2000. In addition to regular activities, one parent organized a Spanish immersion weekend for parents and children each year. Parents put a lot of energy into organizing candy sales to raise funds for their children's field trips and necessary classroom purchases. In spring 2004, the PAC changed its name to *Familias en la Escuela* (FELE) – Families in the School.

In a 1987 article published in *Chicago* magazine, IAMS parent Jerry Sullivan chronicled the battle that he and other parents were waging for the survival of the school. Later, in 1999–2000, both the LSC and the PAC were campaigning for a new building to house IAMS. The Morris school building that IAMS occupied in 1983 had been built in the early 1970s to last a maximum of 20 years. The parents organized a letter-writing campaign and appealed to whatever influential contacts they had, including a U.S. Congressman whose daughter studied at IAMS. As of 2004, however, there were no plans to construct a new site for the school.

Even outside LSC and PAC activities, parent involvement in the school is high, reflecting the school's grassroots history.[3] Parents frequently volunteer in the library, in classrooms, on fieldtrips, during assemblies, and to assist teachers in decorating classrooms. In 2003–2004, when ESL and SSL classes were cut, a group of third-grade parents volunteered to tutor in these areas four times a week. When the school's reading specialist was lost, parents at several grade levels tutored in reading as well. Other parents make use of their professional contacts to secure donations for raffles and other school fundraisers, bring in artists for performances at the school, and locate community members to act as science fair judges. Friendships among parents, teachers, and administrators often extend beyond school activities. At a Chicago Spanish-language theater production I attended in 2003, about a dozen IAMS teachers, administrators, parents, and students in the audience excitedly told me that two parents of IAMS students had starring roles in the play. The many IAMS parents I have met appreciate the sense of family at IAMS and play a very meaningful role in the school and in their children's education.

Conclusions

This chapter has narrated the genesis of Inter-American Magnet School as well as its most recent struggles and successes. It has shown that IAMS students are very successful on mandated state tests in English, and they are also expected to conduct grade-level work in Spanish. However, English "leaked" into the environment and eroded the time and quality of Spanish instruction as well as students' ultimate levels of Spanish proficiency upon graduating, which will be displayed in subsequent chapters. In Chapter 4, I quantify the actual amount of students' Spanish use in a fifth-grade classroom on the basis of over 100 hours of observations and taped recordings of 12 hours of classroom interactions. Chapter 5 attempts to explain students' classroom language through the concept of identity investments (Norton, 2000) in the Spanish language. Chapter 6 presents a similar analysis of language use of the same students three years later in their eighth-grade classrooms. It also offers a linguistic portrait of the Spanish proficiency of the 54 graduating eighth graders. Chapter 7 explores the eighth graders' investments in Spanish.

The study of an environment as complex as a school, particularly one with the linguistic and cultural goals of a dual immersion school like IAMS, could be undertaken from any number of angles. All decisions made in order to limit the research focus necessarily eliminate a host of equally important aspects. An entire volume could be written about the ways in which IAMS embodies multiculturalism and creates a compassionate atmosphere that supports academic achievement for all children through student empowerment and through adult collaboration. This book focuses mainly on Spanish use and proficiency, but an attempt is made to include other voices and aspects of the school that will hopefully create a rich portrait of this successful dual immersion program.

Notes

1. Officially the school does have a sibling lottery, but there have not been enough siblings to require its use. Therefore, all siblings are accepted.
2. All teacher, administrator, and student names used in this book are pseudonyms.
3. However, there is a group of IAMS teachers and parents who feel that politically conservative parents are gaining voice at the school and have opposed and even censored certain activist and social justice elements in different areas of the curriculum that were in fact aligned with the school's original mission.

Chapter 4
Fifth-Grade Language Use and Proficiency

The first stage of this two-year study focused on a fifth-grade classroom. Research has indicated that children in one-way immersion classrooms use considerable amounts of the target language until around fourth and fifth grades, when they begin to shift to English (Blanco-Iglesias *et al.*, 1995; Met & Lorenz, 1997; Tarone & Swain, 1995). Furthermore, Christian (1996) reported that by fifth grade, Spanish language learners in dual immersion score as fully proficient in Spanish on standardized tests. It also seemed that 11-year-olds, unlike younger children, would be able to engage in conversation that revealed aspects of their social identities and their investments in the Spanish language.

As described in Chapter 2, I carried out observations throughout the school at all levels between January and October 1999. In October 1999, I selected Ms. Torres' fifth grade as my focal classroom and began observing there several mornings a week during classes taught in Spanish. I took field notes about language use and about behaviors that appeared to reflect students' attitudes toward Spanish, toward the teacher, and toward one another. I also recorded 53 hours of classroom instruction collected over 22 different lessons between December 1999 and May 2000.[1] Finally, I conducted interviews with the focal students, their mothers, and the teacher. The recordings allowed me to quantify and describe students' language production: how much Spanish they spoke, with whom, and for what purposes. The goal of the observations and interviews was to arrive at an understanding of the reasons behind students' language use.

Ms. Torres' Classroom

The student population in Ms. Torres' classroom was well suited to this study. There were 20 students, 11 who came from Spanish-speaking homes, and 9 who were monolingual English speakers when they arrived to IAMS. The class was divided evenly between girls and boys. Morning classes, which were Spanish language arts, math, and half of the social studies curriculum, were taught in Spanish. Afternoon classes, which were English language arts, science, and the other half of the social studies curriculum, were taught in English. Ms. Torres taught the students the entire day in both languages.

Ms. Torres was an exemplary teacher because of her fluent Spanish use, her alignment with IAMS's goals, and her classroom management skills. She had immigrated to Chicago from Mexico when she was 14 years old and is now a fluent bilingual. She chose to teach at IAMS because seven years earlier, wanting her oldest daughter to maintain her Spanish, Ms. Torres had enrolled her in preschool at IAMS and became increasingly familiar with the school. When completing her education degree, she chose to do her 100 hours of observation in a third-grade classroom and her student teaching in a fifth-grade classroom, both at IAMS. The year of this study was Ms. Torres's second year teaching fifth grade at the school. Her daughter and son both were both attending the school, and her husband, a prominent Spanish-language advertising executive, was president of the Local School Council that year.

Ms. Torres encouraged students to participate actively, to ask questions, and to make connections across subject areas. Shouting out answers and laughter were common in her classroom, yet she maintained sufficient discipline in order to carry out her academic goals. She consistently kept students on task, disciplining them when necessary but not too strictly, yet was also affectionate, often calling them "mijo/mija" or "mi amor." She displayed a firm grasp of the content she was teaching, and her sense of timing and transitioning activities created a clear sense of structure. She made frequent use of groupwork, as was the practice endorsed by the school, and used Spanish more consistently than I had observed in the other two fifth-grade classrooms.

Ms. Torres's students needed a high level of Spanish comprehension in order to be successful in her classroom. She spoke at a native pace similar to what I have observed in Mexican elementary schools, and did not appear to "water down" her vocabulary (cf. Valdés, 1997). In fact, at the beginning of the school year, even L1 Spanish students complained that she spoke Spanish "too fast." The social studies textbook and almost all of the math materials were in Spanish, and the students read three novels in Spanish during the year, had animated discussions about them, and wrote written reactions. Even students who could not produce very fluent or accurate oral Spanish appeared to understand most of what they heard and read in their language arts, math, and social studies classes taught in Spanish.

However, as in the school in general, Spanish was used less often than English in this classroom. Fifth-grade classes were supposed to be taught

60% in Spanish and 40% in English, but Spanish was the official language during a maximum of just 40% of the weeks that I spent in this classroom; some weeks it was even less. The importance of standardized tests was evident as well (cf. Carranza, 1995; Carrigo, 2000). As the time approached for the Iowa Test of Basic Skills and the Illinois State Achievement Test exams, Ms. Torres and many of her colleagues at IAMS had students complete their math journals in English, even though math was supposed to be taught in Spanish, in preparation for the tests.

Additionally, when students spoke to her in English during Spanish lessons, Ms. Torres sometimes required them to repeat themselves in Spanish, but often allowed English use to go uncommented. When I asked her about this, she commented on the challenge of balancing curricular with linguistic goals: whether to pause a lesson to focus on the language of a student's response or whether to accept the English response in order to move the lesson forward. Other IAMS teachers I interviewed expressed the same challenge, one that I experienced myself on several occasions when asked to take over a class for a short time. It is much easier to connect with the students and get a response from them in English.

The Four Focal Students

After observing in Ms. Torres's classroom for ten weeks, I chose four students to be focal students (see Table 4.1). The use of focal students was considered the most effective way to collect naturally occurring data because it permitted me to focus on a subset of the classroom (cf. Heitzman, 1994; Parker *et al.*, 1995). I selected two Spanish L1 and two Spanish L2 students, one boy and one girl from each group. It is important to note that the two Spanish L1 students had arrived to preschool Spanish dominant, but by the time of this study they were English dominant. All four students had at least average levels of oral Spanish proficiency, having been rated at a 3.3 or higher out of a possible 5 by researchers from the Center for Applied Linguistics (CAL)[2] using a modified Student Oral Proficiency Assessment. They were also doing well academically, as measured by the Illinois Goal Assessment Program (IGAP), *La Prueba Riverside* Spanish achievement test, and report card grades. Ms. Torres and I rated all four students "medium" to "high" on their amount of classroom participation during Spanish lessons. A brief narrative description of each student follows.

Carolina (Spanish L1) was a petite, brown-skinned girl whose parents were from Ecuador and Honduras. She was one of the most fluent Spanish speakers in Ms. Torres's class, receiving a rating of 4.9 out of 5 by researchers at the CAL. She spoke Spanish at home with her parents and

Table 4.1 Characteristics of the four focal students

Name	L1	CAL rating, oral Spanish proficiency*	Teacher rating, oral Spanish proficiency**	Teacher rating, participation during Spanish lessons	Grade 4 National percentile, ITBS scores: vocabulary, reading, math	Grade 4 National percentile, La Prueba scores: reading, math (in Spanish)	Grade 4, Percent correct, IGAP (Illinois Goals Assessment Program): social sciences, science
Carolina	Spanish	4.9	5	High	53, 58, 82	82, 62	60, 59
Matt	Spanish	4.9	3+	High	48, 72, 84	82, 80	67, 78
Melissa	English	4.6	3+/4–	Medium/high	80, 94, 95	61, 74	89, 87
Otto	English	3.3	3	Medium/high	36, 51, 74	26, 51	64, 60

* Overall fifth-grade average: Spanish L1 = 4.9, English L1 = 4.1. Based on a scale of 1 to 5.
** Based on a scale of 1 to 5

her maternal grandparents and had no trouble expressing herself orally in class in either language, although she occasionally used English lexical items in her Spanish (e.g. "*Está* wrestling *con un cocodrilo*"). She was one of the most active participants in the classroom in all subject areas, volunteering answers to the teacher's questions and helping other students with vocabulary. Her classmates treated her as a competent peer, and she particularly enjoyed playing soccer.

Melissa (Spanish L2) was a tall, light-skinned European American girl. She spoke only English at home with her parents. Her oral Spanish proficiency, rated at 4.6 by CAL, allowed her to communicate her general ideas, but she often struggled to find words in Spanish. Although she did not often volunteer answers during teacher-fronted lessons, she stood out very early in my observations because, unlike the majority of her classmates, she used a great deal of Spanish during unsupervised peer talk. This Spanish use was occasionally at the expense of socializing and sharing materials with other students, who used English.

Matt (Spanish L1) was an olive-skinned, dark-haired boy whose mother had immigrated from El Salvador as an adult. Matt's mom said that he regularly responded in English when she spoke to him in Spanish. Matt did speak Spanish at home with his maternal grandparents and with his maternal great-grandmother, all of who lived downstairs, but his stepfather was European American and did not know Spanish. Matt's oral Spanish was very nativelike (rated at 4.9 by CAL), although in class he used English words and shifted entirely into English more often than Carolina did. He seemed ahead of his peers in his knowledge of school-related subjects and in his analytical skills, which was corroborated by his grades and standardized test scores, and he participated frequently in class. However, he was beginning to exhibit resistance to homework and to school in general.

Otto (Spanish L2) was a talkative, African-American boy whose parents had emigrated from Africa before he was born. He spoke mainstream U.S. English at home (not African-American English), and CAL rated his oral Spanish proficiency at 3.3, which was lower than the 4.1 average of all the L1 students in fifth grade at the school. He struggled to express himself in Spanish and several of his erroneous verbal forms seemed fossilized throughout the year ("yo estás, nosotros vas"). Although he was not as fluent or as accurate in Spanish as Melissa, he was more fluent than two other students in the class. Despite his relatively low proficiency, he was one of the most participatory students during Spanish lessons. Otto was bright and competitive, sometimes appearing aggressive toward teachers and other students, several of whom requested not to be seated at his table for groupwork.

Source of Language Data

Table 4.2 shows which classes were selected for analysis from the 53 hours of recordings. In Spanish language arts classes, students read novels, analyzed poems, wrote stories, and occasionally did activities focused on verb endings and parts of speech. In social studies they used a textbook written in Spanish to study curricular units including the western movement of the early American pioneers; the Great Migration of African-Americans from the south to the north of the United States; the Aztec empire; and the immigration of Mexicans, Poles, and Chinese to the city of Chicago. During teacher-fronted activities, the teacher was at the front of the room leading classroom discussion. Students were expected to bid to speak publicly (although they often shouted out answers and comments without bidding or being selected) and were not supposed to chat with one another privately. During groupwork, students were engaged in activities at their tables that either required or permitted them to talk to one another freely, although they were occasionally expected to work individually.

The main unit of analysis of students' speech was the *turn,* which has been defined as when an interlocutor stops talking and thus enables another interlocutor to initiate a turn, or when the interlocutor is interrupted by another who initiates another turn (Ellis, 1994; Levinson, 1983). In Example 1, each numbered line represents a separate turn. Matt was assigned a total of four turns in this exchange. I use the transcription conventions outlined in Appendix 4.A, which were adapted from Hatch (1992).

(1)
1 **Ms. Torres:** ¿De qué otros lados vienen las historias y los cuentos?
2 **Matt:** Oooh!
3 **Ms. Torres:** Matt.
4 **Matt:** De...cosas que existen y/

Table 4.2 Classroom recordings selected for analysis

Language arts	8 hours, 46 minutes
Social studies	3 hours, 25 minutes
Transitions between classes*	25 minutes
Teacher fronted lessons	7 hours, 38 minutes
Groupwork	4 hours, 58 minutes
Total	12 hours, 36 minutes

* Short periods before classes had officially begun or after they had ended.

5 **Ms. Torres:**   De cosas que existen pero ¿dónde?
6 **Matt:**   ...y que no existen. Como/
7 **Ms. Torres:**   De cosas que existen/
8 **Matt:**   Uh...como...um...como...son como...como una leyenda, dice de, del sol, and how it was made and, y cosas así.

The procedures I followed for handling turns that were a mixture of Spanish and English, as well as the eight other variables for which I coded each turn, are described in Appendix 4.B.

Spanish Use: Quantity

As shown in Table 4.3, there was a total of 2203 turns produced by the four focal students. After discarding the 112 code-switched turns (66 intersentential code switches and 46 embedded language island code switches; see Appendix 4.B) and the 41 null turns, there were 2050 turns remaining in the corpus for further analysis.

Table 4.4 presents the overall language use of the four students as percentages of their total turns. The students used Spanish for 56% of their total turns, far less than the 100% officially expected during these Spanish lessons.

It was surprising that Spanish was used slightly less often in this classroom with native Spanish-speaking students than has been found in

Table 4.3 Language of all turns

	Monolingual	*Lexeme from other language*	*Total*
Spanish	1059 (48%)	82 (4%)	1141 (52%)
English	878 (40%)	31 (1%)	909 (1%) (41%)
Mixed	n/a	n/a	112 (5%)
Null	n/a	n/a	41 (2%)
Total	1937	113	100% N = 2203

Table 4.4 Overall language use (number of turns)

Spanish	English	Total
56%	44%	100%
(1141)	(909)	(2050)

one-way immersion classrooms that contained no native speakers (Broner, 2000, found 63% Spanish use overall). There may have been significant differences in language rule enforcement and expectations for Spanish use by the teachers in the two studies, but this aspect has not been formally examined. In addition, Broner sat the focal students together for all data collection, which limited peer interlocutors and may have affected the four students' Spanish use patterns. However, the 56% Spanish use of the four focal students in Ms. Torres's classroom was considerably greater than the 33% overall Spanish use found by Fortune (2001), even though in that classroom two focal students spoke Spanish at home.

Table 4.5 displays the language of all turns made by each student. Surprisingly, students' L1 was not related to their overall Spanish use: Melissa (Spanish L2) used Spanish 17% more often than Matt (Spanish L1). It will be demonstrated in Chapter 5 that Melissa had a considerable investment in an identity as a Spanish speaker, while Matt's home language use and somewhat rebellious classroom behavior were reflected in his resistance toward Spanish. However, because Carolina and Matt (both Spanish L1) exhibited very different language use patterns, as did Melissa and Otto (both Spanish L2), further explanations must be sought.

Table 4.5 Overall language use (number of turns) by student

	Spanish L1		Spanish L2		
	Carolina ($N = 590$)	Matt ($N = 527$)	Melissa ($N = 340$)	Otto ($N = 593$)	Total ($N = 2050$)
Spanish	67% (393)	47% (248)	64% (219)	47% (281)	100% (1141)
English	33% (197)	53% (279)	36% (121)	53% (312)	100% (909)
Total	100% (590)	100% (527)	100% (340)	100% (593)	100% (2050)

Table 4.6 Language use (number of turns) by gender

	Girls *(N = 930)*	*Boys* *(N = 1120)*
Spanish	66% (612)	47% (529)
English	34% (318)	53% (591)
Total	100% (930)	100% (1120)

Table 4.6 shows a gender-based pattern of classroom language use. The two girls used Spanish an average of 18.5% more often than did the two boys, regardless of their L1. It appears that these girls were more willing to conform to the teacher's expectations, which has been found in other elementary school classroom research (Toohey, 2000; Willett, 1995). The classroom Spanish use of these two girls seemed related to their investments in identities as well-behaved students, while the two boys were more interested in cultivating identities as rebellious and funny. However, it is important to note that there were six girls in the classroom (two L1 and four L2) who resisted using Spanish, and there were three boys (two L1 and one L2) who seemed to enjoy using Spanish and rarely used English publicly during Spanish time. Therefore, gender explanations of language choice must be tempered by an examination of individual students' classroom behavior.

Language use according to interlocutor

Turns were coded *to teacher* when students answered questions aloud during teacher-fronted lessons or directed turns to her during groupwork, and *to peer* when students directed turns to their classmates. It was usually obvious who the intended interlocutor was, but sometimes it was not entirely clear whether a turn was intended for the teacher to hear. I used the turn's volume as a criterion. If the speech was picked up by the video camera in the corner of the room, it was labeled "to teacher," because it was loud enough for one to assume that the teacher was an intended interlocutor (although the turn was obviously intended for classmates to hear as well). If a turn was picked up only by the tape recorder on the desk, it was not loud enough for the teacher to be a likely intended interlocutor, so the turn was labeled "to peers." If the student was actually talking to the teacher while she was near his or her group, close enough to be picked up by the tape recorder, the turn was coded "to teacher." This criterion relied on some degree of subjective interpretation.

With the teacher

Table 4.7 shows how the students' language choices correlated with the interlocutor (teacher vs. peer). When talking to the teacher, these students used Spanish 82% of the time. Another way to look at this finding is that of the total 1141 Spanish turns in the corpus, 70% of them (794) were directed to the teacher, and of the total 909 English turns in the corpus, only 19% of them (171) were directed to the teacher. These percentages indicate a good deal of effort on the students' part to conform to the teacher's language expectations when addressing her.

In a one-way immersion classroom, Broner (2000) found 98% Spanish use with school adults. However, only 15% of the total corpus included an adult as an interlocutor. My focal students directed fully 47% of their total turns to the teacher, so the 82% Spanish use actually represents a larger quantity of Spanish use. However, greater expectations for IAMS students to use Spanish 100% with their teachers during Spanish lessons would assist them in better meeting the school's goals of language development.

Turns to the teacher were sometimes shouted out loud and sometimes directed to her privately when she approached a student's desks during groupwork activities. I compared language use directed to the teacher under these two conditions (Table 4.8), predicting that students would feel more pressure to use Spanish when speaking publicly and would use more English with her privately.

The students used slightly more English when speaking privately with the teacher (24%) than they did when speaking to her publicly (16%). Because using English during Spanish time could result in a reprimand, it

Table 4.7 Student language use (number of turns) by interlocutor

	Spanish	*English*	*Total*
Speaking to Teacher (47% of corpus)	82% (794)	18% (171)	100% (965)
Speaking to Peers (53% of corpus)	32% (347)	68% (738)	100% (1085)
Total (100% of corpus)	1141	909	2050

Table 4.8 Public and private turns (number of turns) directed to the teacher

Total turns to teacher (N = 965)	Spanish	English
Public (N = 818)	84% (687)	16% (131)
Private (N = 147)	76% (111)	24% (36)

appears that the students tried to avoid a public reprimand by adhering to the language rule more strictly when speaking publicly, relaxing slightly when speaking to the teacher privately. This difference was not large, but it may be an interesting area for future research.

With peers

Returning to Table 4.7, of the 1085 turns directed to peers, 68% were in English and only 32% were in Spanish. This is a considerable drop from their 82% Spanish use with the teacher. Because of the presence of native Spanish-speaking students in dual immersion classrooms, I expected to find greater use of Spanish with peers than had been found in one-way immersion contexts, but this was not the case: although Broner (2000) also found considerably less Spanish use with peers (58%) than with adults (98%), the 32% peer Spanish use produced in my study was less than that in Broner's.[3] As mentioned previously, the limited seating arrangement used in Broner's study may have affected the students' language production.

My findings corroborate those of Carrigo (2000), Fortune (2001), and Carranza (1995) that the presence of students for whom Spanish was an L1 does not guarantee overall higher quantities of student Spanish use than what has been found in one-way immersion classrooms. Many of the Spanish L1 students at IAMS were highly proficient in English and used more English than Spanish in their daily lives. Indeed, in my observations over seven months in all grade-level classrooms, on the playground, and in the cafeteria, English was the preferred language of the majority of the students. Under these circumstances, it may be just as difficult to get Spanish L1 students to use Spanish as it is to get Spanish L2 students to do so. Carranza (1995: 174) suggested that students experienced a "feeling of 'pretense' when two people communicate in one language, knowing that both can be more effective in another." Given Carolina's and Matt's high levels of English proficiency, speaking in Spanish with their peers might have felt just as false as it would have to Melissa or Otto. In Chapter 6, I will discuss the exceptional cases of five Spanish-dominant students who had arrived from Latin America during sixth and seventh grade.

On a positive note, as noted by Fortune (2001), despite the high levels of English use with peers, students in many of today's immersion classrooms do produce a lot of language. Immersion studies done in Canada in the 1980s and 1990s indicated that those classrooms were largely teacher centered, with limited opportunities for students to use French (Allen *et al.*, 1990). In contrast, this classroom was very student centered and offered ample opportunities for students to use language. The problem is getting them to use Spanish, a point to which I will return throughout the book.

Table 4.9 presents language use according to the interlocutor for each student. The students' language use with the teacher was fairly homogenous: all students except Otto used Spanish between 83% and 91% when speaking with the teacher, and even Otto's language use with the teacher was almost three quarters in Spanish.

The students' language use with peers again showed gender variation, with girls using more Spanish than boys, but there are differences that merit description and that the concept of investment may help to explain. Compared with Melissa, Carolina used slightly more Spanish with the teacher but slightly less with her peers. Carolina's high oral Spanish proficiency

Table 4.9 Individual students' language use (number of turns) by interlocutor

	Speaking to teacher			Speaking to peers		
	Spanish (N = 794)	English (N = 171)	Total (N = 965)	Spanish (N = 347)	English (N = 738)	Total (N = 1085)
Carolina	91% (270)	9% (26)	100% (296)	42% (123)	58% (171)	100% (294)
Matt	83% (195)	17% (41)	100% (236)	18% (53)	82% (238)	100% (291)
Melissa	88% (112)	9% (15)	100% (127)	50% (107)	50% (106)	100% (213)
Otto	71% (216)	29% (89)	100% (305)	23% (65)	77% (223)	100% (288)

would have allowed her to use Spanish with her peers more often than she did, but her interview and journal comments, which included worries over being chosen for soccer teams during recess, indicated that she was unwilling to risk social exclusion. Her classmates requested her as a tablemate more often than all the other girls in the classroom except one, indicating that she was very popular. Melissa, however, experienced a degree of social exclusion and mild teasing because of her intense academic focus and her insistence on using Spanish. She often answered her peers' English in Spanish, which no other students in the corpus did, and even occasionally admonished them to use Spanish. It appeared that Carolina satisfied her investment in an identity as a proficient Spanish speaker through her use of Spanish at home and during teacher-fronted lessons; she did not need to insist on using Spanish during groupwork. Because Melissa did not speak Spanish at home, and did not participate very much during teacher-fronted lessons, she insisted on using Spanish during groupwork in part to satisfy her considerable investment in an identity as a Spanish speaker and a good student, which was more important to her than being popular.

Matt's Spanish use with the teacher was only slightly lower than that of the girls, but with his peers he used the least Spanish of all four students. He demonstrated competing identity investments as school-oriented and as rebellious. During teacher-fronted lessons his frequent volunteered answers, offers to help the teacher, and Spanish use reflected his investment in a public identity as a conscientious student. He also wanted to avoid getting in trouble at school, which had serious repercussions at home, so he spoke the minimal amount of Spanish required to stay on good terms with the teacher. However, when talking with his peers out of the teacher's earshot, his comments very clearly sought to identify him as resistant to authority and to the academic demands placed on him. He bragged that he did "buswork, not homework" and often complained about how much he hated school. As will be seen when examining the role of topic, such comments would logically take place in English, the adolescent vernacular of the classroom. Matt was a popular leader and occasionally attempted to subordinate his peers through teasing, which also took place in English. Even Otto, who also often teased his peers, used slightly more Spanish with peers than Matt did, but it will be shown ahead how Otto's English use with the teacher had important negative repercussions.

Finally, it is worth noting that Spanish turns directed to the teacher averaged 8.5 words in length, while Spanish turns directed to peers averaged 5.7 words. Other studies have compared students' L2 use with the teacher to their L2 use with classmates and found that students' peer language use was longer and more complex (Liu, 1994; Willett, 1995). This was not the case in the present study, since peer Spanish turns were even shorter than teacher Spanish turns. The difference may lie in the fact that Willet (1995) and Liu (1994) examined ESL contexts, in which students were acquiring the majority language that held status in the classroom and the community. In other words, those were contexts in which the English-speaking community was "acquiring" the student. When talking with their native English-speaking peers, ESL students may indeed have felt a need to produce longer, socially significant utterances in order to place themselves in the community. On the other hand, in non-English L2 classrooms in the United States, the pattern may be more similar to the one found here, in which English remains the status language and students will only use Spanish when required, such as with the teacher, and will therefore produce long turns only when speaking to her.

Spanish Use: Functions

The previous section documented the overall percentages of Spanish the students produced with different interlocutors and in a variety of contexts. This section explores the communicative functions for which Spanish was used in order to understand this classroom as an environment for L1 and L2 growth.

I used three terms to describe the topic of students' turns: *on-task* when the content of the turn was directly related to the official activity assigned by the teacher; *off-task* when the students were talking about something completely unrelated to the official lesson; and *management* for turns that managed the completion of an academic activity (e.g. while carrying out on-task activities: "You go first," "Let me see that," and "Give me the red marker"). Tarone and Swain (1995) and Blanco-Iglesias *et al.* (1995) used the dichotomy "academic-topics" versus "socializing" when coding turns by topic. It may seem reasonable to equate *on-task* with academic talk and *off-task* with social talk, but, as I will demonstrate, much of the language students use to regulate academically oriented activity (which I have termed *management*) appears more discursively similar to social talk than to academic talk. Broner (2000), Fortune (2001), and others have recognized how difficult it is to decide if a student is on task or off task. The main criterion I used was whether the teacher would likely have approved of the utterance in the context in which it occurred. Turns were coded *unknown* when the preceding turn was not entirely audible, making the topic impossible to determine.

Table 4.10 Overall language use (number of turns) by topic

N = 2050	Spanish	English	Total
On-task (67% of corpus)	68% (935)	32% (436)	100% (1371)
Management (16% of corpus)	43% (144)	57% (193)	100% (337)
Off-task (15% of corpus)	17% (54)	83% (258)	100% (312)
Unknown (1% of corpus)	30% (9)	70% (21)	100% (30)

Table 4.10 shows the amount of Spanish and English used for each topic when speaking to the teacher and to other students. The majority of students' on-task turns (68%) were made in Spanish. These 935 on-task Spanish turns accounted for fully 88% of the entire Spanish corpus, meaning that the great majority of the students' Spanish turns were on task. Management turns were in *English* 57% of the time, suggesting the discursive similarity between management and off-task turns and justifying the separation of management from on-task turns. Students greatly preferred English for off-task topics (83%).

It is also revealing to examine the topic of the turns that the students directed only to other peers in English versus in Spanish (Tables 4.11 and 4.12). They clearly preferred English (89%) when they made off-task comments. The relatively little Spanish that they used with each other was mostly for on-task comments (56%) or to manage an academic task (35%), very rarely to socialize off-task (9%). Noting this trend, I examined the referents of the students' peer English turns and compared them with those of their peer Spanish turns.

Table 4.11 Peer turns by language and topic: Percentage of language total

	Peer English	Peer Spanish
On task	40% (294)	56% (196)
Management	25% (181)	35% (120)
Off task	35% (253)	9% (32)
Total	100% (738)	100% (348)

Table 4.12 Peer turns by language and topic: Percentage of topic total

	Peer on-task	*Peer management*	*Peer off-task*
Spanish	40% (196)	60% (120)	11% (32)
English	60% (294)	40% (181)	89% (253)
Total	100% (490)	100% (301)	100% (285)

Peer English

Peer English was fairly equally spread among on-task (40%), management (25%), and off-task topics (35%). Although these lessons were taught in Spanish, students often asked one another on-task questions in English:

(2)
1 **Eleanor:**   What are delinquents?
2 **Carolina:**   Like, people that do like... criminals.

(3)
1 **April:**   What's "mito"?
2 **Matt:**   Myth is like, something... passed on, century by century, that's either Greek, or Italian, or just... Do you get what I'm saying?

The students also carried out a good deal of management functions in English:

(4)
1 **Eleanor:**   Can I borrow a pen?
2 **Carolina:**   I don't have one. He took mine.

Students' off-task peer English turns were about a wide variety of topics, including music, radio shows, movies, books, and games popular with adolescents (particularly the popular Pokemon cards), and friends' behavior outside of school. Their peer English also served functions like expressing pleasure by saying yes when one's answer was correct, talking about what was "cool" or "retarded," and resistance to school-related activities:

(5)
1 **Eleanor:**   This is the most retarded I've ever drawn.
2 **Carolina:**   Let me see. Oh yeah, that's retarded. [*Laughs*]

(6)
1 **Jesús:**   Should I draw fire?
2 **Melissa:**   That would be cool, yeah.

3 **Jesús:**   Here – fire.
4 **Melissa:**   Cool! Now draw like ice or something. And then plants. Or snow or something.

(7)
1 **P.A.**   [*Public address announcement*]: Queremos recordarles que hoy en la noche tenemos una cena pot luck/
2 **Carolina:**   [*Quietly to tablemates*] I'm not going.
3 **P.A.:**   Va a ser divertido y la comida va a ser rica.
4 **Carolina:**   Whatever.

(8)   [*José threw a piece of paper into the garbage from a distance*]
Otto: [*Imitating a sports announcer*] Tennessee goes for it! Tennessee wins!

(9)
1 **Sharon:**   Otto, stop it!
2 **Otto:**   That's what you do to me.
3 **Sharon:**   I don't go like this. [*Shakes table*]
4 **Otto:**   Yeah you do, see, you're doing it right now. Yeah, you do that. See? You just did it!
5 **Sharon:**   I was just crossing my legs.
6 **Otto:**   Me too.

There were several instances in which Matt's peer English turns responded to a peer's criticism (Example 10) or sought to position him as superior to his peers (Example 11). It also included slang like "dude."

(10)
1 **Otto:**   [*Looking at Matt's drawing*] That looks funny.
2 **Matt:**   *You* look funny. [*Laughs*]

(11)   [*The tape recorder sat between Delia and Matt. Delia reached out to move it closer to herself*]
Matt: Leave it there, Delia. She wants to interview me, not you. I'm smarter than you. I'm smarter than all y'all.

Melissa's peer English was less frequent than that of her peers. She sometimes used English to manage interactions and materials (Examples 12–14). Chapter 5 will expand on how such turns by Melissa positioned her among peers as excessively work focused and mildly antisocial.

(12)   [*Carlos is whistling*]
Melissa: Stop it. I'm trying to write.

(13)
1 **Melissa:**   Heather, um, sorry, but I don't, want to let you borrow that, because I don't want you to lose the top like you, lost yours.
2 **Heather:**   No, I don't want to borrow it anyway.

(14)   [*Melissa had not completed her homework the night before because her father had her backpack. A classmate was collecting homework and reminded her to hand in both parts*]
1 **Melissa:**   I didn't even *do* the other one!
2 **Heather:**   [*Slightly annoyed at Melissa's tone*] Oh, sorry.
3 **Melissa:**   Sorry, I'm kind of crabby this morning.
4 **Carlos:**   You're always crabby.

Some of Otto's peer English turns were made privately to peers during teacher-fronted and appeared to position him as knowing the subject matter:

(15)   [*Students were guessing the title of a story*]
1 **Ms. Torres:**   Se llama "La mujer hambrienta."
2 **Otto:**   I was close.

(16)
1 **Carlos:**   El círculo de la vida.
2 **Ms. Torres:**   Es como el círculo de la vida, perfecto, Carlos.
3 **Otto:**   Mother Nature.

(17)
1 **Ms. Torres:**   Aquí la cazuela, porque está cocinando. So está cocinando, no tenían estufa.
2 **Otto:**   [*To José*] Just like in the movie *Bulldog*. They're roasting him.

Sometimes during groupwork it became evident that Otto had not understood the material. It was typical of him to deny this or blame it on a classmate, as in Example 18:

(18)   [*The class had been discussing "montículos" (burial mounds) for a week*]
1 **Otto:**   Carlos, what are *montículos*?
2 **Melissa:**   What?! You don't know what it is? [*Otto shakes head "No"*]
3 **Carlos:**   Jesus Christ! They're like mountains where they bury/
4 **Otto:**   [*to Melissa*] That's what I asked you and you said no.

At other times he did understand the material and seemed glad to explain it to a tablemate:

(19)
1 **Heather:** Wait, when a person died, they would, um, se quemaban/
2 **Otto:** They would paint them red, then put 'em in a house, burn the house down, then put dirt, and then do it again.

Appendix 4.C contains a summary of 15 different topics and functions that were identified in students' peer English. Peer discourse also forms a large part of the ongoing production of students' classroom identities, which will be further explored in Chapter 5.

Peer Spanish

Compared with students' 738 peer English turns, only 348 peer turns were in Spanish. Peer Spanish was 56% on-task and 35% for management. On-task peer Spanish often related to vocabulary questions (Examples 20 and 21). Other peer Spanish turns served to manage academic tasks (Example 22).

(20)
1 **Melissa:** Caro, ¿qué rima con "norte"?
2 **Carolina:** Corte... ¿Norte? Corte, bote...
3 **Melissa:** ¿Huh?
4 **Carolina:** Bote, um... [*6-second pause*] Yo tengo una lista.

(21)
1 [*Allison is reading José's summary*] La guerra paró y firmaron un contrato y/
2 **Matt:** No. La guerra no paró.
3 **José:** That's what it says.
4 **Matt:** Yeah, la guerra paró *cuando* firmaron el contrato.
5 **José:** Oh.

(22) [*Students are claiming the pages of a novel that they wanted to use as the basis for their illustrations.*]
1 **Jesús:** Yo quiero cuarenta y nueve...
2 **Matt:** ¿Cincuenta y cincuenta y uno?
3 **Jesús:** Hm?
4 **Matt:** Fifty and fifty-one?

Over half of Matt's Spanish peer turns in the corpus were during one social studies class in January, when the teacher had been visiting their table often. Despite her frequent reprimands, the students continued to use a good deal of English (Example 23). On that day, Matt and José made a game out of "correcting" other students' uses of English, and four of his peer Spanish turns that day were like Example 24:

(23)   [*Students were deciding how many times they could vote for the best summary*]
1   **Adam:**   ¿Quién vota para yo?
2   **Matt:**   You can only... tú sólo puedes votar una vez.
3   **José:**   Una vez.
4   **Allison:**   Dos veces.
5   **Jose:**   Who goes for una?
6   **Matt:**   Dos. Dos. Una. Puedes votar una vez.
7   **José:**   Yeah, but we got...
8   **Adam:**   Matty?
9   **Matt:**   No, you can't vote again.
10   **Allison:**   I changed my vote.
11   **Matt:**   No, no, you can't.
12   **Allison:**   Revote!

(24)
1   **Student:**   Right.
2   **Matt:**   No se dice "right," se dice "es verdad". [*Laughter*]

Melissa had the highest percentage of peer talk in Spanish (50%) of all four students. Her peer Spanish was used 50% of the time to manage activities: (Example 25):

(25)   [*Melissa is looking for a black marker*]
1   **Melissa:**   La maestra dije que podemos usar los marcadores normales. ¿Dónde está mi negro?
2   **Jesus:**   Doesn't look like you can.
3   **Melissa:**   Sí, pero la maestra dije que podemos. Yo no sé dónde está mi, mi negro y necesitamos el negro.
4   **Jesús:**   How about a Sharpie? [*brand of marker*]

It was interesting that Melissa sometimes mixed English into a peer exchange that she had begun in Spanish (Example 26). This may have been because the topic was management or off task, as in this example, and also may have reflected a desire to fit in with her peers. Although she used a good deal of Spanish with her peers, perhaps the English that she used with them represented her attempts to invest in an identity as a friendly peer rather than as too much of a rule follower or rule imposer.

(26)
1　**Melissa:**　Hey. Yo voy a tener un *Playstation*.
2　**Jesús:**　Oh, cool.
3　**Melissa:**　Free.
4　**Matt:**　From who?
5　**Melissa:**　Uh, maybe. Last year, mi hermanito y yo estábamos selling chocolate bars para su baseball team, mi hermanito, y despues, y, we sold the most and so we're getting a Playstation.
6　**Matt:**　Does it come with... what games are you going to get?

Of Otto's peer Spanish turns, 40% were made during teacher-fronted lessons. Several of these were quiet repetitions of what others said, which appeared to be a strategy of his that allowed him to produce some Spanish:

(27)
1　**Ms. Torres:**　¿Quiénes eran las personas importantes, Adam?
2　**Adam:**　Los jefes.
3　**Otto:**　[*quietly*] Los jefes.

(28)
1　**Ms. Torres:**　¿Qué otras cosas hacemos de maíz?
2　**Carlos:**　Tortillas.
3　**Otto:**　[*quietly*] Tortillas.

Similarly to the other three students, Otto had only six off-task peer Spanish turns. In one of these turns, he was absentmindedly singing to himself a Cuban song the students had learned in chorus. Two more of his off-task Spanish turns are contained in Example 29 (Lines 3 and 5) on a day when Otto was particularly aware of the teacher's presence:

(29)
1　**Otto:**　José, I'm left handed. I'm left and right handed.
2　**José [Spanish L1]:**　Write "peligroso."
3　**Otto:**　How do you spell "pelig/"?
4　**José:**　Like this, like this. [*Writes the word, shows it to Otto. Otto copies the word with both hands*]
5　**Otto:**　See? I wrote it with my left. Let me write it with my right. [*Students are quietly writing; 6 seconds silence*]

6 **Otto:** Eso es como escribe "peligrosas" con el... *right.* Eso es como escribe "peligrosos" con el *left.* José, mira, "peligrosas."
7 **Ms. Torres:** [*To entire class*] Estoy escuchando a muchos niños hablar inglés.
8 **Otto:** José, mira.

On a few occasions, a student responded to a peer's English in Spanish. Carolina did this 13 times in the corpus, four of which were directed to her classmate Moisés. She appeared to use Spanish to get him back on task and to chastise him for distracting his tablemates (Example 30):

(30) [*Moisés is off task, making a cartoon drawing of a person*]
1 **Moisés:** What color hair?
2 **Carolina:** No importa, no debes de estar haciendo eso ahora.

Additionally, on a few occasions, Carolina told on other students for using English (Example 31). The cases I observed appeared to be motivated by the fact that the other student was off task and distracting her.

(31)
1 **Jesús:** Teos' car, on the back, on the back bumper.
2 **Carolina:** [*To teacher*] Él está hablando, él está hablando inglés.

Melissa responded in Spanish to a peer's English 47 times, much more often than the other three students. However, 79% of those turns were during one lesson in March during which Melissa made several references to the tape recorder at the group's desks. However, the other 21% of her Spanish responses to peer English turns took place on five different days, indicating that it was not an uncommon practice for her. In Examples 32 and 33, we see that as her peers chatted in English, Melissa insisted on using Spanish, both before and after her peers' English turns:

(32)
1 **Matt:** Where's my thingy?
2 **Melissa:** ¿Qué?
3 **Matt:** You don't have to do it exactly like she did.
4 **Melissa:** Ya sé, pero tengo que hacerlo un poco.
5 **Matt:** No, podemos hacer otro... otro *board.*
6 **Melissa:** Tenemos que hacerlos así porque es como un... *filmstrip.*
7 **Matt:** Movies don't go like that!

(33)
1 **Jesús:** Are you done? You're fast. That's because you get a hold of everything before us. That's not fair.
2 **Melissa:** [*Talking about a marker*] Eso no sirve.
3 **Jesús:** Oh cool. You messed up.
4 **Melissa:** No, eso no sirve.
5 **Jesús:** Oh, that's why it looks messed up.

Melissa requested that other students use Spanish (by saying "Español" or "Español, por favor") 10 times in this corpus and seven additional times in my field notes, much more than the other three students. She also corrected another student's Spanish five times (Example 34):

(34)
1 **Ms. Torres:** Otto, busca el tuyo, por favor.
2 **Otto:** No estás en mi escritorio.
3 **Ms. Torres:** ¿No *estás*? Yo sé que yo no *estoy* en tu escritorio.
4 **Otto:** No sé... no estás.
5 **Ms. Torres:** Yo sé que yo no *estoy* en tu escritorio.
6 **Melissa:** [*to Otto*] No *está*.

Some of Melissa's turns presented thus far illustrate her intense academic focus: quieting other students, requesting that they use Spanish, concern over the proper way to carry out a task, and resistance to sharing materials with classmates (which was corroborated one day by Heather after Melissa did not share something with a classmate: "She's been like that since second grade"). These examples also indicate that Jesús, Heather, and Carlos sometimes positioned Melissa as an undesirable tablemate. In Chapter 5, I will expand on the observations that Melissa received a lot of familial support for her Spanish acquisition as well as a great deal of praise for speaking it, and had also developed a strong identification with her uncle's family in Mexico. This may be what prompted her to swim against the peer English tide; she commented that the "whole point" of being at Inter-American was to learn Spanish. In addition to her investment in her identity as a Spanish speaker, she was also an extremely meticulous student who promptly completed all assignments well and who was very concerned with following rules, including those of classroom language use.

Only two times in the corpus did Otto request that a peer use Spanish. Both times were during the same class period when he saw the teacher approaching his group:

(35)

1 **Sharon:** Did you see "Who Wants to Be a Millionaire" yesterday?
3 **Otto:** No, it's "Who Wants to Be... Who Wants to *Marry*."
4 **Sharon:** No, I didn't see that one. Did you see on channel seven, "Who Wants to Be a Millionaire"?
5 **Otto:** He won the million dollars.
6 **Sharon:** He was about to. Man, he's dumb, right? He shoulda, um, he shoulda advanced. It was this question, I don't know/
7 **Otto:** [*Saw the teacher approaching*] ¡Español!
8 **José [Spanish L1]:** Then you didn't see it. You have to know the question.
9 **Otto:** ¡Español!

In summary, off-task peer Spanish, unlike off-task peer English, had a very limited set of functions. Significantly, there were no references to TV, music, or movies, nor any fighting, teasing, or slang in Spanish, and, in fact, most instances of peer Spanish appeared not to carry out an authentic communicative function. That most social talk was conducted in English and most Spanish was used with the teacher and for academic topics echoes Tarone and Swain's (1995) suggestion that a type of diglossia exists in one-way immersion classrooms.[4] In my study, both L1 and L2 students used English for the majority of social functions, although Melissa presented a special case because the identity she sought to promote was precisely that of a Spanish speaker, which, combined with her intense academic focus, outweighed any need to perform social functions such as playing or talking about adolescent themes (Melissa made only 42 off-task comments, compared with an average of 90 for the other 3 students). However, Tarone and Swain also claimed that immersion students use their L1 because they lack the vocabulary to carry out social functions in their L2. They argued that if immersion students knew how to use the L2 for social functions, they would do so.

This study suggests an alternate interpretation. Even if the students had been able to carry out these social functions in Spanish, doing so would have prevented them from establishing themselves within their English-preferring peer group. In other words, it would not be enough for the Spanish-L1 portion of the student body to be able to carry out social functions in Spanish because English was clearly the dominant language for the majority of students and therefore for peer interaction. In fact, my speech samples suggest that Carolina and Matt were indeed proficient enough to have carried out many of these social functions in Spanish except for slang (given the nature of adolescent slang, children who grow up in the

United States are unlikely to know much Spanish slang) although stronger verification such as a translation exercise would be necessary.

Summary

Table 4.13 summarizes the contexts that produced the highest percentages of Spanish use, as well as the percent of the total Spanish turns that they represented. Table 4.14 presents the contexts that saw the lowest percentages of Spanish use. Tables 4.15 and 4.16 do the same for English.

Table 4.13 shows that of all the Spanish turns in the data, the majority were on task, directed to the teacher, and during teacher-fronted lessons. Although groupwork may result in longer turns and more elaborate speech styles for ESL students (Liu, 1994; Willett, 1995), what seemed to promote more Spanish use in this classroom was having the teacher as an interlocutor. Additionally, 95% of all Spanish turns in the data were on task, suggesting that the more students stay on task, the more Spanish they will use. Students used the least amount of Spanish when off task, when speaking to peers, for managing tasks, and during groupwork.

In practically a mirror image of the Spanish data, students used the most English when off task and when speaking to peers, and the least English when they were selected to speak and with the teacher.

Selectedness

When students took public speech turns during teacher-fronted lessons, they could do so in one of three ways. They could bid for the floor and be selected to speak by the teacher, they could shout out an answer without first having been selected, or they could be called on by the teacher even though they had not bid to speak. The first two types of turns are voluntary, and the third type is involuntary. I used the term *selectedness* to code the two

Table 4.13 Greatest Spanish use

	Selected	*Interlocutor = teacher*	*Unselected*	*On task*	*Teacher fronted*
% Spanish use	96%	82%	81%	67%	67%
% of all Spanish turns in corpus ($N = 1141$)	8% (93)	70% (793)	60% (681)	88% (999)	66% (751)

Note: Totals do not equal 100%.

Table 4.14 Least Spanish use

	Off task	Interlocutor = peers	Manage ment	Group work
% Spanish use	16%	32%	36%	42%
% of all Spanish turns in corpus (N = 1141)	4% (51)	30% (347)	7% (81)	34% (390)

Note: Totals do not equal 100%.

types of voluntary turns: *selected* meant that a student had bid for the floor and been chosen to speak, and *unselected* meant the student had shouted out an answer without being selected.

Table 4.17 shows that during teacher-fronted lessons, 87% of the students' turns were unselected and 13% were selected. When shouting out, students used Spanish 81% of the time, but when they had been selected, their Spanish use rose to 96%. I propose that this increase in Spanish use resulted because, after taking the trouble to bid for the floor and winning it over other students' bids, students felt more pressure to use Spanish than if they had just shouted out their answers.

Although selected turns constituted only 13% of the students' turns to the teacher, the fact that 96% of those turns were made in Spanish prompted me to examine the students' bidding strategies and how often they were successful. This seemed important because students who were granted the floor more often were more likely to produce Spanish in this classroom. Table 4.18 shows how often the four focal students made verbal[55] bids to speak and had their bids selected.

Carolina and Matt (both Spanish L1) produced more verbal bids than Melissa and Otto (Spanish L2), which may be because of their higher Spanish proficiency. That is, they may have bid more often because they felt more confident in their ability to give a well-formed answer. However, Melissa was orally more fluent than Otto, yet made only a quarter as many bids

Table 4.15 Greatest English use

	Off task	Interlocutor = peers	Manage- ment	Group work
% English use	84%	68%	64%	58%
% of all English turns in corpus (N = 909)	28% (255)	81% (738)	16% (141)	59% (537)

Note: Totals do not equal 100%.

Table 4.16 Least English use

	Selected to speak	Interlocutor teacher	Unselected (shouted out)	On task	Teacher fronted
% English use	4%	18%	19%	33%	33%
% of all English turns in corpus ($N = 909$)	0.4% (4)	19% (171)	18% (161)	54% (489)	41% (374)

Note: Totals do not equal 100%.

as he did, so Spanish proficiency was not the only factor in bidding frequency. This section presents a brief description of each student's salient strategies for bidding and for keeping the floor. It also illustrates several instances in which the teacher uptook students' contributions. Uptaking, the incorporation of a student's answer into a subsequent teacher question or comment (Cazden, 1988: 85), merits attention because it indicates the teacher's ratification of students' contributions, which may contribute to their continued participation.

Carolina

Carolina's verbal bids were successful 46% of the time. Her bidding strategies may have been partially responsible for her success in gaining the floor. Many students bid by shouting "Ooh!" while raising their hands, and Carolina's "Ooh's!" were often simply louder than those of her classmates. But in Example 36, her use of the Spanish word "Como" as if beginning to produce an answer may be what won her the floor over students who simply raised their hands or shouted "Ooh!":

Table 4.17 Selected turns

Turns directed to the teacher $N = 966$	Selected $N = 124$ (13%)		Unselected (shout out) $N = 842$ (87%)
	Voluntary $N = 97$	Involuntary $N = 27$	Voluntary $N = 842$
Spanish	96% (93)	74% (20)	81% (681)
English	4% (4)	26% (7)	19% (161)

Table 4.18 Verbal bids and selected turns

	Carolina (Spanish L1)	Matt (Spanish L1)	Melissa (Spanish L2)	Otto (Spanish L2)
Verbal bids $N = 74$	28 (38% of corpus)	24 (32% of corpus)	4 (5% of corpus)	18 (25% of corpus)
% of Verbal bids selected	46% (13/28)	61% (14/24)	75% (3/4)	22% (4/18)

(36)
1 **Ms. Torres:** ¿Alguien puede decir lo que es *campesinos*? [*Several students raised hands and shouted "Ooh!"*]
2 **Carolina:** Oh, como/
3 **Ms. Torres:** Carolina.
4 **Carolina:** ¿Alguien que, um, que cuida la tierra?

In addition to frequently selecting Carolina's bids, Ms. Torres accepted being cut off by Carolina during teacher-fronted lessons (Example 37):

(37) [*Ms. Torres was explaining the events leading up to the celebration of* Cinco de Mayo].
1 **Ms. Torres:** Era un grupo pequeño de mexicanos, que este era el general Zaragoza/
2 **Carolina:** Oh, y ellos sabían más la tierra, porque los franceses/
3 **Ms. Torres:** Por eso ganaron.

Carolina was very active during teacher-fronted lessons. In addition to frequently uptaking Carolina's questions, comments, and answers into the lesson, Ms. Torres tended to honor her requests to repeat something or to wait before continuing. Her frequent verbal comments were met with approval by the teacher, who often granted her the floor by either calling on her or letting her cut in. Carolina appeared to be a catalyst for teacher-fronted lessons because she made frequent on-task comments in Spanish.

Melissa

Melissa made only four verbal bids during the lessons in this corpus but was selected to speak 20 times. Three of those four times was she selected in response to a verbal bid, indicating that the teacher responded 17 times to her hand-raising bids. Her few verbal bids consisted of calling out the teacher's name, announcing that she had a question, or shouting "No, yo sé" (Example 38):

(38)
1 **Ms. Torres:** ¿Qué se celebra el cinco de mayo?
2 **Carolina:** La ind{i}pendencia de/
3 **Melissa:** ¡'No!
4 **Otto:** La independencia de México.
5 **Melissa:** No, yo sé.
[*Ms. Torres looked at Melissa, allowing her to continue*]
6 **Melissa:** Um, cuando um/ [*Other students began talking*]
7 **Ms. Torres:** Shh, brevemente, les voy a dar un minuto porque Melissa les explica.
8 **Melissa:** Cuando los franceses, um, vinieron a, a, a, a México y, um, lo tra, como tenían un, una guerra, y, y um, los mexicanos no tenían muchos, um, weapons/
9 **Ms. Torres:** Armas.
10 **Melissa:** Sí, armas, y los franceses tenían muchas. Pero los, um, mexicanos ganaron, con los armas/
11 **Ms. Torres:** Sí, los mexicanos ganaron, pero/

Although the teacher responded to Melissa's hand raising 17 times in the corpus, this was not the most efficient way to get the floor in this classroom. Melissa's hand raising often lost out to a student who shouted out the answer. On other occasions, Melissa did say an answer aloud but it was too quiet for the teacher to hear it. Sometimes it appeared to be Melissa's difficulties with Spanish that caused her to lose the floor. In Example 39, she attempted to give the answer "swamp" but did not know how to say it in Spanish. Preferring to circumlocute in Spanish to describe the concept, she lost the reward of giving the correct answer as another student shouted out the English translation:

(39)
1 **Ms. Torres:** ¿Quién sabe lo que es?
2 **Melissa:** Es como, cuando... [*two-second pause*]
3 **Student:** Swamp.
4 **Ms. Torres:** Sí.
5 **Melissa:** That's what I was trying to say.

On a few occasions, Melissa would resort to English to get her meaning across:

(40)
1   **Ms. Torres:**   La obsidiana, ¿la conocen? Es una piedra suave, negra/
2   **Melissa:**   Si, yo creo. Usan para el... *arrowheads.*
3   **Ms. Torres:**   Lo usan para hacer las puntas de las lanzas.

Matt

Matt made 24 verbal bids, a level of verbal bidding higher than everyone except Carolina, and his verbal bids were the most successful at 61%. Like Carolina, his bidding strategies may have been partially responsible for his success in gaining the floor. In Examples 41 and 42, his use of Spanish words as if beginning a turn in Lines 2 and 5 appears to have won him the floor over students who simply raised their hands or shouted "Ooh!":

(41)
1   **Ms. Torres:**   Y ¿quiénes eran ellos, Delia?
2   **Matt:**   Los que...
3   **Delia:**   Um, vivían en las montañas....
4   **Ms. Torres:**   ¿Vivían en las montañas? [*Several students shout "Oh!" and raise their hands*]
5   **Matt:**   Que... Los, los que..
6   **Ms.**   Torres: Matt.

(42)
1   **Ms. Torres:**   No, no un RE-formatorio. ¿Qué es un OR-fanatorio? [*Otto raises hand and shouts, "Oh!"*]
2   **Matt:**   Que...
3   **Ms. Torres:**   Es diferente.
4   **Matt:**   Que, que, um...
5   **Ms. Torres:**   Matt.
6   **Matt:**   Uh, que cuando, sus... sus... uh, sus papá/
7   **Student next to Matt:**   Padres.
8   **Matt:**   /padres se mueren/
9   **Ms. Torres:**   Exacto, cuando no tienen/
10   **Matt:**   Y no tienen nadie.

Matt employed several of the same strategies for getting and keeping the floor as Carolina, including asking the teacher to wait for him (as in Line

6 of Example 43, which was successful even in English) and interrupting her with increased volume (Example 44):

(43)
1 **Ms. Torres:** Matt, también.
2 **Matt:** Que, ah, de...no me acuerdo su primer nombre...um... Austin. Que/
3 **Ms.** Torres: Moses Austin.
4 **Matt:** Yeah, Moses Austin. Y, um, él, um, fue el que, um/
5 **Ms.** Torres: OK, alguien más que ayude a Matt.
6 **Matt:** *No, no, wait. No.* Después de eso, um, que Marcus y XX Whitman y Henry Elis... Spaldin fundaron una misión de Walla Walla.
7 **Ms. Torres:** No, estás confundido.

(44)
1 **Ms. Torres:** OK, Matt.
2 **Matt:** Porque, el, porque, he locked em... Porque se metió en el cl...eh, closet, y estaban, y no tenían qué comer. Y estaban hartos de comer/
3 **Student:** No, se comían hot dogs.
4 **Ms. Torres:** OK, y ¿cuál/
Matt: Y ESTABA, Y ESTABA, y estaba harto de, estaban los niños hartos de comer lo mismo.

Otto

Table 4.18 showed that Otto made 18 verbal bids, only four of which were successful, and he had only seven nonverbal bids selected. Otto was selected half as often as Carolina and only a third as often as Matt; not only his verbal bids but also his hand raising were more likely to be passed over by the teacher. He did occasionally get his questions uptaken using similar strategies as Carolina and Matt – interrupting, stating that he had a question, or beginning to form a question (Line 2 of Example 45).

(45)
1 **Ms. Torres:** ¿De qué creen que vamos a estar hablando ahorita? Hay tres columnas/
2 **Otto:** Oh, de los/
3 **Ms. Torres:** Otto.
4 **Otto:** ¿De los aztecas?
5 **Ms. Torres:** ¿ Allí dice de los aztecas?
6 **Otto and other students:** No.

Often, like Melissa, Otto's less fluent Spanish appeared to be what caused Ms. Torres to award the floor to someone else. In Example 46, he had to be insistent to get his question answered:

(46)

1 **Ms. Torres:** OK, el exámen va a ser sobre el capítulo cinco y seis, y las palabras, el vocabulario que tienen.

2 **Otto:** Esto vas a ser los... va, um... esto vas/

3 **Ms. Torres:** Sí, Alison.

4 **Alison:** ¿También las palabras de capítulo cuatro?

5 **Ms. Torres:** No, ésas no las contamos.

6 **Otto:** ¿Eso va a ser para el *test*?

7 **Ms. Torres:** No.

8 **Otto:** ¿Qué vas a serlos? [*Probably trying to say, "What will be?"*]

9 **Ms. Torres:** Las palabras que ustedes están haciendo.

Sometimes Otto's enthusiasm to participate during teacher fronted lessons got him in trouble because he lacked appropriateness. Ms. Torres did not usually employ a strict turn-taking system, and students often shouted out answers. But sometimes Ms. Torres did request hand raising, such as in Example 16. She began this lesson by saying, "No quiero empezar lo mismo que ayer. Si saben la respuesta, levanten su mano." Since Otto insisted on shouting out, his turn in Line 14 was reprimanded even though it was in Spanish:

(47)

1 **Ms. Torres:** ¿Thomas Jefferson qué?

2 **Otto:** [*With hand raised, but not selected*] Él era un... pres/

3 **Ms. Torres:** [*annoyed*] Levanten su <u>ma</u>no. ¿Qué hizo, Heather? ¿Qué hizo Thomas Jefferson? [*No answer. Otto still had his hand raised*] Otto.

4 **Otto:** Era un presidente.

5 **Ms. Torres:** Era un presidente, ¿de dónde? [*Carolina begins bidding by shouting "OH!" very loudly. Others are raising hands too*]

6 **Otto:** De Estados Unidos.

7 **Ms. Torres:** OK, en ese tiempo, Thomas Jefferson era presidente de Estados Unidos.¿Y? [*Students are bidding loudly*]

8 **Otto:** Y compró, um, los, um, the Louisiana, la territorio.

9 **Ms. Torres:** El territorio de Louisiana, ¿a quién?

10 **Otto:** De..del, um/ [*Many students shout "¡Oh!"*]

11 **Ms. Torres:** Shh, levanten su mano. ¿A quién, Adam?.

12 **Adam:** A [*English pronunciation*] Napoleon.

13   **Ms. Torres:**   Y ¿quién es Napoleón? Cindy.
14   **Cindy:**   Es el, um, el emperador de España.
15   **Ms. Torres:**   ¿¡De España?! ¿De dónde es Napoleón? Adam.
16   **Adam:**   De Francia.
17   **Ms. Torres:**   Y ¿por qué tuvo que comprárselo a él?
18   **Otto:**   Porque necesitas más/
19   **Ms. Torres:**   ¡Otto, por favor! Contrólate. José.

Although Otto was bright and participated often in classroom activities, in Chapter 5, I will expand on observations that Ms. Torres considered Otto's behavior problematic. This very likely influenced her decisions to grant him the floor. She felt that he talked too much (yet he made approximately the same number of turns as Carolina), used too much English (yet it was exactly the same amount as Matt), and went off task too often (but he was off task slightly less often than Matt). Otto did, however, use the most teacher English (Table 4.9 showed that he used 29% English with the teacher, compared with the other students' 14%), which I argue led to a circular problem when Otto would bid for the floor: the teacher, convinced that Otto would use English or concerned that he would take the lesson off-task, or both, called on him less often than the other students, which denied him the opportunity to practice and improve his Spanish and thus acquire enough Spanish to be able to participate successfully. The perceptions of the teacher were ultimately very important in determining Otto's classroom experience (cf. Jackson & Costa, 1974; Tucker & Lambert, 1973).

In summary, the L1 students Carolina and Matt appeared to be more successful at gaining the public floor than the L2 students. They bid aggressively and loudly and more often used actual Spanish words instead of "Ooh!" Given that language production is a central component of language development (Swain 1985), Spanish L1 students may possibly have reaped more linguistic benefits than their Spanish L2 counterparts in this classroom because they were more successful at creating opportunities to speak it. That the Spanish L2 students were less successful at verbally gaining the floor suggests that this teacher expected and rewarded nativelike participation during teacher-fronted lessons. This finding somewhat contradicts that of Delgado-Larocco (1998) and Valdés (1997), who claimed that dual immersion serves the needs of Spanish L2 students more than the needs of Latinos.

Conclusions

This chapter has illustrated both the quantity and the quality of students' language production during over 12 hours of recorded classroom interactions. Not only did they use Spanish just 56% overall, far less than the 100% expected during Spanish lessons, but the Spanish they produced was for a limited set of functions and topics, supporting Tarone and Swain's (1995) observations that immersion classrooms exhibit signs of diglossia. Why might this be the case?

Merino (1991) proposed that the geographical location of the school could affect language use in classrooms. Reviewing the findings of Chesterfield *et al.* (1983), she suggested that teachers and students in Corpus Christi use less Spanish than their counterparts in Milwaukee because communities close to the Mexican border have greater access to Spanish, causing teachers to feel they should emphasize English instead. On the other hand, the teachers in predominately English-speaking Milwaukee may have purposefully used more Spanish because children had less access to it. Although Inter-American Magnet School is in Chicago, the third largest Hispanic city in the country (which according to this logic might lead to English use in school), it is located in Lakeview, a predominately white, upper-class, and English-speaking neighborhood.

According to Genesee (1987: 96), no direct comparisons have been made of L2 achievement in immersion programs in different geographical settings, although Swain concluded that there was little relationship between the community and L2 acquisition in immersion schools (1981: 118). What was likely more significant in this study than the school's location was that 45% of the Latino students arrived to the school already knowing English. The presence of these bilingual students did not lead to an increase in the student Spanish use found in fifth-grade one-way immersion classrooms (Broner, 2000; Tarone and Swain, 1995). In fact, the student in our study who used the most English was actually Spanish L1. Both L1 and L2 students in this study had more frequent models of native speaker Spanish than if all of students had been Spanish L2, but this did not translate into greater overall use of Spanish.

Another likely factor in students' language use was the bilingual relationship between the students and Ms. Torres (cf. Parker *et al.* 1995). In the "ideal" immersion design described by Cohen and Swain (1976), students had a monolingual Spanish relationship with the Spanish teacher. A future study in a dual immersion classroom in which students have a monolingual relationship with the teacher, such as in sixth-grade social studies at Inter-American, might reveal greater Spanish use than found in my study. This idea will be explored in greater detail in the concluding chapter.

There may be gender explanations for immersion classroom use as well. Among these focal students, the girls used Spanish in 66% of their turns while the boys used Spanish in just 47% of theirs. Gender was more significant than L1, because there was no apparent relationship between students'

L1 and their classroom language use; it was not the case that Spanish L1 students used more Spanish than Spanish L2 students.

Finally, this chapter suggested that the right to speak was not evenly distributed among these four students, with the L2 students being selected to speak more often than the L1 students. McKay and Wong (1996: 578) claimed that the unevenly distributed right to speak was acutely felt by immigrant students who struggled to acquire language proficiency while simultaneously negotiating their identities. I believe that Otto's limited Spanish proficiency created a similar struggle. In the next chapter, I further propose that the language use of the four students in this study was related to issues of their identity investments, and that each student had identity investments that either inhibited or motivated their decisions to use Spanish in the classroom.

Appendix 4.A
Transcription Conventions

Speaker was cut off. Example:

1 **Matt:**   Después, um, um, the plane, como, el avión /
2 **Ms. Torres:** ¿'Aterrizó?

... Short pause, ½ second to 1½ seconds. Example:
La que... Estados Unidos tenía con México.

[*Italics*] The text in italics between brackets is describing the context or actions. Example:
[*Reading Matt's summary*]
[*Laughs*]

Italics Speaker placed stress on the word or syllable. Example:
Yeah, la guerra paró *cuando* firmaron el contrato.
¿Her*mano*? Her*mana*.

XX Speech was inaudible. Example:
Oh, for the fourth-grade XX or whatever?

(*word*) Speech not entirely audible; an approximation of what was heard. Example:
Lo usan para hacer las puntas de las (lanchas).

Appendix 4.B
Variables

Language

There are four main categories under the variable *language*:

Spanish = Turns either 100% in Spanish or containing a single English lexical item.

English = Turns either 100% in English or containing a single Spanish lexical item.

Intrasententiallyl codeswitched = Sentences containing either a matrix language (ML) or an embedded language (EL) island (Myers-Scotton, 1993). Such turns were con eliminated from the corpus.

Null = Nonlanguage bids to get the floor such as "Oh!" as well as turns that consisted of only a name like "Juan" or "Emily."

Class

This refers to whether the interaction took place during Spanish language arts, Spanish social studies, or a transition between classes.

Participant structure

Teacher-fronted = The teacher is at the front of the room leading classroom discussion. Students are usually expected to bid to speak publicly (although in my study they often shouted out answers and comments without bidding or being selected) and are usually not supposed to chat with each other privately.

Groupwork = Students are engaged in activities at their tables that either required or permitted them to talk to one another freely, although sometimes students are expected to work individually and silently.

Interlocutor

Teacher = When students answered questions aloud during teacher fronted lessons (loud enough to be heard by video camera in corner of room), or spoke to the teacher when she was near their desks.

Peers = When students directed turns to their classmates only.

Selectedness

Selected = The student bid to speak and was selected by the teacher.

Unselected = The student shouted out without being called on.

Topic

On-task = Directly related to the academic content of the lesson.
Off-task = Not related to the lesson in any way
Management = Not related to academic content, but manages the completion of an on-task activity.
Unknown = Inaudible or impossible to decide.

Gender

There were two girls and two boys in this study.

L1

One boy and one girl were Spanish L1 and the other boy and girl were Spanish L2.

Appendix 4.C
Functions and Topics of Students' English

Topics

Movies

During academic classes: *Bulldog, Chuckie, Chuckie's Bride.*
When suggesting movies for the class trip bus ride, students used English.

TV shows

"Who wants to be a millionaire," "Reese's"

Popular culture

Pokemon, Power Rangers, Calvin and Hobbes cartoon book, Sony Playstation.

Music/Radio stations

Britney Spears, Savage Garden, B96, Santana, The Beat, OJ.

Addresses and phone numbers

"You live by Albany Street?"
"Hey, Matt, what's your phone number?"

Activities outside of school

"I like going to bed at nine o'clock."
"I watch the news"
Great America ("I've been on every ride like three times.")
"Have you been to St. Louis?" "Of course. Everybody's white. I like the arch."
"What did she give you? She left the price on it!"
Laser tag

Other classes

"I hope we have gym outside."
"Time for lunch."

Computers

"You could print it autoshutdown. Once it's done printing, it will shut down."

Antischool

"That's what I like about music class, I don't even watch the movies."
" I don't need no schoolwork. Buswork, that's all I know."
"I would say, oh, my tummy hurts."
"Oh, my head hurts. I don't care. Four, five more weeks and school's over."

Sports

"Tennessee goes for it! Tennessee wins!"
Wrestlers: The Rock, Vince McMahon.

Other

"Ms. Solis had a baby."
"Your tag is sticking out."
"You got something in your hair."
"Oh my god."

Functions

Fighting/Arguing

"You keep kicking me."
"Stop doing that!"

"Be like that." "Fine, I will."
"Be quiet!"

Teasing/Sarcasm

"I dare you."
"Delia, you sat at the last seat on the ride. There was a hole in your seat. And it went faster. [*Laughter*]"
"I know that, I just found out." "Wow, finally."
"Boogers, where? You probably put it on there. Just kidding."
"You like her." "No I don't." "Yeah you do."

Playing

"José, I'm stuck to the chair."
"Don't do it, don't do it."

Slang/Informal speech

Crabby, gimme, gonna, I don't wanna, cool, that's dumb, dude, boogers, whatever.

Notes

1. I also taped all 4 students during two English language arts lessons and two English social studies lessons, which confirmed my observations that students never used Spanish during English lessons.
2. I would like to thank Liz Howard at CAL for her assistance. This portion of the work reported herein was supported under the Educational Research and Development Centers Program, PR/Award No. R306A60001 for the Center for Research on Education, Diversity & Excellence, as administered by the Institute for Education Sciences, U.S. Department of Education. However, the contents do not necessarily represent the positions or policies of the National Institute on the Education of At-Risk Students, the Institute for Education Sciences, or the U.S. Department of Education, and the reader should not assume endorsement by the federal government.
3. However, such numerical results are not entirely comparable given the differences among researchers in coding language data.
4. However, this classroom did not appear to be entirely diglossic. Academic topics were carried out in English 32% of the time during these Spanish lessons, and 17% of off-task turns were in Spanish. Given that Ms. Torres taught English lessons to these students in the afternoons, they were accustomed to speaking English with her for academic lessons. Spanish, therefore, was not the only "on task" language of this classroom.
5. Nonverbal bids (raising hand) were too difficult to count accurately, so no attempt has been made to determine how often students' nonverbal bids were granted the floor.

Chapter 5
Identity Investments in Fifth Grade

Investment (Norton, 2000) emphasizes that the overriding purpose of social interactions is for people to construct and present an image of who they are. Similarly, Tarone and Swain (1995) noted that peer interactions serve the primarily social function of locating children in a hierarchy. Their language choices in the classroom must therefore be seen as part of their identity performances. In this chapter, I will explore how investment, identity, and power relations may have contributed to the two L2 learners' Spanish language use and to the two heritage Spanish speakers' continued use and development of their L1. That is, following Norton (2000) and McKay and Wong (1996: 591), I have attempted "to link students' classroom language use to the ongoing production of their identities." I sought threads that were common to all students, but given the personal nature of investment and identity, each student had his or her own configuration of sometimes contradictory attitudes and linguistic behaviors, and each student was differently positioned by classmates and by the teacher. Through these descriptions, I suggest explanations for the classroom language use described in Chapter 4.

In order to explore issues of investment, identity, and power, I reexamined the 16 Spanish lessons as well as the four student interviews, the four parent interviews, the two teacher interviews, eight months of field notes, and students' written questionnaires, looking for themes related to the use of Spanish and English at three levels: in the school, in the classroom, and in the lives of the individual students outside of school. Students' classroom identities are a combination of the characteristics they develop in the home, the expectations and positionings they find at school, and the power they have to conform to or resist those expectations. It was not a goal of this study to identify broad "discourses" about different kinds of students that existed in the school (McKay & Wong, 1996; Freeman, 1998), but two interviews with the teacher added to my observations about how she positioned each of the four students. In this section, I will attempt to paint a portrait of the Spanish use expectations in Ms. Torres' classroom (both the teacher's and the students'), how the students responded to those expectations, and the repercussions of their decisions.

The general questions inspired by this construct included the following: What facets of these four students' identities seemed relevant to their classroom language use? How were their relationships to Spanish constructed in their families and outside of school? What were the relevant positionings and resources within the classroom that affected language use? And under what conditions did students' investments in a particular aspect of their identity seem to motivate them to speak Spanish in class or inhibit them from doing so? These questions will be applied to each student in the upcoming sections as I try to highlight how and why each one created, responded to, and resisted opportunities to speak Spanish.

Following McCollum (1994) one of the classroom "resources" that I considered significant was the floor. In Chapter 4, it was seen that Spanish L1 students were generally more successful at getting and holding the public floor than the L2 students. In addition, Melissa, a more academically oriented L2 student, was more successful than Otto, whom the teacher positioned as having problematic participation patterns and lacking academic focus. Speaking Spanish during teacher-fronted lessons, therefore, allowed students to present an identity as a good student, one who participated acceptably (on-task and in Spanish) and was granted the floor as a result. During groupwork, the "floor" at each table was up for grabs among peers, and because groupwork was not closely monitored by the teacher, there was less pressure to speak Spanish. Choosing to do so seemed to be a strong indication of investment, this time directed to one's peers, in an identity as a Spanish speaker and an academically focused student. We saw that the girls used the most peer Spanish and that while they appeared to occasionally influence their peers to use Spanish, Melissa's peers also appeared to pressure her to use English.

In addition, there were four dimensions that emerged as relevant to students' investments: (a) home language use and support for Spanish, as discussed in parent and student interviews; (b) student attitudes toward the dual immersion school and toward Spanish, which I explored in student interviews and a written questionnaire; (c) the teacher's positioning of the student, which I analyzed through my observations and the teacher interviews; and (d) the student's position within her or his peer group, which I constructed through my observations and student interviews.

Classroom Expectations for Spanish Use

A more detailed focus on Ms. Torres's classroom, especially the roles of and expectations for Spanish use, is essential for understanding the context in which the four focal students navigated their classroom language use as described in Chapter 4.

In an interview, Ms. Torres reflected on the difficulties she had getting students to use Spanish and fulfill the school's language use expectations:

> When they get to fifth grade, they don't want to speak Spanish any-more. Maybe because they spend summer speaking English. Even families that speak Spanish at home, the kids watch TV in English. And I think there isn't very much communication at home with the parents. Because their conversations, there's not . . . a way of communicating aside from school-related things. I think they do everything in English. So they get to fifth grade, where I think it's more structured than the previous years. Supposedly we should teach sixty percent in Spanish, forty percent in English. But I think I'm doing fifty-fifty. [. . .] You've seen me, what a struggle it is . . . "Speak Spanish! Speak Spanish!"

When asked if any student came to mind who almost always used Spanish during Spanish lessons, Ms. Torres responded no, that even students with relatively weak English skills used English during Spanish time. In another interview she commented on how "resource" classes diminished overall Spanish use:

> The frustrating thing is that the fun things for them are all in English. Gym, computers, music. So, it's a challenge for the teacher who's teach-ing Spanish. [If these classes were in Spanish] it might help. As soon as they walk out the door, everything is English, English, English.

I sought to understand how the teacher perceived the value of knowing Spanish in the classroom. When asked if knowing Spanish gained any kind of status for students, Ms. Torres replied:

> No, I don't think so. On the contrary, I think those who . . . are weak in English, I think they'd like to get better. I would like the languages to be equal, but I know it's impossible. Spanish will always be underneath. Because they don't use it much. I don't know how they teach the earlier grades, but I imagine that their Spanish isn't at the same level as if we were in a Hispanic country. No, I don't think it's more or less status, it's just that academically they would have problems. [. . .] I think they don't value the language that much.

This quote indicates that English skills are more important to students' sense of academic worth than their Spanish skills. Ms. Torres clearly stated that she believed the students did not value Spanish enough for it to influ-ence their status in the classroom. In other words, it was not a sought-after *resource* (Norton, 2000). I wondered if a lack of Spanish would create social problems for a student and asked whether a student would be made fun of for having poor Spanish skills, to which Ms. Torres replied:

> No, because it's something that, since they're in preschool, it's respect for the two languages and the cultures. They can never draw attention at all to other students' language. And you see them, when they're reading . . . on the contrary, they help each other say the words correctly.

According to Ms. Torres, good Spanish does not provide status among the students, nor does poor Spanish receive negative attention. Students' comments about each other's classroom Spanish corroborated that it was not a large factor in their popularity. However, Spanish did seem to bestow two specific classroom benefits: choosing to speak it seemed linked to an identity as academically successful, and as seen in Chapter 4, proficiency in spoken Spanish seemed to enable students to be more successful at getting the floor during teacher-fronted lessons.

Research has indicated that more Spanish is used in immersion programs among younger students than older students (Blanco Iglesias *et al.*, 1995; Tarone & Swain, 1995). Although she herself had never taught any classes besides fifth grade, Ms. Torres did her student teaching in a third-grade classroom at Inter-American, so I asked her whether it was easier to get the younger students to use Spanish:

> I don't think so. [. . .] Because there are a lot of kids who are just beginning to learn, especially the American and Afro-American children. And even the Hispanics, because often their parents don't speak Spanish at home. Sometimes I start thinking about those kids [with L2 Spanish] . . . they are going through the same thing as kids who come from other countries, learning languages. That challenge, that they have to learn. But I imagine that if their parents are enthusiastic, they will be, too.

Although her experience did not corroborate research findings of greater Spanish use in younger grades, it is interesting that she felt that parental enthusiasm went a long way in determining a student's willingness to learn Spanish. Despite Ms. Torres' struggles to get students to use Spanish and the lack of value she felt they placed on it, she stated that a school in the United States could not really do much more than Inter-American was doing to promote Spanish use and learning:

> No, I don't think so. I think that basically what we do here, activities that are relevant to their daily lives, because what we try to do first, the

family and all that. And work together. They start with their stronger language, and then they eventually blend together.

When asked how she encouraged students' Spanish use, Ms. Torres responded:

> I've tried to do activities in Spanish and speak only Spanish with them. Math, too. Although sometimes when a concept is a little harder for them, I do it in English so they'll understand. Also, the exams they take are in English, the standardized exams. So vocabulary, we have to develop it little by little.

It was mentioned in Chapter 4 that IAMS teachers throughout the school often used greater amounts of English during Spanish lessons when standardized tests were approaching. One day in Ms. Torres's class, a student asked why they were writing math strategies in English. The teacher responded that the test was in English and she wanted them to learn the English terms, but that they could write their strategies in Spanish if they wanted. A general "No!" arose from the students, but Ms. Torres did not even turn around from the blackboard to assess their responses; it had not been a serious offer. On another occasion, a student asked how many of their out-of-class reading logs should be based on Spanish books. Ms. Torres answered that she knew a lot of students had trouble responding in Spanish and therefore their written reactions to Spanish books would be done during class time, not as homework, and would have a less complex format than the one used in English. When I questioned whether this sent a message that Spanish held less value than English, Ms. Torres explained that many students' homes do not have books in Spanish nor support for reading in Spanish, so teachers tried to ensure that students completed reading and journal responses in their home language in order to cultivate reading habits that would help them be successful in school.

Upon hearing a student use English, Ms. Torres would often insist "¡En español!" ("In Spanish") or "Es hora de español" ("It's Spanish time"). Ms. Torres told me that the previous year she charged students 10 cents each time she caught them using English, and the money was used to buy pizza for the class (which seems more festive than punitive). She said this year's group was too immature for that policy, so instead she used a system of *canicas* (marbles). Students could earn *canicas* for finishing their work on time, for using Spanish during groupwork, and for other behaviors the teacher wanted to reinforce. Students lost *canicas* primarily for using English during Spanish time. Ms. Torres would periodically allow students to trade in their *canicas* for items in a prize box – more *canicas* yielded more prizes. As will be seen in the individual student profiles ahead, students were generally excited to earn _canicas_ and disappointed to lose them. However, their true efficacy as motivators for Spanish use is worth examining. According to one student in Ms. Torres's class, "[Students] don't really care about the _canicas_. Because they don't, like, they're not gonna keep them and stuff. And, like, sometimes when they take it away, they like, they get mad, but then they keep talking in English." An examination of my field notes suggested that _canicas_ were more often taken away for English use than awarded for Spanish use.

Another tactic had students act as language monitors. During Spanish reading lessons at the beginning of the year, each student at the table was assigned a "job" such as locating new vocabulary, making predictions, or forming questions about the plot and characters. One of these jobs was monitoring the language use of the group members. That student was responsible for giving two warnings to tablemates for using English. Upon the third infraction, that student was supposed to inform the teacher. One student told me that when she had this job, she sometimes forgot to monitor her tablemates' language use, while at other times she felt peer pressure not to report English use to the teacher: "You know how Teo and Jesús are friends, and then like if I tell something on Teo, to the teacher, then Jesús will be like, 'It's not him, it's not him,' and stuff." The few times I did observe students telling on each other for using English, it appeared to be a retaliation to get the other student in trouble.

One Monday morning in October, during the class' weekly "town meeting," Ms. Torres became very serious as she explained her frustration at students' use of English during Spanish time. Another Spanish encouragement tactic Ms. Torres began using in January was laminated signs held by magnets to the blackboard. During Spanish lessons the sign said "Hora de español" (Spanish time) and during English lessons it was changed to one that read "English time." Once again, the teacher cited students' frequent use of English during Spanish time as she announced the new sign policy. However, perhaps due to the many demands of running a classroom, the signs were quickly abandoned. During morning Spanish classes, the English sign from the previous afternoon would still be displayed.

Despite these attempts to keep a Spanish-language environment, Ms. Torres herself occasionally made a few turns in English during Spanish lessons. Sometimes this was for disciplining, such as during a math lesson when she interrupted her explanation in Spanish of latitude and longitude to reprimand a student in English: "I asked you not to be playing with the compass. Put it down." I rarely observed Ms. Torres using short Spanish turns during English lessons, for example when a Spanish L1 child was looking for a social studies map and she told him, "Búscalo allí, mi amor" ("Look for it over there, my love").

Despite her occasional use of English during Spanish lessons, I always observed Ms. Torres using Spanish with the other two fifth-grade teachers, even the English-dominant one, both in private and in front of the students. This conveyed the message that the official school language was Spanish. But when students from the other fifth-grade classes occasionally came to borrow books during Spanish time, she did not require them to use Spanish. Additionally, and I think significantly, she commented during an interview that she did not know how the other fifth-grade teachers encouraged their students to use Spanish, indicating that it was not something they talked about during their frequent planning meetings.

As seen in Chapter 4, the four focal students in my study showed considerable differences in their language use. When asked how she understood the different dispositions of her students to use Spanish, Ms. Torres said it had to do both with their families and their personal desire. She mentioned Teo, a very bright Spanish L2 boy whose parents fostered academic activities as an example of a hard-working, confident student who used a lot of Spanish:

> I think it has its roots in the family, but also in the philosophy even at this age that each child has about what they want to do. And the respect. [...] Because they are so confident, they have such confidence in who they are, I don't know if that's what helps them. Also, he studies and does his work.

This quote suggests that the teacher linked efforts to speak Spanish with overall academic orientation; it will be shown that the students' interviews revealed a similar connection between Spanish and being a serious student. Ms. Torres also seemed to suggest that it takes a self-confident student to stick with Spanish amid peers' English.

In summary, according to Ms. Torres, knowing more Spanish did not bestow upon students greater prestige in the classroom except perhaps an identity as a serious student. Speaking English during Spanish time did not have severe repercussions; students were often not caught speaking English during groupwork, and if they were, they would get a verbal reprimand and lose a *canica*. They would not be looked upon badly by their classmates, unlike in another classroom I observed, where the prizes were group based and students would chastise one another for causing the group to lose. In addition, the teacher often accepted public uses of English during teacher-fronted lessons.

If "learners invest in a second [or first/heritage] language with the understanding that they will acquire a wider range of symbolic and material resources" (Norton, 2000: 22; content in brackets mine), what "resources" were available to them in this classroom in exchange for their Spanish use and proficiency? And what other identity investments would promote Spanish use? The practices that I observed suggested that overall academic achievement appeared most important to Ms. Torres and the staff at IAMS. She expressed great concern about students who were struggling academically and no specific concern for those who had poor Spanish only. As is the case in monolingual English schools, being a native speaker does not guarantee academic success. There were three Spanish L1 students whose oral Spanish was very proficient but who were not academically successful. There were also two Spanish L2 students who she considered extremely bright, despite their problematic Spanish production.

The Four Students

Each of the four students brought to the classroom differing historical, social, and linguistic relationships to Spanish. Each student was therefore likely to be treated by and react differently to the environment created by Ms. Torres and by the other students, and it is reasonable to posit that their language use[1] reflected those positionings. Several researchers have found that factors such as classroom identity (Willett, 1995), power relationships to native speakers (Norton, 2000), and competing identity agendas (McKay & Wong, 1996) considerably influenced students' willingness and interest in speaking their second language. Although Spanish was actually a first language for two of the students in my study, both of them used English more frequently in their daily lives, and used it exclusively with friends. Spanish was therefore to a large extent the "minority" language for all four students.

To restate a central concept, a person's identity includes not only how she views herself, but also how others view her and the roles they create for and allow her to display. All four of these students were very bright, friendly, and participatory. As seen in Chapter 4, they differed in their willingness to use Spanish in the classroom. Returning to Norton (2000), the term "power" refers to the socially constructed and constantly renegotiated relations among individuals, institutions, and communities through which symbolic and material resources in a society are produced, distributed, and validated. In this classroom, Ms. Torres controlled several resources, including the assignment of grades and classroom discipline, who got the floor during teacher-fronted lessons by selecting students or cutting them off, and how *canicas* were distributed and taken away. We have seen that the "right to speak" was not evenly distributed among these four students; we will see how power relations among peers enabled or constrained the expression of students' investment in Spanish. The analyses of these four students attempt to contribute something of significance to our understandings of dual immersion classroom processes.

In this section, I present qualitative interpretations of my observations and interviews with the four students, their mothers, and the teacher. I conducted one interview with each student and each mother. The teacher was interviewed formally twice, and I asked her questions informally during the six months I spent in her classroom.

Carolina: "Sometimes you keep talking all this English and you start forgetting your Spanish"

At home, Carolina spoke mostly English but some Spanish with her mother, who had immigrated from Ecuador at the age of five, and mostly Spanish with her father, who had immigrated from Honduras after high school. All members of the household used Spanish with Carolina's grandparents, who also lived there, but Carolina used only English with her older sister Natalie and both Spanish and English with her three-year-old sister. The family watched television and listened to the radio predominantly in Spanish. On more than one occasion I heard Carolina chatting with Ms. Torres about the latest plot in a *telenovela* (soap opera). Mrs. Padilla commented that she wanted her daughters to be "really bilingual. Not just in speaking, but in writing and so forth," and she cited her own success in the job market as proof of the importance of these skills. She exhibited positive attitudes toward Spanish and felt secure in her daughters' appreciation of their family's Hispanic heritage. When asked if she thought that Carolina would speak Spanish to her own children in the future, she responded, "She knows it's important for me that they learned Spanish. She has enough cousins that haven't, and when they go to South America, it's a shame, their Spanish is atrocious. And she knows that's not good."

Despite these positive attitudes, Mrs. Padilla showed considerably more concern about her daughters' English development than her Spanish development. When it was discovered that Natalie's English grammar was a bit deficient, their mom enrolled both Natalie and Carolina in English tutoring sessions. She also admitted that although Carolina's English regularly contained new vocabulary that she learned in school, her Spanish did not. Carolina mentioned that because Natalie's school record listed her as "limited English proficient" when she entered kindergarten, her parents used more English with Carolina in order to avoid the same classification. It seems accurate to say that for Mrs. Padilla, Spanish development was important as long as her children's English did not suffer, a very reasonable response to mainstream educational demands in the United States. I argue that Carolina's classroom language use reflected these competing demands.

Carolina enjoyed IAMS, indicating that she would not be happy in a school that taught only English because she "might forget Spanish." According to Mrs. Padilla, she and her husband once considered sending their youngest daughter to a school that was more academically rigorous than IAMS, but "Carolina said no, it's a family tradition, you can't send her to another school." On the written questionnaire, she indicated "true" for all statements about enjoying hearing the two languages, the importance of knowing them in Chicago, and a desire for her hypothetical future children to know both languages. The only questions to which she answered "kind of true" were about enjoying the way the languages were taught in school, wanting to marry someone who speaks Spanish, and the need to know Spanish to get a good job.

Although Carolina earned good grades, Ms. Torres and Mrs. Padilla agreed that Carolina did not like to write in either language. She postponed writing assignments as long as she could and put very little effort into them. Her mother indicated that she resisted using the Spanish dictionaries her parents bought her, which amounted to several per year because she regularly "lost" them. Since her writing would not go far in earning Carolina good grades, I argue that she used as much Spanish as she did with the teacher in order to maintain an identity as a good student. In other words, her high Spanish proficiency combined with her level of classroom participation positioned her as a successful student during Spanish language arts and social studies classes. In fact, Ms. Torres and all of the other three focal students named Carolina when asked which students spoke Spanish well.

Socially, Carolina was successful in that she was well liked by her classmates. Ms. Torres allowed all students to write the names of three classmates with whom they would like to sit, and six students chose to sit with Carolina; by this measure, she was the second most popular girl in the class. As seen in Chapter 4, she used English 58% of the time with her peers, including the functions of presenting her knowledge of popular music, radio stations, and television shows, as well as occasionally engaging in antischool discourse (e.g. complaining that she did not want to return to class after a field trip), all functions which serve to position her among her classmates. She was aware that she used English during Spanish time, indicating that it was because she forgot or because outside class, "I talk English most of the time. I don't really, like, use Spanish that much." When asked how students reacted to Ms. Torres's discipline of their English use, she responded, "Sometimes we just don't talk because we are afraid that we might start speaking English." My observations confirmed that the students sometimes preferred to remain silent rather than speak Spanish with one another.

Carolina's identity as a good Spanish speaker was displayed enough during teacher-fronted lessons – where she used Spanish with the teacher 91% of the time – that she did not feel the need to insist on using Spanish during groupwork. In addition, her journal entries indicated that she did not want to risk exclusion from social talk with her peers, which took place in English. Also noteworthy is Carolina's reluctance to accept a position as a superior Spanish speaker by virtue of coming from a Spanish-speaking family. She commented, "People keep on like judging me that I should really know a lot of Spanish since I come from a Spanish family. But sometimes it's not true, because sometimes you keep talking all this English and you start forgetting your Spanish." In my discussion of Melissa, I will suggest that Melissa did just the opposite: she enjoyed receiving praise for her Spanish precisely because it was not expected of her as a nonnative speaker.

Matt: "Buswork, that's all I know"

Matt's mother, Mrs. Castillo, came to the United States from El Salvador when she was 18 years old. Matt's father died when he was eight years old. Mrs. Castillo's husband, Matt's stepfather, was European American and did not speak Spanish. Mrs. Castillo told me that when she spoke to Matt in Spanish, he almost always answered her in English or indicated that he did not understand what she said, so she repeated herself in English. She noticed that his Spanish vocabulary and syntax had declined over the past year, and noted that he spoke only English with his younger sister (with whom she used Spanish). However, Matt used Spanish every day before and after school with his grandparents and great-grandparents, all living downstairs. The only other people with whom Matt said he used Spanish outside school were two friends at church. Both Matt and his mother said that the television programs he watched and the music he listened to were all in English – Matt left the room whenever his mother put on Spanish television programs – but he did watch an occasional soccer news program in Spanish. Although half of the library books that Mrs. Castillo regularly brought home for her son were in Spanish, she said that he read more in English. Yet Matt was not interested in abandoning Spanish entirely. When his parents mentioned the possibility of moving to the suburbs and told him that he would only find English-speaking friends there, he said, "I'm not going to speak Spanish or what?" and that "He was pensive, like he didn't like the idea very much." His mother also said that Matt paid attention to Latino entertainment figures and could identify their countries of origin.

Matt's mother chose IAMS based on a recommendation from a family friend. She commented that the bilingual programs in other schools did not teach Spanish well, whereas at IAMS "el primero es español" ("Spanish is first"). She said this was important in her decision because

> sometimes it's very difficult for someone who works to teach them . . . one can teach them to speak, but to write it well and read it well, it's quite difficult. They don't learn that in these schools around here. English, they're always going to learn. But the second language, which is the one of the family and where one comes from, it's very difficult because we're in an environment where more English is spoken.

Mrs. Castillo said that her son and his friends identified more with English than with Spanish, but she wanted Matt to know Spanish because it was "his background, his culture." Despite her positive feelings about IAMS, Mrs. Castillo did express some of the same concerns as did Carolina's mother about her children's English development. These parents may not need to worry, because Matt and Carolina had no noticeable accent in English and did very well in school and on standardized tests. Yet their fears about their children's English development may have been part of the reason why they did not push their children to speak Spanish with them.

Matt was successful and well adjusted at school. According to his mother, "He feels like he's in a family, he identifies with everyone." His enjoyment of learning was reflected in his comment that he liked that the teachers at IAMS were strict because students could get work done. Matt exhibited positive attitudes toward Spanish, both personal and school related, when he wrote that it was important to know Spanish, "because it's the language of your culture, and there are things in Spanish that we have to read." On the questionnaire, he indicated that Spanish was important on various levels (for a good job, for his future spouse and children, and in Chicago), but that he liked speaking Spanish slightly less than speaking English. When asked in the interview what was important to succeed at the school, Matt was the only focal student who mentioned "knowing Spanish and English."

Despite these positive written responses about Spanish, in his interview Matt expressed quite the opposite. He said that there was "too much Spanish" at the school, particularly because the standardized math tests were in English: "Sometimes [having math class in Spanish] is bad, because in the Iowa tests, there's these words in English that they never told us, and like at the last minute they give us these sheets with the words in English." He also said he would prefer that science be taught in English because it would be easier. He then commented that learning Spanish was important at school only for Spanish class, nothing more, and that Spanish class was so boring that he "almost fell asleep once." When asked why he used English during Spanish class, Matt, like Carolina, replied that he was "used to talking in English." Melissa made the astute observation that "Matt knows lots of words in Spanish but he doesn't use them that much. When I was at his table, he goofed around a lot, so lots of times when he probably did know the words I was asking him about, he didn't say them." We saw in Chapter 4 that "goofing around" took place almost entirely in English, so Matt's inclination to do so would naturally lead to English use. But equally as important is the fact that Matt was more proficient in Spanish than he let on.

When I asked Ms. Torres at the beginning of the school year to name students with high Spanish proficiency, the first student she mentioned was Matt, saying that he was "fabulous." However, later in the year she commented about his underutilized Spanish skills, stating that he used too much English and often falsely told her that he did not understand or know how to say things. She said that he wrote surprisingly well in Spanish ("even better than Carolina" in regard to spelling and other conventions) although the content was limited to "the basics." His mother confirmed that he did not like to write in either language, preferring to finish quickly rather than plan and revise his work.

Although Ms. Torres felt that Matt had a solid level of Spanish proficiency, she did not consider his attitudes toward Spanish very positive. It was while discussing Carolina's attitudes that Ms. Torres revealed her opinion about Matt's:

> I think that Carolina likes Spanish. And she feels proud to be able to speak it. But Matt is different. [*Laughter*] He refuses it more. But it's because of their age right now, I think he's more rebellious.

This echoes the gender-related findings of language use presented in Chapter 4: Mrs. Torres seems to be saying that, in general, boys at this age exhibit more rebellious behavior than do girls. In fact, Matt was one of the five students Ms. Torres mentioned from whom she most frequently took away *canicas* for speaking English. When asked how students felt when a *canica* was taken away, she replied:

> They don't like it. "Oh, but I wasn't talking." "No, but he asked me in English." They deny it. Ay, especially Matt. He's always fighting.

You can see the anger on their faces. I see it very clearly, especially in Otto. And of course Matt, I don't have to see it. He tells me. He's very defensive. He's always defending himself.

There are indeed several examples of Matt resisting the loss of a *canica* in the corpus. Although he seemed to dislike being publicly reprimanded for speaking English, Ms. Torres said that when he was caught he did not make an effort to speak Spanish, which was also evident in the corpus. However, Matt did use Spanish 83% of the time with the teacher, indicating a general willingness to conform to the public language rules. This willingness may have been motivated by the fact that his mother kept in touch with Ms. Torres about her son's behavior and academic performance and imposed negative consequences if either one was unsatisfactory. Given that in this classroom, being a good student involved staying on task and following the language rules, Matt did enough of each to avoid getting into any serious trouble. Ms. Torres said she was happy with Matt's level of participation in both Spanish and English lessons. Perhaps for this reason, she selected his bids as often as she did. As was shown in Chapter 4, Matt made more verbal bids and had a higher percentage of them accepted than the other three students. Like Carolina's strategies, Matt's bidding strategies may have been partially responsible for his success in gaining the floor, which, in addition to providing him opportunities to use Spanish, represented a positioning by the teacher as a competent classroom participant.

Matt indeed wanted to be perceived publicly as a conscientious and helpful student, which was evident in his frequent participation during class and his consistent volunteering to assist the teacher with tasks such as moving the overhead projector or collecting lunch money. Matt was also very intelligent and often provided his classmates with instructions and correct answers. However, once he had completed the assigned academic task, he clearly sought to position himself among his peers as popular and as resistant to school activities. Ms. Torres noted that he was a classroom leader and that he was aware of his increasing popularity with the girls. There are multiple examples in the corpus in which Matt attempted to subordinate his peers through playful teasing (such as several of the examples in Appendix 4.C), made jokes, and indicated that he hated school and homework: " I don't need no schoolwork. Buswork, that's all I know." Matt used the least amount of Spanish with peers of all four focal students, which is understandable given that teasing and making jokes are off-task activities, which in this classroom took place in English. In addition, Matt's resistance to school would naturally include an avoidance of Spanish, which was arguably the language for on-task school activity only.

Melissa: "En español, por favor"

Melissa Butler's home was English speaking. Her parents were of Irish and German descent, and her mother did not know Spanish. Her husband had learned some Spanish by taking courses in college and speaking it daily at work. The Butlers decided to send Melissa to IAMS primarily for her to learn Spanish, which they considered "the second language of the world," and for her to learn diversity and cultural sensitivity. In addition, Mrs. Butler's sister was married to a man from Mexico, which they felt provided an important family connection to the Spanish language and Mexican culture.

Mrs. Butler described Melissa's first four months in kindergarten at IAMS as horrible because she could not understand Spanish: "She was in tears. That's probably why she learned Spanish as quickly as she did, because she couldn't stand to sit there and have a story be read and not understand it." Mrs. Butler recalled how later that year, Melissa excitedly announced to her parents that she would be learning to read in Spanish before English. Her parents placed labels on items around the house with their names in both languages. The family's home library had picture dictionaries and children's music in Spanish.

Although English was the language spoken in the Butler household, Spanish played a positive role in the family as a source of pride, entertainment, and connection to the community. Mr. Butler would occasionally organize "Spanish-speaking night" in the house and play Spanish word games with his children. Mrs. Butler indicated that in the past, Melissa and her younger brother Mark would spontaneously declare "Spanish only" time on Sunday afternoons, although during fifth grade, Melissa said that she only used Spanish with Mark when helping him with homework. Mrs. Butler also said that Melissa would sometimes unknowingly slip into Spanish while talking with her. She also spoke Spanish with a Latino neighbor and with parents at her brother's baseball games. Mrs. Butler commented that because her daughter looked up every word she did not understand, they bought her an expensive electronic translator. Her children also received periodic visits from a family friend from Spain who gave the children Spanish books, read to them in Spanish, and talked with them about Mexico. Mrs. Butler required Melissa to open her first bank account in Spanish with a Spanish-speaking teller, which proved to be an eye-opening experience:

> At first she was very mad at me. And walking home from the bank, she goes, "Mom, I get it! If somebody in the bank only knows English, and a person in the bank who wanted to do their banking only knew

Spanish, I could help them understand each other." And I was almost in tears, because that's exactly it. And from that point on, she noticed all the places that she could use Spanish outside of the school. We'd be in restaurants, and those people don't think that we're a bilingual family sitting here. And [our kids] have befriended every chef and every waiter in every restaurant on the North side. They all know our kids, and they love it when they come, they totally speak in Spanish in every restaurant that we go into. And that's a wonderful connection for them.

This quote also reveals the pride that Mrs. Butler felt from the connections that her family could make with people in the community through the Spanish skills of her children. She also seemed to enjoy the challenge that her children's Spanish presented to people's perceptions about the family based on their physical appearance, which was echoed by Melissa in her interview.

Perhaps the strongest indication of the role of Spanish in Melissa's life came from her mother's claim that she had "adopted" a Hispanic identity through her uncle from Mexico. Her Uncle Paco lived in a Chicago suburb but returned monthly to his hometown in Michoacán, Mexico. When the Butlers visited him there, the governor took them for a four-day tour of the state, which Melissa enjoyed so thoroughly that, for her math project on how she would spend a million dollars, she detailed how she would pay for the entire school to visit Mexico. According to Mrs. Butler, Uncle Paco was very proud of Melissa's Spanish, particularly because his two sons had not learned it. It is significant that Melissa called Paco's mother *abuela* (grandma), who according to Mrs. Butler was happy to "finally" have grandkids like Melissa and her brother who spoke and appreciated the Spanish language. Mrs. Butler commented that this "grandmother" was also encouraging Melissa to have a *quinceañera* party in Mexico, which contributed significantly to Melissa's self-identity:

> She will now tell you that she is also Hispanic, because of her uncle, by marriage. She has added that to who she is. The fact that she's going to go down there and celebrate turning 15. It's like this was her legit way to take it on. I think she has always wanted to fit in in that way, at Inter-American.

I do not know how many Latino students at IAMS talked about having *quinceañera* parties – and we will see in Chapter 8 that Carolina was not the least bit interested in having one – but clearly Melissa relished the idea. Overall, Mrs. Butler commented that Melissa felt like a group member at the school. When the Butlers considered transferring her to another school because of concerns that the sixth- through eighth-grade program at IAMS was not academically rigorous, Mrs. Butler recalls that "Melissa totally freaked out. She goes, 'You rip that [application] up right now, Mom. I am not going to another school, [Inter-American] is the best school in the world.'" When asked why she liked IAMS, the first thing Melissa mentioned was that she was able to learn Spanish. She wrote that it was important to know Spanish to help other people and when in countries where Spanish is spoken. Ms. Torres noted that Melissa had "enormous respect for the language and the culture" and was aware that her parents were proud that she and her brother could speak Spanish, although Melissa's questionnaire results were not as consistent as might have been expected. She said it was only "kind of true" that she wants to marry someone who spoke Spanish and "false" that it was important for her children to know Spanish and that it was important to know Spanish to get a good job.

Recall from Chapter 4 that, of the four focal students, Melissa used the greatest amount of Spanish with her peers (50% of the time). Mrs. Butler said that, according to Melissa, the other kids used English because they were lazy, but that Melissa did so because she got tired of drawing attention to herself for her Spanish. However, Melissa said that she used English because "I'm just not used to really speaking Spanish in conversations very much." This was the same reason given by Carolina and Matt. She added that when the teacher reprimanded the class for using English, "I feel like I should have been speaking Spanish, I feel kinda guilty."

Despite her classroom English use, why did Melissa use so much Spanish with her peers? Ms. Torres noted that Melissa was extremely focused on her academic performance. Mrs. Butler corroborated that her daughter was a perfectionist with her schoolwork and felt that she would be letting the teacher down if she did not complete it perfectly. In addition, Ms. Torres felt that Melissa's desire for her Spanish to be as strong as her English was so powerful that it caused her stress. When the class was reading the Cuban-American novel *Kike*, Ms. Torres said that Melissa cried because she did not understand everything:

> When I talked to her I made her see that she was good [in Spanish], because she wants to be as good as she is in English. But I tell her, you can't, because Spanish isn't spoken in your home. You'll do it one day, but it takes time. Maybe if at some point you want to live in Mexico or in Spain, or any other country, where the language is constant in your life.

I did not observe in any other students a similar interest, which for Melissa was practically a compulsion, for developing Spanish abilities. She showed a similar intensity for schoolwork, which, combined with her reluctance to share answers and materials with classmates and her enthusiasm for Spanish, led to a mildly negative reputation among her peers. Both Ms. Torres and Mrs. Butler commented that Melissa generally enjoyed groupwork but would feel stressed when her classmates did not do an equal share of the work, which I observed on several occasions as she quieted her tablemates or expressed concern over the proper way to carry out a task. Several times I heard her respond to a peer's question with "You should know that" and saw her refuse to lend art supplies. Melissa was just as popular a tablemate as the other three focal students, having been selected by four students, but she did experience a degree of marginalization. Several classmates made comments about her being "crabby," teased her for her interest in music class, and expressed pleasure when she made mistakes (although she sometimes did share materials and engage in friendly conversations with her classmates).

Both Matt and Otto stated that Melissa used "mostly Spanish" during Spanish lessons. As shown in Chapter 4, she did not make public turns very often, so groupwork was her main opportunity to practice Spanish. She was the only focal student in the corpus that requested that her tablemates use Spanish and, more notably, she often responded to her peers' English comments in Spanish. An additional benefit to insisting on Spanish during groupwork was that it reduced the chances that her peers would direct social talk to her – since social talk usually took place in English – thus allowing her to remain on task.

It was unclear to me whether Melissa knew that her classroom language use was different from that of her classmates. She commented that the "whole point' of being at IAMS was to learn Spanish, and she was willing to swim against the tide of peer English use. Her investments in her familial connections to Mexico, being perceived as a good student, following rules and completing schoolwork properly, and in developing her Spanish combined to create very strong investments in speaking Spanish in class.

Otto: "I keep forgetting to speak Spanish, and I'm not getting it that much"

Otto lived with his mother and two siblings. His parents had immigrated from Africa before he was born: Mrs. Solomon was from Liberia and spoke English fairly well, and his father, who lived in Chicago and whom Otto saw regularly, was from Guinea and spoke English and French fluently. Otto and his family spoke mainstream U.S. English, and both he and his mother commented that they watched English television programs and listened to English religious radio programming. Otto said that he used

Spanish outside school only when "in a store and someone doesn't speak English." Otto's mother felt that her son's Spanish was "good, for somebody who, it's not spoken at home, like other kids who already know it." He received weekly after-school help with his homework from college student volunteers at a local Baptist church. When I asked if these tutors also helped with his Spanish homework, his mother replied, "No, but he knows how to do his homework in Spanish, because he can speak it." However, we will see later that Otto often did not understand classroom tasks, and even when he did, he frequently lacked the Spanish skills to carry them out very well. Mrs. Solomon spoke little and seemed less knowledgeable about U.S. school culture compared to the other three mothers I interviewed, but she was clearly satisfied with her son's academic development and with his Spanish skills.

Mrs. Solomon learned about IAMS through a brochure about Chicago's nontraditional public schools and said that she liked the family environment, that the teachers were nice to the students, and that it was not as crowded as other schools. She said that Otto loved the school, describing how he woke up early every morning and waited for the bus well before it was due to arrive. His mother and father had each considered switching Otto to another school, and on both occasions he said he did not want to leave IAMS. His expressed positive attitudes toward Spanish, stating that he liked the school "because you learn a different language and if I go to a place and they only speak Spanish I'll know what they're saying." On the questionnaire, he indicated that it is important to know Spanish and that he will use it when he grows up. However, he indicated that he liked speaking Spanish less than speaking English and that he would have preferred to have math classes in English.

When asked about Otto's attitude toward Spanish, Ms. Torres sighed: "He likes it. He knows that it's good for him, but he doesn't have the support at home. He's trying, but he's not as fluent as he should be." Although she noted that Otto's Spanish had improved since the beginning of the year, his was the first name she mentioned when describing students who "constantly" used English in class. Ms. Torres considered Otto academically strong and very enthusiastic, but complained that he shouted out answers without thinking first, talked too much in class, and was often aggressive:

Otto is a good kid, but he's something else [*tremendo*]. {*Laughter*} His mouth doesn't stop all day long. They say he was the same way last year. The good thing is that he knows when he did something wrong, and he immediately apologizes. But he continues the same way afterwards. Sometimes in his spontaneity, he disrespects people and hurts them, his classmates and even his teachers. He can overwhelm even very good students.

During groupwork, Otto often looked at his tablemates' written answers and compared them with his own – sometimes annoying them by copying directly – and asked them questions if he did not understand. When he thought he was right and a classmate was wrong, he said so, and when his competence was called into question, he usually tried to blame his tablemates for misdirecting him. He also frequently teased them. Despite Otto's competitive, sometimes aggressive, behavior, four students chose to work with him. He was also popular on the playground, where I observed classmates vying for his participation on their football and soccer teams.

Although Otto struggled to produce complete sentences in Spanish, he sought to appear competent by offering to help to other students when they had lost their place during a Spanish read-aloud or when they mispronounced a word. If he knew the answer to a vocabulary question, he would call it out, and he provided English translations of Spanish words that he understood. When the teacher called attention to the class' English use one morning, he quickly stated, "Yo estaba hablando español con José" ("I was speaking Spanish with José"). On another morning, after Ms. Torres read a story in English, he announced, "Colorín, colorado, este cuento se ha acabado" (a common phrase signaling that a story has ended).

In addition to volunteering frequently to plug in the overhead projector, carry books, or distribute rulers and calculators, Otto sought to display his knowledge of content whenever possible by frequently calling out answers to the teacher's questions. Despite his overall good intentions, Otto used considerably more English with the teacher than did the other focal students. His lower oral Spanish proficiency was undoubtedly partially responsible. Otto said that, overall, during Spanish classes he spoke half Spanish and half English, "Because I keep forgetting to speak Spanish, and I'm not getting it that much." But perhaps equally important were his strong needs to give the correct answer accurately and quickly, and to joke, tease, and argue with his peers, which, like Matt, he did on many occasions in the corpus. I suggested in Chapter 4 that Otto's English use with the teacher contributed to his being called on less often than his classmates. His investments in an identity as knowledgeable and accepted by his peers, which he could do in English, appeared more important to him than developing his oral Spanish proficiency. A researcher working with the concept of motivation might mistakenly conclude that Otto used less Spanish than the other students only because he was less motivated to learn it, unaware of the fact that he was sometimes silenced by the teacher and that his investments in an identity as generally knowledgeable and socially accepted by his peers were more important to him than developing his oral Spanish proficiency.

Conclusions

Norton's (2000) work encourages an exploration of how students' identity investments relate to their classroom language production. This framework emphasizes that language learning "is not simply a skill that is acquired with hard work and dedication, but a complex social practice that engages the identities of language learners in ways that have received little attention in the field of SLA" (2000: 132). I have highlighted the identity investments of these four dual immersion students and sought to show how those investments either encouraged or discouraged their Spanish use in the classroom, because language production cannot be separated from contextual and historical factors. This study supports the idea that favorable investments in an identity as a Spanish speaker lead to greater Spanish use in the classroom.

According to Norton (2000), learners invest in a language when they feel they will acquire a wider range of symbolic and material resources and expect the "return" to be worth the investment. The investments of these four students can be summarized as follows: by using Spanish with the teacher, Carolina received favor beyond what her academic production alone might have earned, Melissa fortified her identity as a Spanish speaker and an academically focused student, and Matt was able to stay out of trouble, but Otto experienced a conflict with his investment in presenting himself as knowledgeable and aggressive. No one besides Melissa felt enough return on his or her investment to use Spanish with classroom peers, although at just 50% of her peer turns, her Spanish use was lower than what one might expect.

Second language acquisition (SLA) theories like Schumann's acculturation model (1978) recognize the importance of regular contact between language learners and speakers of the target language. However, similarly to that of Norton (2000), our study suggests that contact alone does not guarantee L2 use. Half of the students in this classroom were native blingual Spanish speakers, yet Spanish was used among peers just 32% of the time, and in fact the L2 girl used more Spanish than the L1 boy. The sociolinguistic characteristics of the classroom and the school in general suggested that although Spanish was reserved for academic topics, English was the language of greater status (cf. Freeman, 1998; McCollum, 1994). While the field of applied linguistics has not yet developed formal theories of heritage language development, investment can also make an important contribution to understanding how bilingual Spanish speakers decide whether to communicate in their first language, in English, or in code-switched language. For example, Matt appeared more interested in presenting an identity as funny and rebellious than as an on task Spanish speaker, and he used the least Spanish of all four students.

I agree with Freeman (1998) that dual immersion is an attempt at language planning. According to Fasold (1984), a successful language planning policy includes measures to influence how people identify themselves so that the identity of the target language population becomes desirable. If bilingual youth are to maintain their Spanish language skills to a sufficient degree for them to transmit the language to their own future children, this study suggests that they need to be presented palatable identities as Spanish speakers (cf. Fasold, 1984). Dual immersion educators need to explore ways to cultivate students' investments in identities as Spanish speakers. Despite IAMS' possible weaknesses in this area, I believe that the L1 Spanish speakers maintained their Spanish abilities in this dual immersion school far more than they would have in other program types. Since they were highly proficient in English, they most definitely would have been transitioned out of bilingual education after three years (or fewer) into mainstream all-English classes, where they would do no reading, writing, listening, or speaking in Spanish. Similarly, the Spanish L2 students at IAMS were likely far more proficient in Spanish than their counterparts in traditional FLES programs that teach Spanish for only 40 minutes per day, three to four times per week.

In Chapter 4, we saw that gender appeared to be more significant than L1 in overall language output. This echoes ESL research findings (Toohey, 2000; Willett, 1995) that girls are often more inclined to follow classroom rules. In Ms. Torres's classroom, the rules included that Spanish be spoken during Spanish lessons. In addition to positioning them as compliant students, using Spanish during Spanish lessons was advantageous to these two girls' identities as academically solid students. The qualitative data corroborated, particularly for Melissa, that such an investment in academic standing was indeed exerting a strong influence on her behavior. The data further suggested that the two girls had other identity investments outside of the classroom that made them more interested in using and developing Spanish than the boys.

Melissa, although not from a Spanish-speaking family, had "adopted" an identity as a Spanish speaker through her family's pride in her ability to speak it, which was often put on display in her community and while she visited her uncle in Mexico. She also came from an academic family and was intensely concerned with academic achievement, which meant that she stayed on task and took care to use Spanish when it was the official language of the lesson. Carolina spoke Spanish daily with her family and was one of the most fluent Spanish speakers in the class. She appeared very comfortable with her bilingual, bicultural identity, and stated that it was important that students used more Spanish at Inter-American than at other bilingual schools in order that she would not forget her Spanish.

The boys earned good grades but generally showed more resistance to school. They engineered ways to leave the classroom when they could and sometimes argued with the teacher, two behaviors not exhibited by the girls. Matt engaged in a good deal of antischool commentary with his peers (about hating school, doing homework on the bus, etc.), which took place in English, given that Spanish was used mostly (88% of the time) for official, academic activity. However, Matt did use enough Spanish with the teacher to avoid getting into any serious trouble. Otto's lower Spanish proficiency combined with his zeal to participate and his sometimes aggressive, off-task behavior undoubtedly contributed to his higher levels of English use. Both boys had reputations as intelligent, capable students, which did not appear to be jeopardized by their English use during Spanish lessons.

Unlike the girls, the boys seemed to have few identity investments outside of school that required developing or demonstrating high Spanish proficiency. Matt used Spanish at home with his grandparents who lived downstairs, but since his stepfather did not know Spanish, his nuclear family tended to use English. Otto's family did not know Spanish and received no support for his Spanish development outside of school.

The next chapter visits these four students and their 48 classmates during their eighth-grade year in 2002–2003. I again describe their classroom language use, in addition to reporting on measures of their Spanish proficiency upon graduation from IAMS. In Chapter 7, I will describe the identity investments that appeared related to their language use as teenagers in eighth grade.

Notes

1. McKay and Wong (1996:606) insisted that what impels a learner to certain language use behaviors is much more complex and much less conscious than implied in terms such as *choice*, but researchers select such terms for lack of better alternatives.

Chapter 6

Language Use in Eighth Grade

Chapter 4 described the general expectations for Spanish use throughout the school building, as well as the expectations for and actual use of Spanish in the fifth-grade class that I observed. We saw that the four focal students used Spanish with the teacher on average 82% of the time, but only 32% of the time when speaking with one another. The present chapter investigates the classroom Spanish use of the same four students three years later, in eighth grade, as well as the language use of their classmates. I will begin by describing the school's official policy for Spanish use in eighth grade, followed by what I learned from my observations and interviews. Next, I present a detailed analysis of actual Spanish and English use during a typical eighth-grade Spanish social studies class. The chapter concludes with what I saw as the "unofficial" expectations for Spanish use in eighth grade, and to what extent they were met by both students and teachers.

Official Eighth-Grade Language Policy

During the 2002–2003 school year, the students' eighth-grade year was set up in the following way. The 55 students were divided into three groups and spent approximately two hours per day with each of three teachers. English language arts was taught totally in English by Ms. Gingiss. Math and science were taught by Ms. Castro, and were supposed to be taught half in English and half in Spanish. That is, half of the textbooks were in English and half were in Spanish, and lessons were supposed to be divided equally between the two languages. Spanish language arts was taught 100% in Spanish three days a week by Ms. Maas, who also taught social studies half in English and half in Spanish. Just as in fifth grade, all "resource" classes (music, gym, and computers) were taught in English. Eighth graders participated in district-wide history and science fairs, as well as a Young Authors competition, all of which took place in English.

Ms. Castro's math and science classes

Ms. Castro, the math and science teacher, was in her seventh year at IAMS. She was of Puerto Rican background and spoke only Spanish until she was five years old; she was 13 before she learned that her mother spoke any English. Her classes were supposed to be taught half in Spanish and half in English. On the two days I visited Ms. Castro's math and science classes, however, I did not hear her use any Spanish. The twelve eighth-graders that I interviewed indicated that Ms. Castro "sometimes" used Spanish, usually when explaining something to one of the five students who had recently arrived from Latin America, but that the great majority of her classes were taught in English. Ms. Castro herself admitted, "If I teach 25% of my curriculum in Spanish, it's a lot." She said that not only did students resist all efforts to use Spanish – for example, groaning and pleading whenever she would ask them to use the Spanish version of the textbook – in her opinion it was more important that they understand the content she was teaching, even if that meant presenting it in English:

> I teach mostly in English but I shouldn't, but when their frustration is high, I move on. My goal is not to teach you Spanish, my goal is to teach you math. I don't have the time. They should have had the Spanish already. I don't like any kids to be lost, because their level of frustration goes up. I don't have time to figure out whether they deciphered their second language correctly. Also [the administration] says they don't care about test scores, but then they tell you, look, the scores went down.

She confessed that although she speaks, reads, and writes Spanish, and has certification to teach Spanish, that if she were to teach it, "it would be a disservice. I am not a Spanish teacher." In fact, when the school was reorganizing the structure of eighth grade and proposed that Ms. Castro teach math, science, and Spanish, she refused to teach Spanish and threatened to leave the school if forced to do so.

Ms. Castro pointed out during her interview that students could fail everything in eighth grade except math and English and still graduate. The students were perfectly aware of this, as demonstrated by an action research project that Ms. Maas, the Spanish language arts and social studies teacher, completed as a professional development activity. All eighth graders answered a questionnaire that she designed. They reported that they completed their math, science, and English homework much more frequently than their Spanish homework, which they did rarely if at all.

One student said directly to Ms. Maas, "Ms. Castro said, 'I don't care if you get an A in Spanish, you have to pass my class in order to graduate,'" which was echoed by other students on different occasions. All 12 students that I interviewed claimed that math was their most important class and that Spanish was the least important. When I asked them why, some of them said that they did not need to pass Spanish in order to graduate. Clearly, the students were receiving and internalizing this message.

Judging from my observations and interviews, Ms. Castro was a favorite teacher of many students, who truly enjoyed her class and her company. They also respected her and followed her rules, which was evident by how orderly they behaved in her classroom (in stark contrast to Ms. Maas's classroom, which will be described in a later section). When a brand new student arrived to IAMS and Ms. Maas asked his classmates to offer him advice about being successful at the school, one unruly student shouted out, "Don't mess with Ms. Castro, she don't play."

Despite how successful Ms. Castro was at connecting with many students, math and science were supposed to be taught half in Spanish, so I sought the opinions of other teachers and administrators about the fact that they were not. One teacher commented angrily, "Just because she is unapologetic about not using Spanish, doesn't mean it's right." This teacher claimed that the administration had asked Ms. Castro on several occasions to use Spanish, but suspected that Ms. Castro did not because, in addition to her belief that the students would become confused if math and science were taught in Spanish, she herself lacked the Spanish proficiency to do so. Although this teacher generally supported the administration's stance of allowing teachers the freedom to make important decisions, she was very frustrated that a language use decision like this was left to the judgment of Ms. Castro. A member of the administrative team corroborated that Ms. Castro had been approached about using more Spanish, but this administrator appeared resigned to accept the status quo regarding language use, stating only that "[Ms.Castro] wants her students to do well in her class. But there's a culture in eighth grade that needs to change. And it will, little by little, especially if we use positive recognition and rewards."

One example of such rewards was the trips to Mexico that were occasionally organized for seventh- or eighth-grade students. The administrator who organized these trips said that she did so in order to promote Spanish use in the upper cycle, and that many students years later recalled the wonderful art, drama, music, and sports activities during their two weeks in Mexico. Unfortunately, only some ten trips had taken place since 1986, and by 2003 it had been several years in a row since a group had gone. Moreover, it is unclear whether the possibility of such a trip would override the eighth-grade students' clear resistance to using Spanish, which will be described in greater detail in the next sections. In any case, IAMS administrators were clearly aware of the lack of Spanish use in eighth grade math and science, but were unwilling to press the issue.

A bit of background context about the upper cycle (sixth through eighth grade) at Inter-American will shed light on the language use that took place there. Several teachers claimed that the upper cycle had been weak for many years, particularly in Spanish instruction. One teacher blamed the fact that an upper-cycle teacher had retired several years previously but had not been replaced, so the remaining five upper cycle teachers were "spread thin." Two other teachers complained that more resources were invested in the lower grades than in the upper grades. One teacher claimed that there had been "rumblings that the school would go to K-6 only, that maybe we should cut our losses and stick to what we do well." Indeed, there were two high-achieving students during the fifth-grade year of my study whose parents transferred them to a different middle school for sixth through eighth grade, something that both Melissa's and Carolina's moms had also considered, stating that they were worried that IAMS could not prepare their daughters to be academically competitive. It should be noted that in Chicago, many parents opt to send their children to public magnet high schools that require high standardized test scores from seventh and eighth grade.[1]

Teacher turnover was another problem mentioned in the upper cycle. For example, the seventh-grade Spanish language arts and social studies teacher during 2001–2002, a new hire, left the school after one year. Ms. Maas, too, stayed in eighth grade just one year. The teacher hired to replace her, also a new hire, left after one school year as well. Perhaps realizing what a difficult job it was to teach Spanish in the upper cycle, the administration decided to select a teacher from within IAMS and asked Ms. Torres, the highly successful fifth-grade teacher described in Chapters 4 and 5, to switch to eighth grade. While I did not observe her teaching in eighth grade, she told me that when she first started, it was a significant challenge for her. She said that "adolescents are bored by almost everything except hanging out with their friends" and when she announced that they would be reading three books in Spanish during the year, they complained that they had not read a book in Spanish in two years. The students resisted almost every kind of activity she proposed, but since she had already been the fifth-grade teacher of a third of the class, and the rest of the students had some contact with her in school, she was able to gently force the students into compliance. Some students admitted to her that they only completed her assignments "because it's for you." In addition to already having students' respect and solid classroom management techniques, it was of enormous help that Ms. Torres had solid relationships with many of her students' families and could count on them for support.

In summary, math and science were taught almost 100% in English instead of 50% in Spanish. The math and science teacher stated that the students resisted Spanish and that it was more important that they know the concepts well in English for standardized tests, for passing eighth grade, and for academic success in high school. The administration was aware of this issue, but unwilling to force a change. This meant that the entire responsibility for eighth-grade instruction in Spanish fell upon the Spanish language arts and social studies teacher. During the year of this study, that teacher was Ms. Maas, a first-year teacher with no prior professional experience with teenagers or with teaching.

Ms. Maas's Spanish language arts and social studies

Ms. Maas held what is known as an Illinois Type 29 provisional bilingual certification. Owing to an extreme shortage of bilingual teachers, these certificates were issued to any college graduate who passed a Spanish proficiency test. They were valid for five years, during which time the individual had to become formally certified in order to continue teaching. This means that such individuals could be hired to teach without ever having taken courses in teaching methods, lesson planning, or child development, or ever having completed a student teaching practicum. This was exactly the case for Ms. Maas. She had just returned from an extended period living in Chile and, in part owing to the tight job market in Chicago, decided to try teaching: "I thought it was within the realm of possibilities. If I liked it, I would study and continue." She was offered two teaching positions and chose IAMS because "I liked the mission, not trying to wean kids from their first language, and the promotion of biculturalism."

Ms. Maas had graduated from a prestigious university, spoke fluent, educated Spanish, and was exceptionally bright and creative. However, IAMS hired her for one of its most challenging positions despite the fact she was almost entirely unprepared to carry it out. Exacerbating this situation was the fact that she was provided with no fixed curriculum (she said later with a chuckle, "I was told I would have a tremendous opportunity to create my own curriculum") and very little mentoring. For the social studies curriculum, she simply followed the textbook that she found in the classroom. For Spanish language arts, she exchanged emails with a teacher friend in Chile and chose to focus on narratives, poetry, and plays, although the class barely moved past the narratives. She chose the texts from an anthology she had used during her own high school years. Although IAMS had a Spanish language arts textbook for eighth grade, Ms. Maas "wasn't fond of it because there wasn't a lot of stuff by native speakers. It was mostly translated."

Ms. Maas admitted that she had no preparation in lesson plan or curriculum development. However, some of her classroom activities were very well designed and well received by the students. For example, one day she had pairs of students do a role-play activity in which Andrew Jackson and John Calhoun argued about national policy toward Native Americans. Students often became interested in a particular topic of conversation, such as the legend of La Llorona or the impending war in Iraq, although they usually shouted out their opinions in English. Overall, however, Ms. Maas's pedagogy and assessment were uneven. Oftentimes during groupwork, students were not given concrete tasks to complete, or the tasks were not particularly engaging. Social studies tests were often in a multiple choice format that required rote memorization, with questions asked in random order instead of presented in thematic sections such as "La compra de Louisiana," "La independencia," and "Los pioneros exploradores." Vocabulary tests consisted of uncontextualized lists of words pulled from a recently read story that students had to define.

Ms. Maas was told to pick a mentor at the beginning of the year, even though she did not yet know her colleagues. Once she had picked one, however, no mentoring happened: "I was told that if I needed help, I would have to ask for it. The problem was that I was so overwhelmed, I was unable to verbalize my questions. I had so many. I didn't even know how to write a lesson plan." In January, the school librarian, as part of her regular assistance to social studies teachers prior to the history fair, taught four lessons to Ms. Maas's class about Internet research and choosing a research topic. Ms. Maas recalled, "One time she walked into my class and saw the bedlam, and that I was at my wits' end. I asked her if anyone had ever just walked out and never come back. She knew I was in deep trouble."

Classroom management was one of Ms. Maas's biggest challenges. The students sensed early on that Ms. Maas was unable to discipline them, and during my very first visits to her class during the third week of school, I noticed that many students were off task, unruly, and sometimes very rude to her and to one another. During teacher-fronted activities, I routinely observed them doing their math homework, chatting about popular music artists, yawning loudly, or putting their head on their desks. They would get up whenever they wanted, knocking over chairs and yelling to one another. Often there were public displays of boredom or disinterest.

On one occasion a student shouted out, "What time do we leave here?" and another said, "Mmm that chicken smells good." Ms. Maas responded angrily, "Excuse me! Class is not over yet." The second student replied, "It's not?" and another chimed in, "It will be in two minutes." When asked to read stories and answer questions in groups, usually only one or two groups out of six would complete the assignment. The others either did homework for other classes, played tic-tac-toe, chatted about things of interest to them, walked around the room, or performed their identities by shouting things at one another.[2] Students would also taunt the teacher by laughing when their classmates were disciplined.

At the beginning of the school year, Ms. Maas's response was to yell at the students. By November, she began waiting for them to quiet down. She also began issuing "warnings" that would lead to further discipline, such as having to stay in during recess. However, this ended up being more of a punishment for the teacher than for the students: "I'd be losing my lunch period. Another period of me trying to discipline these kids, how torturous." Although I had committed myself to observing the school environment without affecting it, I was upset by the lack of respect and abusive treatment that Ms. Maas endured. On several occasions I asked Ms. Castro and Ms. Gingiss (the English teacher) to allow Ms. Maas to observe their classes two or three times and take note of their management practices, and offered to cover Ms. Maas's classes myself while she did this. However, this idea never materialized. By April, Ms. Maas had given up, telling me, "This really won't be a class anymore. The harder I try, the ruder they are with me." Later she said, "I was burning out. [A colleague] gave me a copy of *Assertive Discipline*, but you can't always benefit from written resources, you have to talk to somebody. Every Sunday night, I got a knot in my stomach, thinking, Do I have to go back there? I was often bawling after school."

Despite the curricular and discipline problems, there were no complaints from parents about Ms. Maas. She attributed this to their overall lack of concern with their children's Spanish development. The only parents who contacted her during the year were those whose children got grades much lower than usual. For example, one girl was given the first C she had ever received in her life because she did not complete a single journal assignment. After a parent-teacher conference, she began producing some journals. On the other hand, the mother of focal student Carolina mentioned how much she appreciated Ms. Maas's quick and regular responses to her email inquiries about her daughter's progress, stating that she was the only teacher who did so.

These descriptions of Ms. Maas's difficult situation are a necessary background to the patterns of student language use and behavior that I observed in her classroom. Classroom management is intimately tied with language use in immersion environments, specifically the ways in which Spanish use is rewarded and English use is sanctioned, because it is difficult to get students to use the minority language. Aside from her very infrequent uses of English to discipline students, Ms. Maas herself used Spanish almost 100% during instructional time, most admirably even after she had given up on herself as a teacher. However, she did not possess the experience or skills necessary to keep the students using Spanish consistently.

Language Use during Spanish Language Arts and Social Studies: General Observations

I observed a total of 48 lessons taught by Ms. Maas over a period of five months, including 12 Spanish language arts lessons, 21 social studies lessons, and 15 Fridays on which students presented their current events news articles. Of these 48 lessons, 20 were recorded using a digital voice recorder. The recorder was sometimes left on a group of students' desks and was sometimes carried around the room by me during classroom discussions.

The general pattern of language use I observed was that students used exclusively English with one another, and mostly English when speaking aloud during a whole-class activity (referred to in Chapter 5 as *public turns*). The following general description of student language use during Spanish language arts and social studies classes is divided into two categories: use of Spanish and resistance to Spanish. Then, I will present a more detailed quantification of language use during one class period.

Use of Spanish

Although students would often make their public contributions to a discussion in English or, even more notable, give a presentation in English that they was supposed to be done in Spanish, there are many examples in the corpus of students completing presentations in Spanish, answering the teacher's questions in Spanish, and even following a classmate's public English turn with a Spanish turn. When students were involved in a teacher-fronted activity, they seemed as likely to make their contributions in English as they were in Spanish. Even Otto, who had a relatively low level of Spanish proficiency and use, occasionally attempted to make public turns in Spanish, such as "Los indios estaban peleando con los white men."[3] When students used English, the teacher would often request that they use Spanish, which was sometimes successful, even if only for one turn. In Example 1, the teacher asked the student to use Spanish in Line 2, and in Line 5 the teacher translated the student's English turn in another attempt to prompt her to use Spanish:

(1)
1 **Student:**   My article is about this Muslim lady, she . . .
2 **Teacher:**   ¿Puedes decirlo en español?
3 **Student:**   Una mujer que, um, she beat her kids, um, con las manos.
4   She had two kids, one was five and one was two.
5 **Teacher:**   Tenía dos niños, uno de cinco anos y otro de dos.
6 **Student:**   Entonces ahora el papá tiene custodia de los niños y ella va a la cárcel.

One interesting use of Spanish that appeared fairly often was what I will call mock discipline. This happened 12 times in the corpus among a group of three boys in one classroom. On one occasion, two of the boys were misbehaving and Ms. Maas chastised them in Spanish. The third boy followed her turn by saying, "¡Niñas! ¡No se rompan las medias!" ("Girls! Don't rip your pantyhose!") On another occasion, the teacher requested that one of the boys throw out his gum, to which another of the boys shouted out, "Bótalo" ("Throw it away"). If one of them spoke aloud in English, another might yell out, "¡En español!" ("In Spanish!"). These were clearly intended to imitate a teacher's use of Spanish and probably served to antagonize the interlocutor, and perhaps the teacher as well, although when I asked one of the three boys about these Spanish uses, he simply replied, "'Cause the words, in Spanish . . . to say something like that, they're funny." Other specific examples of students' Spanish use will be presented in the detailed analysis of the current events lesson.

Resistance to Spanish

There are at least two ways in which students can show resistance to something they are asked to do: they can do the opposite, or they can complain about it. This section describes examples of both types of resistance to Spanish that I encountered during my observations of eighth-grade Spanish language arts and social studies classroom. An actual quantification of students' English use will be offered in the analysis of the current events lesson later in this chapter. It will be seen that students used English two-thirds of the time, which is a clear resistance to using Spanish. Here,

I will describe students' other behaviors and statements that can be interpreted as resistance to using Spanish.

Clearly the use of English constitutes a resistance to using Spanish. But sometimes, instead of using English outright, students would claim they did not know how to say what they wanted to say in Spanish. When the teacher would request that they use Spanish, they often did, but would switch back to English before very long, as in Example 2.

(2)　**T**　= Teacher, **M.H.** = L2 student

T:　A ver, M., ¿qué estabas diciendo?
M.H.:　I can't say it in Spanish.
T:　Por supuesto que lo puedes decir en espanol.
M.H.:　[*Laughing*] Bush and an Illinois senator . . .
T:　Bush y un senador de Illinois.
M.H.:　Bush y un Senador de Illinois estaban hablando off the record, y, um, Bush dijo algo sobre, um, que iban a asesinar a Saddam Hussein. Y después él se fue y se lo dijo al *media*, y ahora todos los saben y Bush *is mad at him*.
T:　Y Bush está . . .
M.H.:　Enojado con él.

Current events classes, which will be described in greater detail in the following section, saw the greatest use of Spanish by the students. However, even during current events, students often began in English and only switched to Spanish when repeatedly asked to do so by the teacher. It was also clear that many students did not prepare for their presentations. Some would use relatively simple words like "people" or "twin brother" in English instead of looking up the equivalents in Spanish. One day in October, Otto went to the front of the room to give his presentation and stated to the teacher, "I'm gonna say it primero en inglés, después en español." However, he never followed his English presentation with a Spanish version. Ms. Maas simply stated, "Me hiciste trampa" ("You tricked me"). Even Melissa once gave a presentation about a review of a play, but did not look up in advance several words that she needed to say in Spanish. During her presentation she asked, "¿Cómo se dice *review*?" and "How do you say *version*?" On many days, and particularly in Group 1, only a handful of students even brought an article and volunteered to present. The rest took a zero for the assignment, and the period was spent without a lesson. I often observed students writing their article summary – that is, completing their Spanish current events homework – while other students were giving their presentations.

In another example of students' resistance to Spanish, I observed some of them questioning outright the school's language policy. One day in October, a boy asked Ms. Maas defiantly, "Why are we doing history in Spanish? In high school, they ask us for English." The teacher replied, "Porque ésta es una escuela bilingüe" ("Because this school is bilingual"). Otto called out in response, "I'm not going to be taking Spanish in high school." On another afternoon in December, a third-generation Puerto Rican student, with very low Spanish proficiency, began her current events presentation in English. When the teacher asked her to use Spanish, she retorted, "It doesn't matter, estudios sociales [social studies] shouldn't be in Spanish anyway." The teacher replied, "It is in this school," prompting the student to claim, "This school is stupid." Although hers appeared to be a minority opinion, there were at least a handful of students who were willing to express dissatisfaction with the school's expectations for their Spanish use.

Another way in which students expressed resistance to Spanish was through their reactions to classmates who were recent immigrants from Latin America and who spoke it fluently and quickly. J.S., a humorous and studious Cuban boy who had arrived to the United States in fifth grade, would be a few sentences into his current events presentations when the rest of the students would erupt in a chorus of "Huh? I don't understand him." It may be that some of his classmates were unaccustomed to a Caribbean accent, but he was perfectly comprehensible. These reactions indicate that students did not expect or appreciate when their peers spoke to them in Spanish.

Language Use during a Typical Social Studies Current Events Class

For the fifth-grade analysis of classroom language use presented in Chapter 4, I coded every utterance produced by the four focal students during twelve and half hours of language arts and social studies classroom recordings. In the eighth-grade year of this study, I did not conduct the same type of analysis. There are two reasons for this. First, one of the four focal students was not in the same eighth-grade classroom group as the other three students, which would have required double the recordings and interpretations of the two different classroom contexts. Second, from the beginning of my observations in eighth grade, I noticed that students used very little Spanish with the teacher and practically none with one another, making a detailed turn-by-turn analysis unnecessary.

What I did instead was analyze a typical class, calculating the number of teacher turns and student responses in each language. The class I chose to analyze was a particular kind of social studies class called current events, which happened each Friday. The reason I chose current events is the following. The majority of Spanish language arts and social studies classes began with teacher-fronted explanations, followed by a period of groupwork, and ending with teacher-fronted evaluations. Research has shown that most teacher-fronted classes follow the "initiation-response-evaluation" pattern, in which the teacher initiates an exchange with a question, students respond, and the teacher evaluates their response. In this type of participant structure, students tend to produce relatively short turns, which was indeed the case in the classes I observed. In addition, all groupwork that I observed during the eighth-grade year took place in English. Therefore, it was difficult to find student Spanish turns of sufficient length for analysis.

The solution was to analyze a current events period. Each Friday, as part of their social studies curriculum, students were required to bring in a news article from the current week and read aloud to the class a written summary in Spanish that they had prepared about the article. They were also supposed to pose a question to the class based on what they had reported. Although Ms. Maas claimed that this assignment was an attempt to unite Spanish and social studies, she did not require that the news article be written in Spanish,[4] which often led to the following scenario. A student would go to the front of the room and begin summarizing an article in English, and only upon repeated requests from the teacher would he or she use Spanish. It also meant that the students often did not prepare in advance the vocabulary they would need to present the article in Spanish. However, the current events class of March 7, 2003, had good levels of student presentations and participation, and was also typical enough to merit analysis.

The current events period that I analyzed was 45 minutes long. Owing to the expository nature of the participant structure during current events, many of the students' turns were relatively lengthy, some lasting up to two minutes. I could identify the specific student in most turns because I recognized their voices on the recordings, but approximately 10% of the student turns could not be attributed to any particular student. As mentioned earlier, students used English very frequently, sometimes mixing in a single Spanish word, other times switching completely to English after starting to speak in Spanish. I used Myers-Scotton's (1993) definitions of code switching in the following way. First, I divided each of the students' turns into sentences. "Sentence" is defined loosely as a unit of speech that, in writing, would likely be marked with a period. This obviously involved some degree of subjective interpretation. Examples 2 and 3 show how turns were divided into sentences. Each sentence is marked with a number.

(2)

1   Mi artículo es de algo que pasó el miércoles... este miércoles. (2) Um... fue una protesta de estudiantes de... um, de secundaria y de colegio... um, que protestaron, uh... against la guerra... que no querían que la guerra pase. (3) Um, y... uh... this was like, nationwide. (4) Habían protestas en San Francisco y en Nueva York, um..y en otras partes. (5) Yo pienso que esta protesta es... es algo bueno... porque como un estudiante dijo, es más importante... esto es más importante que la escuela, por ahora. / (6) Um.... porque mucha gente va a morir si la guerra empieza. / (7) That's my article.

(3)

1   También además... tienes más a tu lado... (2) Tienes más como, like, just like... (3) Everything that you need for a war. (4) Like I don't know, weapons and stuff.

Next, each monolingual sentence was coded as either English or Spanish. When there was a switch from one language to another within the same sentence (known as intrasentential code switching), it was coded according to the following categories: Spanish base + English lexical item (such as "Todos los hombres necesitan ir al *war.*"); Spanish base + English island[5] (such as "Ellos estan pensando a darles como algunos pequenos de sus, um, de sus *weapons, or whatever*"), English base + Spanish lexical item (there were no examples in this recording), or English base + Spanish island ("They need to get rid of *sus armas, um, de ma... de poder... de* , like, sus armas"). Determining the base language was sometimes complicated, as demonstrated by the four sentences in the turn shown in Example 4.

Example 4 Difficulties determining the base language
(1)   Ellos no van a, like... (2) They're not gonna... (3) Como que ya sabemos que no vas a solucionar nada con fighting. (4) Pero también cuando they're like talking they're not doing anything, so they're probably better off just fighting.

(1)   Spanish base + English lexical item
(2)   English
(3)   Spanish base + English lexical item
(4)   English base + Spanish island

Often, the language in which a sentence begins is the base language. However, according to Myers-Scotton (1993), the language that provides the majority of the content morphemes is the base language. In the case of Sentence 4, the greater number of content morphemes are in Spanish, so it was coded as a Spanish base + English island, even though the sentence began in English.

Findings

Table 6.1 displays the findings of language use by students and teacher during this 45-minute class period that, in theory, was supposed to take place 100% in Spanish.

As Table 6.1 shows, the teacher used Spanish almost 97% of the time during this current events class. Although during my observations she occasionally used English to discipline the students, during this particular class period, her uses of English were always to give English equivalents of content that the students did not understand in Spanish, such as "United Nations Security Council" or "enlist in selective service."

Students' sentences were in Spanish approximately one third of the time (39%) and in English two thirds of the time (62%). Public Spanish use during this eighth grade class period, then, at almost 40%, was slightly less than half of the 84% public Spanish turns that students had produced in fifth grade. Some students used Spanish for extended turns, such as in example 5, and other times they used English for extended turns, such as in example 6. I was unable to determine any pattern in students' language choices during this current events lesson.

Example 5 Extended Spanish turn

M.H. (L2): Yo no estoy completamente a favor pero no estoy completa-mente en contra. Porque como han sido . . . creo que doce años que han dicho a Sadam Hussein que se tiene que quitar todas sus armas. Que ya es tiempo, que se tienen que hacer algo más de hablar y escucharle dar mentiras. Y si hay una posibilidad de sacar a Saddam Hussein, será mucho más fácil.

Example 6 Extended English turn

C.P. (L1): OK, I have a question. Why is it that Bush wants to bomb them and not another place like . . . Didn't like, the U.S. like him or something, used to help Iraq when, like . . . before, and then, like, they did something that like got him mad and so now. . . .

Table 6.1 Spanish and English turns during a typical eighth-grade current events class

	Spanish				English			
	Monolingual Spanish	Spanish base + English lexical item	Spanish base + English island	**Total Spanish**	Monolingual English	English base + Spanish lexical item	English base + Spanish island	**Total English**
Teacher	93.3%	1.4%	1.8%	96.5%	3.5%	0	0	3.5%
(*n* = 283)	(264)	(4)	(5)	(273)	(10)			(10)
Students	28.3%	5.5%	4.9%	38.7%	60.1%	0	1.2%	61.9%
(*n* = 328)	(93)	(18)	(16)	(127)	(197)		(6)	(203)

Table 6.2 Six students with greatest number of turns during this class period

	M.H.	*C.P.*	*L.D.*	*J.S.*	*A.M.*	*I.G.*
Number of turns	73	54	27	26	25	19
Percent of total number of student turns in corpus ($n = 328$)	22%	16%	8%	8%	8%	6%

It is worth noting that 68% of all the coded student sentences during this class were produced by six students. Table 6.2 displays this information. By this account, the language use data presented here is representative of only one third of the class. The other two-thirds of the students made relatively few public turns and, therefore, used even less Spanish than what is reported here.

Except for the periods of time during which students presented their articles, this class resembled many other social studies and language arts classes that I observed. Students used English among one another, only switching to Spanish when speaking publicly to the teacher. Even then, the teacher usually had to insist on Spanish use several times before the students would speak it, and they would often switch back to English very quickly.

"Our success is our undoing": Faculty responses to fifth and eighth-grade language use findings

After I analyzed the eighth-grade classroom language use data, I interviewed the three eighth-grade teachers, two teachers in other grades, and three administrators. I wanted to know whether they were aware of the students' persistent use of English that I had found in both fifth grade and eighth grade and, if so, what understandings they had of the situation.

A complaint mentioned in response by several individuals was the fact that the school was not allowed to select students based on language dominance. One teacher explained that most magnet school lotteries were structured according to racial category. That is, a certain percent of students must be African American, Hispanic, or white. Although Inter-American is permitted to admit a higher percentage of Hispanic students than many other magnet schools in order to promote their dual language mission, they were not allowed to use home language use as a lottery selection criterion. This teacher claimed that IAMS had tried to do so, but was forced to stop. She also explained that magnet schools are not permitted to go into any neighborhoods and recruit students, but that a certain amount of recruitment in Latino neighborhoods did happen surreptitiously. A different teacher stated, "We talked about recruiting down on 18th street [in the heart of the largest Mexican neighborhood in Chicago] but then they cut our bussing. They eliminated our preschool buses, and our other buses can only pick up kids who live six miles away or less. And besides, even if students come to preschool as Spanish dominant, by third grade they're very bilingual."

The school's cofounder, Adela Coronado-Greeley, echoed this sentiment by stating unequivocally: "Too many of our students are already bilingual and more dominant in English than in Spanish. 50% of our kids should be Spanish dominant when they begin at the school." She argued that the school used to be permitted to select students based on language proficiency and that they should fight to regain that ability: "You can't wait for things, you have to do them." She also noted that some English-dominant children were accepted to the school after third grade although there was a policy against it, and suggested that the school stop doing so.

A related issue, which has been found in heritage language communities across the country, is that younger siblings tend to use less of the heritage language than older siblings. Older siblings often spend their early years in a monolingual Spanish-speaking home. They then learn English at school, and eventually speak it at home with their younger siblings. Because of this English use in the home, the younger siblings usually develop less Spanish than the older ones. Two teachers admitted that Inter-American's sibling policy, although an important part of their mission to a create family-oriented school, "works against us linguistically." Adela noted that the sibling priority policy was developed for families to maintain *Spanish* competency, but that students were so successful at acquiring English at Inter-American that their younger siblings were no longer Spanish dominant. In addition, the school had built such a strong reputation that it was attracting middle-class, English-dominant families. Looking pensive, she pronounced her conclusion about the school's role in students' English and Spanish development: "Our success [in English] is our undoing [in Spanish]."

Other individuals cited the increasingly middle-class constitution of the IAMS community as responsible for the waning enrollment of Spanish-dominant students. As Adela told me, "We couldn't get any English speakers when we first started out. We used to put flyers up in welfare offices, hospital waiting rooms, Jewel [a grocery store]. Now we have very educated people applying for the school." Referring to the recent push to move the school to a new building, and referencing the requirement that 30% of the student body live in the immediate vicinity of the school, one teacher stated: "We're so desperate to get out of Lakeview and into a working-class neighborhood. We've become so well known that many middle-class types with pull are in here. This has become a school of privilege." The school's other cofounder, Janet Nolan, expressed concern that instead of being a dual immersion program with a 50% to 60% Hispanic population, the school seemed on its way to becoming a one-way Spanish immersion program. She noted that the school used to be a port of entry for Latino parents who "developed their voice" there. However, she said that she no longer saw many less empowered Latino parents at the school, and that the number of English Language Learning children had decreased (Kirk, 2000, provides quantitative evidence that this is indeed the case).

Although I asked the people I interviewed to respond to my findings of language use in two classrooms, one fifth- and one eighth-grade, clearly students' language use patterns are not isolated there. They have their roots in practices and expectations throughout the students' years at the school. One teacher told me that the year before, the teachers' organization:

> sat down and analyzed how many minutes of Spanish students were really getting at each grade level. We all found surprises. It's a constant topic of conversation, we're always worrying about it. Through a grant, we spent time in the summer working on projects that carried over from year to year, including professional development for teachers. For a few years, we worked on integrating Spanish grammar into our units. But there are always so many interruptions. And you need to get momentum. We would do a few lessons, the whole faculty would be involved, we'd look at the scope and sequence, but it was frustrating because you need to spend massive amounts of time. Grammar has been a pressing issue that comes up periodically among teachers and parents. Last year we said, an even more pressing issue than grammar is social use of Spanish. We set up a sequence of four activities per year such as games, movies, songs. First we would present them to the faculty. We would play then together, then people would come back with more games. But then the momentum runs out.

Various individuals I interviewed also mentioned the importance of students' attitudes in their language use. Although I address this topic in greater depth through the concept of investment in Chapters 5 and 8,

I will mention here these individuals' responses during our interviews. According to one teacher:

> Spanish is something the teachers want you to do, so by definition you don't want to do it. Students are willing to go with it until social considerations are more important to them. It's getting worse in some ways. It's become more shamelessly blatant, like "We won't do it and we're proud of it." It feels that way to me.

She felt that in general, students' motivations to use Spanish were not strong enough, and that if Inter-American could create a strong enough *need* for students to speak Spanish in order to get what they want, they would do it. For example, she noted that in sixth grade, students get a grade for speaking Spanish, a practice that she felt should be implemented at additional grade levels. This teacher also tied Spanish use with academic achievement, claiming that the students most willing to use Spanish tended to be those who achieved the most academically (a trend I noticed among the fifth graders, see Chapter 5). Another teacher commented that in general, the school's expectations for Spanish use were not high enough, but also that "students are insecure about their Spanish, which becomes habitual as they move through our classrooms." In my two years of observations, I often noticed students who would rather be silent than speak in Spanish, saying "never mind" after the teacher made repeated requests that they use Spanish.

School cofounder Adela Coroando-Greeley commented specifically about the eighth grade language use findings. She noted that in their early teenage years, students might not value Spanish very much, but that "the seed, the sprout is there." Each year, several Inter-American graduates return to compete for a college scholarship named after Adela's daughter and, according to Adela, at that point the students clearly understand the value of Spanish and appreciate the opportunities that IAMS provided for them. She called this "delayed appreciation." Adela also mused on the needs of the students and the important role of the dedication and skill of the teachers:

> The school shouldn't be a total Spanish immersion, that would be a detriment to the children who need to learn English. I would far prefer what we have. I don't say it's perfect. I do believe that some young teacher is going to have the answer for it. We have wonderful teachers in the primary grades who don't allow a word of English in their classrooms. In our upper grades, children are in adolescence, so perhaps the teachers let them get away with more.

Commenting on the same phenomenon of resistance to Spanish, Janet Nolan said that most people, including IAMS students, do not want to be a part of a group that is discriminated against. She described past campaigns at the school to build the status of Spanish, including a weeklong fair. It included carnival games that the older students made for the younger students, such as booths where children could guess the number of beans in a jar. For the older students, speakers from a local Spanish-language radio station came to speak in Spanish about how important the language was. There were contests involving giving speeches, spelling bees, and writing competitions, all in Spanish. This seemed to me an excellent way to involve the entire school in Spanish-language activities, and also responded to the numerous schoolwide and district-wide competitions that took place in English. Unfortunately, there were no such school-wide activities during the two years I spent at the school.

Janet added that one year, the teachers were going to produce a book of children's games in Spanish that was to be used in classrooms, on the playground, and in physical education classes. In order to gather material, they began to ask teachers about the games they used to play in their home countries. However, Janet did not know if the book was ever completed. Despite the difficulties in carrying out new ideas, a current teacher noted, "We're lucky because teachers come here with a purpose. We constantly get new blood, and there are enough of us oldies but goodies who never say die. We're easy to reinspire."

The assistant principal, considering ways that Spanish use could be increased in IAMS classrooms, pondered the suggestion that teachers have only monolingual relationships with students. For example, in fifth grade, instead of having Ms. Torres all day long for all of their subjects, students would have her in the morning for Spanish language arts, math, and the half of social studies that was taught in Spanish, and they would have a different teacher in the afternoon for English language arts and for the other half of social studies taught in English. This way, students could only use Spanish with certain individuals. However, he decided that such a practice would lead to "departmentalization," or a separation of teaching efforts, which he felt was not a good approach for teaching primary and intermediate grades.

In conclusion of this section, at various levels, the school community was conscious of the need to actively and consistently promote the Spanish language, and had produced many good ideas for doing so. However, many of these ideas had either ceased being promoted or were not completed. Among the six teachers and administrators I interviewed at the end of 2003, I noted enthusiasm and a desire to improve from four of them, and a more resigned and negative attitude from two of them. However, based on two years of observations and informal conversations, the positive responses are more representative of the school community in general. What appear to be necessary are a focused drive to make improvements, the willingness to decide on a group plan, and the support necessary to carry the group's ideas out to fruition over the long term.

Conclusions: Language Use in Eighth Grade

This chapter has shown that actual Spanish use in eighth grade was not in accordance with the official 50% policy. Math and science were taught almost 100% in English, and although Ms. Maas, the Spanish language arts and social studies teacher, used Spanish almost exclusively during Spanish lessons, students used Spanish an average of 40% of the time for their public turns during her Spanish lessons, which is less than half of the 84% of public Spanish turns they had used in fifth grade.

Young people at the age of 13 and 14 tend to demonstrate resistance to authority on many levels as they seek to negotiate and develop their individual identities. Therefore, it is no surprise that this eighth-grade class resisted using Spanish, particularly when there were no sanctions against using English. In addition, the students' upcoming transition to high school, where Spanish is not necessary for entrance or for success therein, influenced their practices and their discourse regarding the importance of Spanish.

It certainly would not be fair or accurate to assume that the school year 2002–2003, during which an inexperienced teacher bravely attempted to teach eighth-grade Spanish language arts and social studies, indicates a regular practice of the school. It is beyond the scope of this book to analyze the ways in which the teachers before and after Ms. Maas understood their task and to what degree they met the school's official goals for eighth grade. However, the fact that such an inexperienced teacher was hired for arguably one of the most difficult positions in the school speaks to the low expectations held by the administration during this period for eighth-grade Spanish instruction.

The ultimate Spanish linguistic proficiency attained by IAMS students upon graduation was built long before they set foot in Ms. Maas's classroom, and may in fact be a more reliable indicator of the schools' expectations for students' Spanish development. Students' Spanish proficiency upon graduation will be the focus of Chapter 7. In-depth interviews with the four focal students and their parents, as well as with eight of their classmates, are presented in Chapter 8 as additional context for understanding the students' language choices and development. As seen in Chapter 5, individuals' identity investments cannot be ignored when trying to fully understand issues of language use.

Notes

1. It should be noted that the concerns described here about academic rigor in the upper cycle apply only to this particular school. In general, dual immersion programs are designed to be highly academically challenging.
2. However, when the assigned groupwork task was to produce a story, most groups would complete the activity, even though they talked about it in English and translated the story into Spanish as the final step.
3. The insertion of English lexical items or switches between languages was very frequent, as will be seen in the detailed analysis of the current events class.
4. Ms. Maas said that students complained vociferously that they could not understand news articles written in Spanish that they found on the Internet or in Chicago's free weekly Spanish language newspaper.
5. Embedded language islands were discussed in Chapter 5.

Chapter 7
Spanish Proficiency in Eighth Grade

Chapter 6 demonstrated that during eighth-grade classes that were taught in Spanish, students used even less Spanish publicly (39%) than they had in fifth grade (84%), and they used English 100% of the time when speaking with peers. Given these relatively low levels of Spanish output, a logical question to ask is, To what degree does students' Spanish proficiency develop during their years at the school? In the remaining sections of this chapter, I will describe the results on several measures of students' Spanish proficiency administered during their eighth-grade year (age 13–14), presenting findings on students' overall oral and written Spanish proficiency, their production of various grammatical forms, including the subjunctive, the conditional, and tense and aspect, and their sociolinguistic proficiency.

Table 7.1 presents information about the 52 eighth-grade participants, including the age at which they began learning Spanish and English. All students in this graduating class began learning their L2 upon entering the dual immersion school, except for the nine Spanish L1 students who began learning English and Spanish simultaneously in the home. The majority of the Spanish L1 students began learning English in preschool. Most Spanish L2 students began learning Spanish in kindergarten or first grade, followed by those who began in preschool.

The five students labeled "Recent Arrivals" had immigrated to the United States from Latin America during sixth or seventh grade, only one to two years before this study. They were native Spanish speakers who received English as a Second Language support at school. Although after a year or two in the United States they were technically no longer monolingual Spanish speakers, we will compare the L1 and L2 students' performance to theirs. Unfortunately there were not enough Recent Arrivals, nor enough students in each category of age of first exposure to the L2, to make statistical comparisons between all groups and subgroups. Therefore, in this study we will compare statistically only students in the categories of "L1" and "L2." We will then comment on the performance of recent arrivals in comparison to the other two groups of students.

Table 7.1 Student participants

	Age began learning Spanish	*Age began learning English*
Spanish L1, heritage speakers $n = 30$		In home since birth $n = 9$
	In home since birth	4 years old (preschool) $n = 14$
		5–6 years old (kindergarten or 1st grade) $n = 5$
		8–9 years old (3rd–4th grade) $n = 2$
Spanish L2 $n = 17$	4 years old (preschool) $n = 6$	In home since birth
	5–6 years old (kindergarten or 1st grade) $n = 8$	
	8–9 years old (3rd–4th grade) $n = 3$	
Spanish L1, recent arrivals $n = 5$	In home since birth	10–12 years old

Measures

I sought to examine dual immersion students' overall oral, written, and reading proficiency, as well as specific aspects of their sociolinguistic and grammatical production, using a variety of measures, some of which were modeled after those used in by researchers in Canadian immersion classrooms (Harley *et al.*, 1990). Table 7.2 displays the measures used, and a description of each measure follows.

Spanish proficiency in speaking, writing, and reading

Two measures were used to rate students' oral Spanish. One was the Spanish Language Assessment Scales-Oral (LAS-O), a standardized exam consisting of identifying vocabulary items displayed in 10 drawings, a multiple-choice listening comprehension section, and listening to a story and then retelling it while viewing picture prompts (see Appendix 7.A for the story text). All portions of the LAS-O were graded by an independent

Table 7.2 Measures

	(A) Oral	(B) Written	(C) Multiple choice, sentence completion and translation
(1) Grammar	Story retelling LAS-O	Narrative story from	Sentence completion (24 items); translation (13 items)
(2) Sociolinguistic competence	Role plays (6 situations)	Letter of persuasion to a landlord; letter from parent to child	Multiple choice (10 items)
(3) Reading	n/a	n/a	*Logramos* test
(4) Writing	n/a	Narrative story	n/a
(5) Speaking and listening proficiency	1. LAS-O 2. FLOSEM	n/a	LAS-O

consulting firm authorized by the publishers of the exam. I also used the Foreign Language Oral Skills Evaluation Matrix (FLOSEM), an upgraded version of the Student Oral Language Observation Matrix developed by the California Department of Education (Lindholm-Leary, 2001). The FLOSEM assesses oral language proficiency in five domains: comprehension, fluency, vocabulary, pronunciation, and grammar. It is not a test, but rather a matrix that is filled out by individuals who have had extensive interaction with students in a number of contexts. For this study, FLOSEM ratings were completed by two people: myself, who spent two days per week with the students, and the students' classroom Spanish teacher. Overall ratings never differed more than one point, in which case we averaged the two ratings.

To elicit a writing sample, we used a prompt similar to the one used by Canadian immersion researchers (Harley *et al.*, 1990). Students were given the first two lines of a story about a cat and some dogs, and were asked to complete the story. Their narratives were evaluated using a rubric based on the one developed by the Northwest Regional Laboratory (2002), which was designed for the evaluation of Spanish language narratives. A trained assistant and I rated the written narratives independently and came to an agreement on a final score.

Students' reading abilities were measured through the *Logramos* test (2002), a norm-referenced achievement test that assesses the academic progress of Spanish-speaking students. Two sections of the *Logramos* reading test were regularly administered to all IAMS students. The vocabulary portion includes multiple-choice questions that present words in the context of a phrase or short sentence, and students choose the answer whose meaning is closest to that of the given word. The reading comprehension portion consists of multiple-choice questions about reading passages that include poetry, fiction, biographical sketches, social studies selections, and topics of general interest.

Sociolinguistic appropriateness

Three measures, modeled after those used in French immersion contexts in Canada (Allen et al., 1983), were used to determine whether students could identify and produce appropriately polite Spanish. The first measure involved the production of two letters. In one, an informal task, students were asked to write a note from their mother instructing the student to clean their room before the arrival of company. In the other, a formal task, students were asked to pretend they had a dog and write a letter convincing a potential landlord to allow their family to rent an apartment that did not permit animals. The tasks were scored in the following way (based on Allen et al., 1983, with some modifications):

Tempering verbs. One point was given for any "tempering" uses of the imperfect subjunctive, the conditional, or the future (e.g. "Si *podrían* hacer un favor y dejar nuestro perrito..." or "*Quisiera* tener en su casa a mi perro"). One point was awarded for one or more such uses. Uses of the chronological future or conditional (such as "Les prometo que el perro no hará daño en el apartamento") were not counted here.

Polite pronouns. Two points were given if the letter used "usted" or "ustedes" more than once. One point was given if "usted(es)" was used only once or irregularly (that is, appearing along with "tú"). Zero points were assigned if there was no use of "usted(es)" or if one sole use of usted/ustedes was accompanied by more than one use of "tú."

Closing. One point was assigned if the letter had a closing that was moderately formal (such as "Gracias por escucharme" or "Atentamente"), while zero points were given if the closing was missing.

Respectfulness of arguments. This involved a subjective determination of how respectfully the students presented their points to support their request, and the level of respect implicit in their arguments. Two points were given if the letter was very respectful (including language like "Les quiero pedir un favor muy grande," or "Se lo suplico"), 1 point if it was moderately respectful, and zero points if the letter was not particularly respectful.

Two raters scored each letter independently – a trained assistant and I. Differences in scoring were minimal, and when this happened, we arrived at an average score. The maximum score on each letter was 6, indicating a very formal use of Spanish. After calculating the score for each letter, we calculated the difference in scores between the two letters. This is called the difference score, which demonstrates sensitivity to the different register level required in each letter (Allen *et al.*, 1983).

The second sociolinguistic measure involved oral role plays of requests. These conformed to Kasper and Dahl's (1991) definition of closed role plays, in which actors respond to the description of a situation. Students were asked to envision a situation and say aloud in Spanish how they would carry out the appropriate request. Three situations were formal: inviting an unknown man to sit down, asking a professor to explain an assignment, and asking a police officer for directions. The other three situations were informal: telling a dog to sit down, asking a younger sibling to turn off the television, and asking a friend to lower their voice. Each request could receive a maximum of 4 points: one point for any use of a politeness markers (such as "señor," "por favor," or "profesora"), 1 point for the use of "usted," 1 point for the use of a question ("¿Puedes bajar la voz?") or an indirect request ("Estás hablando muy alto"), and 1 point for the use of the conditional or the future ("¿Me podría indicar el camino?" or "¿Será que me puede ayudar?").[1] Thus the request "Profesora, ¿me podría explicar la tarea?" would receive 4 points, one in each of the scoring categories.

The third and final sociolinguistic measure was a set of 10 multiple-choice items. Appendix 7.B displays the written instructions provided for the students as well as the 10 question items. The option considered correct is underlined. These items attempted to determine whether students could identify the most appropriate utterance in each situation. Of the three possible answers, one is considered too informal and the other is either too formal or is more appropriate in a written context. The correct answers were based on the responses of five Spanish-dominant adults in a pilot study. However, as will be seen in the results, the multiple-choice measure did not appear to be reliable.

Grammatical production

The production of six forms was targeted by this study. Three of them were elicited using sentence completion prompts: the present subjunctive, the past subjunctive, and the conditional.[2] The instructions requested that students focus on the content of their response, which was to come from their opinions or their imaginations, and that there were no right or wrong answers. Two forms were elicited through a translation task: *gustar* and the use of the infinitive (vs. the gerund) in subject position. These two forms were chosen because they often show variation from normative monolingual use. The portion of the study examining these five forms was exploratory in nature in that I used only six to eight items per form and did not include distractor items. The sixth and final grammatical area was the correct production of the tense/aspect distinction between the preterite and the imperfect. This was analyzed through the verbs produced in oral and written narratives already described.

The sentence completion prompts are displayed in Tables 3 through 6. In Table 7.3, the subjunctive prompts appear with a description of the type of syntactic constructions (adjectival, adverbial, or nominal clauses) and semantic criteria (existential status, potential events, doubt, attitude, etc.) they represent. All are typically considered obligatory contexts for the subjunctive.

Table 7.3 Subjunctive sentence completion prompts

Present subjunctive	(1) "En la escuela, no me gusta que los maestros..." *Nominal/attitude* (2) "Mi mamá siempre me pide que..." *Nominal/command* (3) "Voy a estar feliz cuando..." *Adverbial/potential event* (4) "Es imposible que este año mis amigos..." *Nominal/attitude* (5) "Los papás trabajan para que sus hijos..." *Adverbial/potential event* (6) "Busco un novio/una novia que..." *Adjectival/[+/−]existential status*
Imperfect subjunctive	(7) "La semana pasada, me parecía muy mal que..." *Nominal/attitude* (8) "El año pasado, un amigo me pidió que..." *Nominal/command* (9) "Mis hermanos y yo compraríamos un nuevo televisor si nosotros.." *Apodosis* (10) "Anoche mi mamá me dio $10 para que yo..." *Adverbial/potential event* (11) "La semana pasada mi papá no quería que yo..." *Nominal/command* (12) "Mis primos vendrían más a mi casa si ellos..." *Apodosis*

Table 7.4 Conditional sentence completion prompts

(13) "Si yo tuviera mil dólares, yo . . . "
(14) "Si los maestros no dieran nada de tarea, nosotros . . . "
(15) "Yo___a esa muchacha si ella me diera su número de teléfono."
(16) "Si todas las computadoras tuvieran acceso al Internet, la gente . . . "
(17) Si estudiaras más, tú . . . "
(18) Mis amigos___si ellos tuvieran más tiempo."

The next set of questions focused on the conditional (see Table 7.4 for the prompts). However, many dialects of Spanish permit the imperfect or the past subjunctive in these contexts (e.g. "Si yo tuviera mil dólares, yo *compraba/comprara/compraría* una mansión"). Therefore, all three forms were coded as correct.

Table 7.5 shows the translation prompts for the *gustar* and gerund items. While translation tasks can be criticized as proficiency measures because they force students into what Grosjean (1998) calls a bilingual mode, these items are likely reflective to some degree of students' underlying grammatical systems.

Table 7.5 *Gustar* and gerund prompts

Gustar	1. Penelope likes Tom.
	2. Eighth graders like good teachers.
	3. My sister likes boys.
	4. My cousins like Coca-Cola.
	5. Mexicans like tacos.
	6. Adults don't like noise.
	7. My friend likes parties.
	8. People like watching good movies.
Gerund	1. People like watching good movies.
	2. Mary was arrested for stealing.
	3. Smoking is bad for your health.
	4. Having friends is important; they are someone you can talk with.
	5. The only thing he cares about is making money.

Results

Overall oral and written Spanish proficiency

Results of the LAS-O and the FLOSEM oral proficiency measures, the written measure, and reading scores are presented in Table 7.6. I have

Table 7.6 Students' oral, written, and reading Spanish proficiency

	L1 mean *N = 31* *(sd)*	*L2 mean* *N = 16* *(sd)*	*Recent arrival* *mean*** *N = 5* *(sd)*
Oral LAS-O, Total *(Max = 100)*	85.5* (6.99)	64.9* (8.06)	89.5 (5.92)
LAS-O, Story retelling[3] *(Max = 5)*	3.9* (0.61)	2.7* (0.47)	4.2 (0.45)
FLOSEM *(Max = 6)*	5.08* (0.71)	3.10* (0.82)	6.00 (0.00)
Writing: Global rating *(Max = 30)*	24.9* (3.27)	17.5* (5.00)	26.0 (3.53)
Reading: *Logramos* vocabulary (National percentile rank)	48.9 (sd = 24.8)	33.6 (sd = 22.7)	79.2 (sd = 10.7)
Logramos reading comprehension (National percentile rank)	66.7 (sd = 24.3)	58.1 (sd = 31.4)	77.4 (sd = 17.3)

* $p < 0.0001$.
** Not submitted to statistical analysis.

included the scores of the five Recent Arrival students for comparison, but these were not submitted to statistical analysis in this study owing to the low *N* size.

Overall, as might be expected, the L1 students were significantly superior to the L2 students on all measures except reading, where they scored better but not significantly so. In addition, L1 students were not far behind the Recent Arrivals on the oral and writing measures, indicating that L1 heritage Spanish speakers raised in the United States and attending this two-way immersion school have maintained strong levels of Spanish proficiency.

We see a relationship between scores on the LAS-O and on the FLOSEM, the two tests of oral Spanish proficiency. The L1 students scored proportionally very similarly on the LAS-O story (3.9 out of 5) as they did on the FLOSEM (5.1 out of 6). The same is true for the L2 students on the LAS-O story (2.7 out of 5) and the FLOSEM (3.1 out of 6). However, a few L2 students actually outscored L1 students on the LAS-O and on the FLOSEM, and not all Recent Arrival students got perfect scores on the LAS-O. This is likely because most standardized measures are biased for overall academic ability, rewarding what Cummins (1979) refers to as Cognitive Academic Language Proficiency, or CALP. The scores on the FLOSEM, however, more closely match what are called Basic Interpersonal Communication Skills (BICS); all of the Recent Arrivals did achieve the highest possible score on the FLOSEM. The high level of CALP expected on the LAS-O probably explains why some L2 students actually outscored a few L1 students, but does not explain why some L2s outscored L1s on the FLOSEM. The BICS/CALP distinction may also explain why the Recent Arrivals scored perfectly on the FLOSEM but not on the LAS-O or the writing measure; the only Recent Arrival student who got a 5 on the LAS-O story retelling came from a more highly educated home background than the other 4 Recent Arrival students.

In order to get a better sense of students' oral Spanish production, Appendix 7.C displays six story texts, representing both L1 and L2 students at the high, medium, and low level. Some errors are present in all but the highest rated L1 story, particularly the lack of "a" marking the object of the verb "gustar" ("Maria Elena le gustaba trabajar en su jardin"). L1 student C.D.'s highly rated story contained slightly more sophisticated vocabulary such as "placer," "pretender," and "cariñoso," as well as the conditional tense. L2 students showed some subject-verb agreement difficulties such as "ella dije" and "unos hombres le vinó". The lower rated stories were shorter, often contained switches to English, were missing definite articles ("hombres querían casarse con ella"), and showed numerous number and gender agreement problems. It is interesting that the high-scoring L2 student had the same ratings as the low-scoring L1 student, a difference that may be related to students' investment in developing their Spanish (which will be explored further in Chapter 8).

Appendix 7.D displays the story prompt and the written narratives of the same six students, again representing three levels of proficiency for both L1 and L2 students. Both L2 and L1 students evidence sufficient vocabulary and verb forms to make themselves understood, although the L2 students show problems with subject-verb agreement and with prepositions. Again, L2 student M.B. outscored L1 student M.C., although M.C. was grammatically more correct. For example, these two students produced contexts that required the subjunctive, and while M.B. did not produce the subjunctive ("Hizo que el gato era muy pareado"), M.C. did produce it all three times that it was required ("... para que *tiren* balazos para que los perros se *caigan*." And "... que causo que toda la gente se *moviera* al rio.")

Finally, students' national ranking on the *Logramos* reading comprehension test (displayed in Table 7.6) shows that the difference between L1 and L2 students' percentiles (66.7 and 58.1 respectively) did not reach significance, and both groups scored lower than the Recent Arrival students (77.4). These findings, although not statistically significant, stand somewhat in contrast to those found in Canadian immersion, where the immersion students scored equally well as native speaker controls on tests of reading comprehension. It may be that this reading measure was very difficult, given that even the Recent Arrival students did not score perfectly, although the CALP limitations of these particular Recent Arrival students mentioned earlier likely played a role in their reading scores. Students' vocabulary percentile rankings show a slightly bigger gap between L1 and L2 students (48.9 and 33.6 respectively) and an even bigger gap between L1 students and Recent Arrival students (79.2) than on the reading comprehension measure.

Sociolinguistic appropriateness

Results on the written letters show substantial differences between L1, L2, and Recent Arrival students (see Table 7.7).

As stated earlier, a high difference score between the formal and the informal letters is assumed to indicate a high level of sociolinguistic proficiency, specifically for making polite requests. The Recent Arrival students, whose formal letters were rated at an average of 5 out of 6 points, had the highest difference score (4.0) of all three groups, followed by the L1 (3.1) and then the L2 students (0.59). The formal and informal letters written by the

Table 7.7 Written letters of request

	L1 (n = 30)	L2 (n = 17)	Recent Arrival (n = 5)**
Formal letter Max. score = 6	3.83* (sd = 1.51)	1.82* (sd = 0.73)	5.0
Informal letter Max. score = 6	0.73 (sd = 0.52)	1.24 (sd = 0.66)	1.0
Difference score between formal & informal letters	3.10* (sd = 1.75)	0.59* (sd = 1.23)	4.0

* Significant at $p < 0.001$.
** Not submitted to statistical analysis.

Table 7.8 Oral role plays

	L1 (n = 30)	L2 (n = 17)	Recent Arrival (n = 5)**
Formal Max = 12	6.7* (sd = 1.75)	4.65* (sd = 1.32.)	7.6
Informal Max = 12	1.9 (sd = 1.37)	1.7 (sd = 59)	1.6
Difference score between formal and informal role plays	4.8* (sd = 1.75)	2.94* (sd = 1.44)	6.0

* Significant at $p < 0.001$.
** Not submitted to statistical analysis.

Spanish L2 students were rated almost equally (1.82 and 1.24 respectively), resulting in a very low difference score. This means that L2 students were unable to produce sufficiently formal written requests. Their informal letters were also more formal than those of the L1 and the Recent Arrival students. Similarly to the conclusions in Canadian immersion (Harley et al., 1990), these students seem to produce one level of language that is too formal in informal contexts, and not formal enough for formal ones. One consistent problem among the L2 students was the lack of consistency with polite verb forms. They often mixed "tú" and "usted" for the same addressee in both the formal and informal letters.

The oral role plays (Table 7.8) again showed considerable differences among the three groups of students.

All groups received approximately equal scores on the informal role plays. It was on the formal role-play task where differences among the three groups of students were apparent. As with the letters, the Recent Arrival students produced the most formal speech for the formal role plays and the most informal speech for informal role plays, resulting in the largest difference scores. The L1 and L2 students did display knowledge of register by using more formal Spanish for the formal contexts than in informal ones, but their difference scores were smaller than those of the Recent Arrivals. L2 students again produced the least formal language on the formal task, although their difference scores were greater on the oral role play than on the letters. This suggests that the L2 students had slightly greater ability to produce formal language in a face-to-face interaction than in writing.

Several role-play situations did not result in the type of language we expected. For example, even highly proficient L1 students used "tú" with the "Professor". This may be because these relatively young students do not have experience with professors, only with their primary school teachers, with whom in my years of observations they used "tú" exclusively. There were also some Recent Arrivals and some L1 students whose Spanish dialects use "usted" with typically informal addressees, such as younger siblings and dogs. During visits to the homes of two of the L1 students, I noticed that their parents regularly used "usted" with their children. Despite these anomalies, the role plays, like the letters, appeared to be a reliable measure of students' ability to adjust their Spanish according to the level of formality.

Finally, Table 7.9 displays the accuracy rates for each of the 10 multiple-choice items.

A *t* test revealed that there were no significant differences between the L1 and the L2 students on the multiple-choice items. The Recent Arrivals' responses were not submitted to statistical analysis, but they scored overall even less accurately than the L1 and the L2 students, leading me to doubt the validity of this measure. It is interesting to note that the three questions most often missed by the Recent Arrival students were questions #4, #7 and #10, which sought to elicit formal written Spanish (item 7 was missed by a large number of L1 and L2 students as well). This may be because

Table 7.9 Accuracy on multiple-choice items

Question #	L1 (n = 30)	L2 (n = 17)	Recent Arrival* (n = 5)
1	57% (17)	6% (1)	80% (4)
2	90% (27)	94% (16)	80% (4)
3	53% (16)	53% (9)	80% (4)
4	87% (26)	53% (9)	40% (2)
5	83% (25)	71% (12)	80% (4)
6	47% (14)	29% (5)	40% (2)
7	30% (9)	35% (6)	20% (1)
8	70% (21)	88% (15)	60% (3)
9	67% (20)	65% (11)	60% (3)
10	70% (21)	53% (9)	40% (2)
Average % correct	65.4%	54.7%	58.0%
Average # correct	6.53	6.06	5.80
sd	1.69	1.81	1.30

* Not submitted to statistical analysis.

Table 7.10 Production of elicited forms on open-ended items

Group	Present subjunctive (max = 6)		Imperfect subjunctive (max = 6)		Conditional/ imperfect (max = 6)	
	Mean	sd	Mean	sd	Mean	sd
L1 (n = 31)	4.39*	1.87	3.16*	1.61	5.00*	1.59
L2 (n = 16)	0.31*	0.793	0.50*	0.632	1.19*	1.33
Recent Arrival** (n = 5)	6.00	0.000	3.00	0.000	6.00	0.00

* Significant at $p < 0.001$.
** Not submitted to statistical analysis.

these students left their countries of origin before acquiring skills in formal written academic Spanish.

Some of the multiple-choice items, notably questions 2, 5, and 8, resulted in very frequent selection of the correct answer. However, in general, these did not appear to be reliable indicators of sociolinguistic proficiency. It has been noted that it is difficult to construct multiple-choice options that isolate pragmatic alternatives, making it impossible to determine the exact reason for which respondents opted for a given answer (Kasper & Rose, 2002: 97).

Grammatical production

The frequency of production of the present subjunctive, the imperfect subjunctive, and the conditional (or the imperfect subjunctive) is presented in Table 7.10.

Subjunctive

All 52 students completed the 12 subjunctive prompt items for a total of 676 tokens. Nine students, eight of whom were L1, on at least one item either produced no verb (e.g. in response to "Busco un novio que...," one student wrote only "guapo") or produced one uninflected infinitive. There were a total of 26 such responses, or 4.2% of the corpus of these 12 questions. The other 95.8% of responses included inflected verbs.

Table 7.11 Use of the present subjunctive by item

	L1 (n = 31)	L2 (n = 16)	Recent Arrival (n = 5)
(1) "En la escuela, no me gusta que los maestros... ,"	28 (90%)	0 (0%)	5 (100%)
(2) "Mi mamá siempre me pide que... "	25 (81%)	1 (6%)	5 (100%)
(3) "Voy aestar feliz cuando... "	17 (55%)	1 (6%)	5 (100%)
(4) "Es imposible que este año mis amigos... "	21 (68%)	0 (0%)	5 (100%)
(5) "Los papás trabajan para que sus hijos... "	26 (84%)	1 (6%)	5 (100%)
(6) "Busco un novio/una novia que... ."	19 (61%)	2 (13%)	5 (100%)

Table 7.10 shows that L1 students scored on average 4.39 correct (i.e. they produced the present subjunctive) out of a possible 6. This was lower than the scores of the Recent Arrival students, who produced the present subjunctive 100% of the time, but it represents fairly regular production of this form. The L2 students rarely produced the present subjunctive at all. Table 7.11 shows students' use of the subjunctive on each item.

The three items most often missed by the L1 students were 3 ("Voy a estar feliz cuando," to which 39% of L1 students used the present indicative), 4 ("Es imposible que este año mis amigos"), and 6 ("Busco un/a novio/a que") yielding 32% present indicative responses each. It may be that these three contexts, one referring to the future, one to impossibility, and one to something being sought, are semantically more certain and therefore prone to the use of the indicative than the other items ("no me gusta que," "pide que," and "para que"). However, a greater number of test items in each semantic field are necessary to make firm conclusions.

The L2 students were significantly less accurate than the L1 students, averaging only .31 correct. The item that resulted in the greatest use of the subjunctive among L2 students was 6 ("Busco un/a novio/a que... "), where two L2 students (13%) used the subjunctive. In two items ("no me gusta que" and "es imposible que") not one L2 student (0%) produced the subjunctive. Although the majority of their incorrect responses were in the present indicative, the L2 students produced a wider range of forms for these items than did the L1 students, including the infinitive, the future, and the imperfect, indicating very little control over the verbal system in these contexts.

On the six items designed to elicit the imperfect subjunctive, Table 7.10 showed that the results were fairly similar to those for the present

Table 7.12 Use of the past subjunctive by item

	L1 (n = 31)	L2 (n = 16)	Recent Arrival (n = 5)
(7) "La semana pasada, me parecía muy mal que..."	4 (13%)	0 (0%)	1 (20%)
(8) "El año pasado, un amigo me pidió que..."	20 (65%)	1 (6%)	2 (40%)
(9) "Mis hermanos y yo compraríamos un nuevo televisor si nosotros..."	12 (39%)	2 (13%)	1 (20%)
(10) "Anoche mi mamá me dio $10 para que yo..."	21 (68%)	3 (19%)	4 (80%)
(11) "La semana pasada mi papá no quería que yo..."	25 (81%)	2 (13%)	3 (60%)
(12) "Mis primos vendrían más a mi casa si ellos..."	16 (52%)	0 (0%)	4 (80%)

subjunctive for L1 and L2 students, but not for Recent Arrival students. The Recent Arrival students did not use the imperfect subjunctive 100% of the time as we had expected. On items 7 and 9 they reached just 20% use of this form, where they used the present subjunctive ("Me parecía muy mal que me *grite* la maestra") or other forms ("Mis hermanos y yo compraríamos un nuevo televisor si nosotros *subimos* las notas/no nos *hablamos/tendríamos* dinero/*teníamos* dinero"). Table 7.12 breaks down students' performance on each past subjunctive prompt.

Interestingly, the L1 students produced a higher percentage of past subjunctive forms than did the Recent Arrivals, although they were less accurate with the past subjunctive (mean = 3.16 out of a possible 6) than they were with the present subjunctive (where they had averaged 4.39 out of 6). Like the Recent Arrival students, the L1 students produced the least past subjunctive in response to items 7 and 9. Regarding item 7 ("Me parecía muy mal que"), it is worth noting that 15 L1 students produced preterite responses, as did two Recent Arrival students, supporting other findings (Blake, 1983; Lavandera, 1984) that the semantic context of attitudes is open to speaker interpretation in mood selection. The L1 students were most accurate on items 11 ("La semana pasada mi papá no quería que yo..."), 10 ("Anoche mi mamá me dio $10 para que yo..."), and 8 ("El año pasado, un amigo me pidió que..."). The L2 students produced relatively little past subjunctive, reaching a maximum of just three students (19%) on item #10 ("Anoche mi mamá me dio $10 para que yo..."), and no student (0%) on two items. Yet they showed greater use of the past subjunctive than of the present subjunctive, which was unexpected.

Conditional

The prompts in this section were designed to elicit the conditional tense. However, in many dialects of Spanish, an apodosis permits the imperfect or the past subjunctive in addition to the conditional ("Si los maestros no dieran nada de tarea, nosostros *jugaríamos/ jugábamos/ jugáramos*"). In fact, the imperfect subjunctive was produced by the Recent Arrival students on these items, so both forms – the past subjunctive and the conditional – were coded as correct (no student produced the imperfect indicative). Table 7.10 displayed the general results, and Table 7.13 shows individual items. Although this measure was not successful in isolating the conditional, these results are reported because they do suggest accurate production of the past subjunctive, which was also part of this study.

Table 7.10 showed that the L1 students produced a greater number of the conditional or the past subjunctive (mean 5 out of 6) than of the past subjunctive (3.16) and the present subjunctive (4.39). Item 15 resulted in the lowest written use of the conditional/ past subjunctive for L1 students, but at 74% it was still relatively high.

The L2 students produced as few instances of the conditional/ past subjunctive (mean 1.19 out of 6) as with the present and past subjunctive. We gained some insight into a few L2 students' abilities when, on a different oral task, they began a response in English that contained a conditional, but did not use the conditional when they switched to Spanish. Two examples of this are "She would reject him . . . ella dice no" and "They wouldn't have much in common . . . no va a tener mucho en comun." This suggests that some students understood that the conditional was required, but were unable to produce it in Spanish.

Table 7.13 Use of the conditional (or past subjunctive) by item

	L1 *(n = 31)*	*L2* *(n = 16)*	*Recent Arrival* *(n = 5)*
(13) "Si yo tuviera mil dólares, yo . . . "	27 (87%)	5 (31%)	5 (100%)
(14) "Si los maestros no dieran nada de tarea, nosostros . . . "	28 (90%)	1 (6%)	5 (100%)
(15) "Yo____a esa muchacha si ella me diera su número de teléfono."	23 (74%)	2 (13%)	5 (100%)
(16) "Si todas las computadoras tuvieran acceso al Internet, la gente . . . "	26 (84%)	5 (31%)	5 (100%)
(17) "Si estudiaras más, tú . . . "	25 (81%)	4 (25%)	5 (100%)
(18) Mis amigos____si ellos tuvieran más tiempo."	26 (84%)	2 (13%)	5 (100%)

Table 7.14 Correct translation of sentences requiring *gustar* (8 items)

Group	Mean	sd
L1 (n = 30)	2.9*	1.99
L2 (n = 16)	0.0*	0.00
RA (n = 5)	5.6**	2.07

  * Significant at $p < 0.001$.
** Not submitted to statistical analysis.

Gustar

Students completed eight written translations and were instructed to use some form of *gustar* in all of them. An item was coded as incorrect for any of the following errors: missing or overused "a" (both of which are exemplified in "Gloria le gusta a Emilio" as a translation of "Gloria likes Emilio"), lack of agreement between the pronoun "le/les" and the corresponding indirect object (such as "A mis primos le gusta"), or lack of agreement between gusta/gustan and the subject (such as "A mi hermana le gusta los chicos" or "A primos les gustan la Coca-Cola"). The mean number of correct translations by each group of students appears in Table 7.14, and the accuracy on each item in Table 7.15.

As with the preceding verb forms, the L1 students were significantly more accurate than the L2 students with *gustar* translations. Not a single L2 student in this graduating class translated any of these sentences correctly, without a missing "a" or agreement errors. The L1 students were more inaccurate on this item than on any of the others presented until now. However, even the Recent Arrival students translated some of these items incorrectly, particularly items 1, 2, 5, and 6. Possible explanations include that this translation task was not a valid measure, or that their grammar of this structure was beginning to attrite.

Table 7.15 Correct translations of each *gustar* item

English text	L1 (n = 30)	L2 (n = 16)	RA (n = 5)
(1) Penelope likes Tom.	13 (43%)	0 (0%)	3 (60%)
(2) Eighth graders like good teachers.	6 (20%)	0 (0%)	3 (60%)
(3) My sister likes boys.	7 (23%)	0 (0%)	4 (80%)
(4) My cousins like Coca-Cola.	8 (27%)	0 (0%)	5 (100%)
(5) Mexicans like tacos.	11 (37%)	0 (0%)	3 (60%)
(6) Adults don't like noise.	10 (33%)	0 (0%)	2 (40%)
(7) My friend likes parties.	5 (17%)	0 (0%)	4 (80%)
(8) People like watching good movies.	13 (43%)	0 (0%)	4 (80%)

Table 7.16 Frequencies of correct gerund translations

	L1 (n = 30)	L2 (n = 16)	RA (n = 5)	Chi-square (df = 4)
(25) People like watching good movies.	28 (93%)	8 (50%)	5 (100%)	0.007
(26) Mary was arrested for stealing.	17 (57%)	1 (6%)	4 (80%)	0.006
(27) Smoking is bad for your health.	10 (33%)	1 (6%)	5 (100%)	0.010
(28) Having friends is important.	11 (37%)	3 (19%)	5 (100%)	0.021
(29) The only thing he cares about is making money.	23 (77%)	5 (31%)	2 (40%)	0.023
Average	59.4%	22.4%	84%	

Infinitive in subject position

Students completed five translations of prompts that in English used the gerund but that in monolingual Spanish require an infinitive. Items were coded as correct if the infinitive was used in the Spanish translation, incorrect if the gerund was used, and "other" if some other translation was used. The frequencies of correct translations are displayed in Table 7.16.

There is a clear correlation between overall proficiency and accuracy on this item: students with higher levels of Spanish proficiency correctly translated the English gerund into Spanish more frequently. The overwhelming majority of L2 students used the Spanish gerund, such as "Fumando es malo para la salud" and "Teniendo amigos es importante." Only one Recent Arrival student produced the gerund in one item (the other non-infinitive translations produced by these students were coded "other"), indicating that the use of the gerund in place of a subject infinitive was uncommon among this group of students. The use of the gerund in subject position, then, clearly distinguishes the heritage speakers from the monolingual Spanish speakers and, to a lesser extent, the L2 speakers from the L1 speakers.

Tense/aspect

An analysis of the students' oral and written narratives was undertaken to see how accurately they produced the preterite/imperfect distinction. An abbreviated version of the methodology and principal findings of that analysis will be presented here, but the reader should consult Potowski (2005) for greater details. The difference between the preterite and the

Table 7.17 Morpheme distribution by lexical aspect in oral story prompt

	Imperfect	*Preterite*
Stat	9 (69%)	0 (0%)
Act	1 (8%)	0 (0%)
Acc	0 (0%)	0 (0%)
Ach	3 (23%)	8 (100%)
Total	13 (100%)	8 (100%)
	13/21 = 62%	8/21 = 38%

imperfect is one of *aspect*. Aspect, as defined by Comrie (1976), is the internal temporal structure of a situation. The two categories of aspect are bounded, which looks at the verbal activity from outside as having a beginning and an end, such as the preterite, and unbounded, which looks at the verb activity from the inside, without specifying a beginning or an end to the activity – as is the imperfect. The selection of preterite or imperfect morphology, such as "comió" vs. "comía," corresponds to a *grammatical* encoding of aspect. Use of tense and aspect is thought to be correlated with overall Spanish proficiency, because knowledge of aspectual distinctions in Spanish comprises knowledge of both morphosyntactic paradigms as well as the semantic interpretations associated with each form (Montrul, 2002).

In order to study students' production of tense and aspect, I analyzed the two narratives that they produced, one oral and one written. The entire story text that the students heard appears in Appendix 7.A, with preterite and imperfect verbs labeled according to inherent lexical aspect. Table 7.17 displays the distribution of past tense morphemes in the oral story prompt.

The story was like most narratives in that the imperfect was used mostly for descriptions and background details, while the preterite moved the action forward. The story was somewhat unique in that there were three achievement verbs in the imperfect (*entraba, preguntaban, respondía*), accounting for 23% of the imperfect morphology. The majority of imperfect verbs were used for stative verbs, as would be expected.

In both narratives produced by the students, each past tense verb was classified as preterite or imperfect and coded for its inherent lexical aspect (state, activity, accomplishment, or achievement). They were also marked as correct or incorrect uses of the preterite and imperfect. A total of 1445 verb tokens were produced by the students in the oral and written narratives. See Table 7.18 for a summary of these two measures and some examples of stative, accomplishment, activity, and achievement verbs that were produced by students in each one.

Table 7.18 Examples

Oral narrative	Written narrative
Prompt: Story about a girl who worked in her garden and, after rejecting many suitors, agreed to marry Vicente. See Appendix 7.A for full text. Students were asked to retell the story in their own words.	Prompt: *"Era una tarde soleada de junio y en el balcón de la casa de los Sánchez dormía un gato tranquilamente. De repente, tres perros..."* Students were asked to fill up 13 lines to complete the story.
Le gustaba trabajar en su jardín = stative	*Porque los perros estaban sueltos* = stative
Plantaron juntos = activity	*Los perros ladraban* = activity
Fui al jardín = accomplishment	*Se subió en la cima de un árbol* = accomplishment
Se quitó la máscara = achievement	*Salió el due no* = achievement

According to the lexical aspect hypothesis (Shirai & Andersen, 1995), we would expect the distribution of past tense morphemes to correlate with students' overall proficiency. That is, the more proficient Spanish L1 students would evidence a spread of the preterite to stative verbs and of the imperfect to achievement verbs, while the less proficient Spanish L2 students would not. We would also expect the highest level of accuracy in the use of preterite and imperfect forms from the recent arrivals, followed by the heritage speakers and lastly the L2 learners (see Montrul, 2002).

Oral story retelling

The original story heard by the students was 261 words long. There were no major differences between students on the length of their oral story retellings. Figures 7.1 and 7.2 show the frequency distribution of preterite

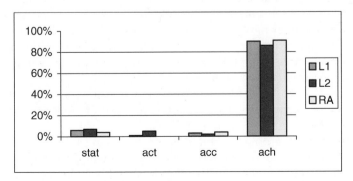

Figure 7.1 Distribution of preterite in oral task

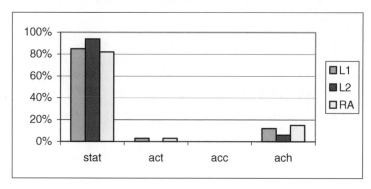

Figure 7.2 Distribution of imperfect in oral task

and imperfect, respectively, with each of the four kinds of predicates produced by the students. The percentage and number of tokens for this and all subsequent figures appear in Appendix 7.C, following Salaberry's (2000: 87) claim that reporting raw scores is necessary because low token counts can generate meaningless percentages.

Overall, there were no notable differences among the three groups in terms of frequency of distribution. Thus, it appears that both L2 learners and L1 heritage speakers in this class have approximated a native aspectual system when asked to narrate an oral story. Achievement verbs constituted 41.8% of all tokens, as would be expected in narratives (Bardovi-Harlig, 2000). L2 students used slightly more stative imperfect and slightly less achievement imperfect than the other two groups.

Written narratives

There were no major differences between L1 and L2 students on the length of the written stories. Unlike in Hasbún (1995), the written task did not generate longer narratives than the oral task, although students took more time for the written task. They had 10 minutes maximum for the written task; there was no time limit on the oral story retelling, but no student took more than 4 minutes to retell it.

Figures 7.3 and 7.4 display the frequency distribution of preterite and imperfect, respectively, with each of the four kinds of predicates produced by the students on the written narratives.

Again, there were no notable differences among the three groups in terms of frequency of distribution. The preterite was overwhelming used with achievement verbs and the imperfect with stative verbs in both

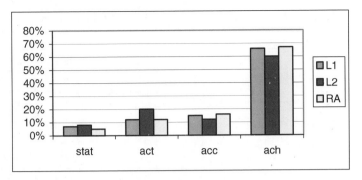

Figure 7.3 Distribution of preterite in written task

types of narratives. Thus, the hypothesis that L2 students would exhibit a different morpheme distribution than the bilingual students (who would, in turn, be different from the native speakers) was not sustained.

Tables 7.19 and 7.20 show students' accuracy on both the oral and written measures. On the oral task, L1 students were only 69% accurate on the use of the preterite with stative verbs, and L2 students were even less accurate at 57%. On the written task, L1 students showed higher accuracy (95%) with preterite statives, while the L2 students were slightly less accurate at 78%. Errors in preterite statives were also found by Montrul (2002) among bilingual adults. In addition, L2 students showed erroneous usage with oral preterite activity verbs (80% correct), such as "Y eso era todo lo que hizo" (instead of *hacía*). There were a total of three errors (oral and written) in achievement imperfect, all produced by L2 students (such as "*Era matado" and "*Se escondía debajo del árbol").

Figure 7.4 Distribution of imperfect in written task

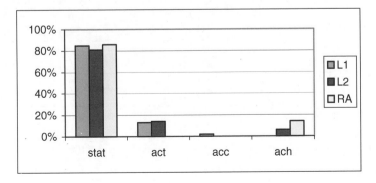

Table 7.19 Percentage accuracy on oral task by predicate type

	L1		L2		RA	
	Preterite	Imperfect	Preterite	Imperfect	Preterite	Imperfect
Stat	69% (9/13)	100% (301/301)	57% (4/7)	100% (125/125)	100% (2/2)	100% (50/50)
Act	100% (2/2)	100% (10/10)	80% (4/5)	– (0/0)	– (0/0)	100% (2/2)
Acc	86% (6/7)	100% (1/1)	100% (2/2)	– (0/0)	100% (2/2)	– (0/0)
Ach	100% (195/195)	100% (43/43)	99% (84/85)	88% (7/8)	100% (41/41)	100% (9/9)
Total	98% (212/217)	100% (355/355)	95% (94/99)	99% (132/133)	100% (45/45)	100% (61/61)

However, there were so few error tokens in our study that a percentage comparison is not very revealing. For example, Table 7.19 gives the impression that when L1 students used the preterite with stative verbs, they were accurate only 69% of the time. However, there were only four errors in total, and all of them were produced by one individual student (e.g. "*El árbol fue alto"). In addition, the L2 students appear to be incorrect with preterite statives 57% of the time, but two of the three errors were produced by one student. Similarly, we feel that no conclusions can be drawn in contexts where a 0% accuracy rate is due to one or two erroneous tokens (such as

Table 7.20 Percentage accuracy on written task by predicate type

	L1		L2		RA	
	Preterite	Imperfect	Preterite	Imperfect	Preterite	Imperfect
Stat	95% (18/19)	100% (47/47)	78% (7/9)	97% (28/29)	100% (2/2)	100% (6/6)
Act	100% (33/33)	100% (7/7)	100% (23/23)	80% (4/5)	100% (5/5)	– (0/0)
Acc	100% (44/44)	0% (0/1)	100% (14/14)	– (0/0)	100% (7/7)	– (0/0)
Ach	100% (183/183)	– (0/0)	100% (70/70)	0% (0/2)	100% (28/28)	100% (1/1)
Total	99.6% (278/279)	98.2% (54/55)	98.3% (114/116)	88.9% (32/36)	100% (42/42)	100% (7/7)

L1 accomplishment imperfect and L2 achievement imperfect on the written task). Overall, Tables 7.19 and 7.20 show very high percentages of accurate use (similarly to Montrul, 2002, and Silva Corvalán, 1994).

Given that stative verbs were relatively problematic for both L2 and bilingual students, we examined how many types were present in the stative tokens of the oral corpus. A total of 24 different stative verbs were used, the most frequent being *ser* (19%), *querer* (18%), *gustar* (14%), *haber* (11%) and *tener* (8%). This stands in contrast to the findings of Barvodi-Harlig and Bergström (1996) that 81% of all stative verbs in their corpus were *être* and *avoir*. This indicates that, although they may not always mark them correctly for tense and aspect, these dual immersion students have a wide range of stative verbs in their productive systems.

In conclusion, all three types of students, bilingual Spanish L1, Spanish L2, and Recent Arrivals, produced similar distributions of preterite and imperfect by aspectual category. Therefore, in our data there was no correlation between morpheme distribution and Spanish proficiency, which may constitute further evidence against the Lexical Aspect Hypothesis. However, the three groups of students were differentiated by accuracy, with higher levels of Spanish proficiency resulting in more accurate production of preterite and imperfect.

For the Spanish L2 students, who were the most inaccurate in tense/aspect production, we may conclude that the tense/aspect system is not completely acquired by the time they graduate from a dual immersion program, although it is fairly advanced. In order to determine whether the bilingual students' systems display incomplete acquisition, or whether it is a case of attrition after having been completely acquired, longitudinal studies beginning with younger students are necessary (cf. Silva-Corvalán, 2003). As Montrul (2002: 41) claims, "Attrition of a primary language forces us to look deeper into the role of input in L1 acquisition, both the kind of input and the frequency required to maintain language skills." Dual immersion is considered the program type that uses the greatest quantity of Spanish input than any other elementary school program. How well students in dual immersion, both L1 and L2, produce tense and aspect may reflect the quality of input they receive and, ultimately, how well these schools contribute to Spanish heritage maintenance and Spanish L2 acquisition.

Conclusions and Pedagogical Implications

Performances on the FLOSEM, the LAS-O, and the writing measure indicate that all but a handful of students were capable of getting across their ideas in Spanish. In other words, they are able to communicate in Spanish far more than what they are unable to communicate. The examples of L2 students' oral and written narratives presented here provide greater detail about the Spanish that they had acquired upon graduating from this dual immersion school. These findings also highlight the facts that language comprehension usually outstrips performance, and that form, function, and task interact in complex ways.

As might be expected, the Spanish L2 learners performed significantly less well than their L1 heritage speaker classmates and their Spanish-dominant Recent Arrival classmates on all sociolinguistic and grammatical tasks. The L1 students were not far behind the Recent Arrival students on the written and oral sociolinguistic measures, and scored on average one or two points behind them on the production of the present subjunctive and the conditional, indicating that they had developed or maintained strong levels of Spanish. However, L2 students' performance on these tests of grammatical and sociolinguistic production are relatively low after nine years in a dual immersion school.

Although this study does not formally examine students' English proficiency, there are several indications that their English was far stronger than their Spanish. Their scores on standardized tests administered in English were above the city norms. No students in this class aside from the Recent Arrivals had received ESL pullout classes since third grade. And although I regularly spotted spelling errors in their English work, these were very common for students their age in urban contexts, and my conversations with the eighth-grade English teacher revealed that IAMS students' English was no worse than that of students at other schools in the district. However, it is perfectly logical to assume that these students reached a level of Spanish proficiency that they would not have been able to achieve had they attended typical Chicago public elementary schools, where English is used 100% of the time.

Regarding the sociolinguistic findings, Koike (1989) contends that learners' pragmatic knowledge may not be fully represented in their production, particularly if they have not acquired the verb forms necessary to carry out a particular function. However, our scoring procedures awarded just one point for verb forms, giving students other opportunities to score points for politeness through strategies such as pronouns and indirectness. Therefore, judging by the very low politeness scores of the L2 students on both the oral role play and on the written letter, we may conclude that these students are not developing high levels of pragmatic competence (at least for making polite requests) in this dual immersion program. In other words, the interactions in which these students are participating appear to be insufficient for the development of politeness.[4]

Harley (1984: 59), attempting to explain the Canadian immersion students' insufficiently polite performance, stated that such sociolinguistic inadequacies are related to students' grammatical problems as well as to the fact that their social interactions with native French speakers is extremely limited. Although in this dual immersion school 60% of the students are in fact native bilingual Spanish speakers, they quickly become English dominant and use mostly English with their peers (Delgado Larocco, 1998; Fortune, 2001; Potowski, 2004). The collaboration and collective scaffolding (Donato, 1994) in Spanish among students that could lead to pragmatic development, therefore, do not take place with great regularity. In other words, the mere presence of native speakers is not sufficient for the development of this type of proficiency. Students need regular communication with individuals with whom they have a monolingual relationship in Spanish. Researchers such as Bardovi-Harlig (2001) have argued for the usefulness of explicit instruction in pragmatics. Dual immersion teachers would likely welcome the development of well-designed lessons focusing on politeness and other pragmatic targets. They might also explore ways to make pragmatic elements more salient in their day-to-day interactions with students, including an insistence that students address teachers and administrators with the polite "usted" form.

On the grammatical production items, the heritage Spanish speakers produced significantly more of the forms than did the Spanish L2 students; the almost nil use of the subjunctive and 0% accuracy in translating sentences requiring *gustar* by L2 graduates of this dual immersion school are particularly notable. The heritage speakers were less accurate than the Recently Arrival Spanish speakers, particularly in the production of the present subjunctive. However, the fact that the recently arrived students did not score perfectly on all items points to the difficulty of the items, the inadequacy of the test prompts, or perhaps to a change in progress in their mood system (cf. Silva-Corvalan, 1996). Although we lack thorough studies of the characteristics of the input that dual immersion students receive, Inter-American students are exposed to a great deal of native Spanish from teachers and instructional materials. What is unclear is the degree to which students are expected to *produce* language, and the feedback they receive on their output. Immersion teachers and students are held more accountable for content than for language, which often means that language is not focused on in any systematic way. This study suggests that activities designed to highlight the forms and functions of the subjunctive and conditional – that is, tasks that require the use of these forms in extended discourse and providing students with feedback on the use of the forms, while still being contextualized and related to academic content – are a worthwhile area of pursuit.

Any comparisons with findings from one-way French immersion class-rooms must be made cautiously. Aside from differences in the linguistic structures in the two languages, French in Canada and Spanish in the United States present very different constellations of factors that undoubt-edly affect language use and development. But what about a future study comparing L2 students' proficiency in Spanish one-way immersion vs. in two-way immersion in the United States? Or a study that compares L1 heritage speakers in a dual immersion program with their counterparts in transitional bilingual education programs taught mostly in English? For example, it is plausible that heritage speakers in a dual immersion pro-gram, by virtue of the amount of Spanish they must read and speak each day, produce and comprehend Spanish (including the subjunctive and the conditional) to a greater degree than their peers who receive all of their education in English. While a large-scale study comparing a great num-ber of schools might yield interesting trends, numerous program variables can substantially influence classroom language acquisition, including the percentage of heritage speakers and their levels of Spanish proficiency, the amount and quality of Spanish used by the teacher, and how much Spanish is actually used by the students.

There are clear limitations to the ways in which the proficiency data were collected and analyzed. Instead of discrete sentence completion items, ana-lyzing the grammar produced within structured interviews and from oral and written narratives (cf. Harley *et al.*, 1990, and represented by cells 1A and 1B in my Table 7.2), might give a more accurate picture of students' grammatical production. In addition, the present study did not utilize the discourse or strategic competence measures that were used by Harley *et al.* (1990), yet Romaine (1995: 270) contends that discourse tests yield a more accurate measure of the students' skills because they involve stretches of speech. Grammar elicitation measures should contain a greater number of tokens as well as distractor items in order to make more valid conclu-sions. Finally, sociolinguistic multiple-choice items should result in greater consensus among native speaker control groups.

Dual immersion contexts also offer many possibilities for future research on pragmatic development. Most research on L2 pragmatics has focused on adults, who are normally fully pragmatically competent in their L1. However, children have to develop not only accurate representations of pragmatic knowledge, but also linguistic control over those representa-tions. A dual immersion school that spans a number of years offers a rela-tively controlled environment in which to conduct longitudinal studies. In addition, very little is known about teacher talk and the quantity and qual-ity of input that students receive in dual immersion classrooms, which are primordial in any examination of classroom acquisition. Finally, the pragmatic development of heritage Spanish speakers is a completely unexplored yet potentially interesting area for research.

Results indicate that dual immersion students, both L1 and L2, would benefit from more assistance in acquiring tense and aspect. In a study on one-way immersion, Harley & Swain (1984) proposed that problematic L2 features may not be salient or frequent enough in the classroom talk of immersion teachers, and that teachers may not be providing enough feedback about students' errors. However, Krashen (1982) claimed that input alone was enough, and that grammar teaching would not improve acquisition. Harley (1989), setting out to test Krashen's hypothesis and based on findings that French immersion students were not mastering the functions and uses of the *passé composé* and the *imparfait*, designed an eight-week bank of materials focusing on these two forms and their uses. The experimental students performed significantly better than the control students on two out of three measures, but three months later there were no differences between the groups. Harley (1989) suggested that teachers use a functional approach to grammar at a younger age, in grades 3 and 4. As Chapter 4 showed, fifth-grade students in this school used Spanish just 56% overall —82% with the teacher and 32% with peers. Problems in acquiring tense and aspect, therefore, may also be due in part to a lack of output (Swain, 1985).

Swain and Lapkin (1982: 50), discussing French one-way immersion students in Canada, stated that "Once the children have reached a point . . . there is no strong social incentive to develop further towards native speaker norms." The question of "incentives" to develop Spanish is related to the construct of investment that I have been utilizing in this study to explain students' decisions to use and develop their Spanish. Chapter 8 revisits the four focal students and their classmates as they negotiate the multiple demands of their adolescent identities, including their friends, their schoolwork and upcoming transition to high school, and their families.

Appendix 7.A
Oral Story Text, "La jardinera," with Verbs Identified for Inherent Lexical Aspect

Reproduced from Language Assessment Scales, Oral, by permission of CTB/ McGraw Hill LLC. Copyright © 1990 by Sharon E. Duncan, Ph.D., and Edward A. DeAvlia, Ph.D. All rights reserved. LAS is a registered trademark of DeAvila, Duncan and Associates, Inc.

Había[stat] una vez una joven que *se llamaba*[stat] María Elena. El único placer del que *disfrutaba*[stat] esta muchacha *era*[stat] trabajar en su jardín.

Todos los días se le *veía*[act] plantando y sembrando y cuando *entraba*[ach] a su jardín *parecía*[stat] olvidarse de todos los demás.

A sus amigas les *extrañaba*[stat] que no tuviera novio y que nunca hablara de casarse. "Pobrecita María Elena. Siempre estás con la cara sucia y tu ropa manchada. Nunca tienes tiempo para divertirte. ¿Quién querrá casarse contigo?" le *preguntaban*[ach].

"Eso a mi no me importa," les *respondía*[ach] María Elena. "Estoy muy contenta y me encanta trabajar con las plantas."

En efecto, *había*[stat] muchos jóvenes que *querían*[stat] casarse con ella, pero María Elena a todos les *dijo*[ach] que no. Y, desilusionados, se *marcharon*[ach]. Todos menos uno, el que *se llamaba*[stat] Vicente.

Un día, Vicente *regresó*[ach] al jardín de la joven, disfrazado como una anciana y le *dijo*[ach], "María Elena, debes casarte con Vicente. Es muy guapo y fuerte y te quiere mucho. Además, es inteligente y un buen jardinero." Y ella le *contestó*[ach], "Tiene usted razón, abuelita. Vicente es inteligente y guapo y parece saber mucho sobre las plantas y las flores. Pero es solo un hombre." "¿Solo un hombre?" *dijo*[ach] la vieja. "Los hombres y las mujeres se necesitan, igual que tus plantas necesitan del sol," *dijo*[ach], quitándose el disfraz. "Igual que Vicente necesita de ti, María Elena."

"Muy bien, Vicente," *dijo*[ach] la muchacha, riéndose y abrazándolo con cariño. "Me has convencido. Me casaré contigo, pero solamente si me ayudas a plantar." "Con todo gusto, mi amor."

Appendix 7.B
Multiple-Choice Instructions and Test Items

Instructions

Selecciona la mejor respuesta.
Ejemplo: En la escuela, un alumno le dice a otro:

(a) *La maestra castigó a Elena hoy.*
(b) *Hoy, Elena fue castigada por la maestra.*
(c) *Hoy, Elena ha recibido un castigo por la maestra debido a su mala conducta.*
    La respuesta correcta es (a) porque (b) es demasiado formal para un amigo, y (c) pertenece más a la lengua escrita que a la lengua hablada.

Test items (Correct answersare underlined)

(1) En una reunión de trabajo, dice un adulto a las demás personas:
    (a) Cierren la puerta.
    (b) *¿Podrían cerrar la puerta, por favor?*

(c) ¿Tendrían ustedes la amabilidad de cerrar la puerta, por favor?

(2) En la parada del autobús, dice Silvia a su hermana:
   (a) Anoche se me presentó la oportunidad de ver a Jorge.
   (b) No lo va a creer usted, anoche vi a Jorge.
   (c) *No lo vas a creer, anoche vi a Jorge.*

(3) En el restaurante, un mesero de 35 anos de edad les dice a dos jóvenes de 20 anos:
   (a) Como nuestro helado es delicioso, permítanme recomendárselo.
   (b) Pidan el helado como postre porque es delicioso.
   (c) *De postre les recomiendo el helado, es delicioso.*

(4) Un reporte en la primera pagina de un periódico nacional:
   (a) La guerra no va a estar mucho tiempo.
   (b) Creemos que la guerra no va a durar mucho.
   (c) *Las autoridades indican que la guerra no será larga.*

(5) En una oficina, un señor que visita por primera vez le pregunta a la recepcionista:
   (a) ¿Tendría usted la bondad de indicarme donde están los baños?
   (b) ¿Dónde están los baños?
   (c) *Disculpe señorita, ¿me podría decir donde están los baños?*

(6) Entras a la oficina de la directora de tu escuela y le dices:
   (a) *¿Usted quería verme?*
   (b) ¿Querías hablar conmigo?
   (c) He acudido a su oficina porque me informaron de su deseo de verme.

(7) En un libro de texto de estudios sociales:
   (a) *Los trabajadores, cansados de las pésimas condiciones, organizaron un sindicato.*
   (b) Los trabajadores estaban cansados de las pésimas condiciones y por esto organizaron un sindicato.
   (c) Las condiciones eran muy malas entonces los trabajadores organizaron un sindicato.

(8) En la biblioteca, un estudiante de 8° grado les dice a un grupo de estudiantes de secundaria (*high school*):
   (a) ¿Serían tan amables de prestarme ese diccionario durante unos momentos?
   (b) *¿Me pueden prestar ese diccionario?*
   (c) Préstenme ese diccionario.

(9) En Walgreen's, le dice la farmacéutica (*pharmacist*) a una señora desconocida:
   (a) Toma esta medicina dos veces por día.
   (b) *Usted debe tomar esta medicina dos veces por día.*
   (c) Se le ruega que tome esta medicina dos veces por día.

(10) En su reporte para el fiscal (*prosecutor*), escribe la abogada defensora:
   (a) Como ustedes no tienen muchas pruebas contra mi cliente, su caso es muy débil.
   (b) *Dada la escasez de pruebas contra el acusado, su caso no demuestra mucha validez.*
   (c) Dejen el caso ya, no tienen muchas pruebas y vamos a ganar nosotros.

Appendix 7.C
Oral Narrative Texts of Six Students

M.B. (high L2), LAS story score = 3, overall LAS score = 3

"La jardinera. Había una vez una jardinera que se llamaba María Elena. Ella le gustaba plantar y jardinar en su jardín. Y, pero eso es, era todo lo que his, hice. Um, sus amigas dicieron por qué, por qué no tienes novio y por qué nada más eh um . . . trabajas con tus plantas en vez de tener una vida con un hombre. Y ella dicía que, que no quería tener un novio y . . . Pero muchos hombres querían casarse con ella pero um ella dice, dijo a ellos no, porque uh, no eran interesados en lo que ella gustaba. Pero había un hombre que se llamaba Vicente que, uh, que amaba mucho a ella. Y una, un día, uh, se vino disfrazado en, como una abuelita a su jardín. Y ella creía que estaba hablando con algo totalmente diferente. Y dis, dije a María Elena que debes casarse con V porque él es muy guapo y fuerte y le gusta jardinar. *Is that a word?* Y ella dijo sí, él es todos esas cosas pero solamente es un hombre. Y la abuelita dijo sí, es un hombre, pero um . . . quiere casarse con ti. Y ella dije en, oh, y después él ah uh, . . . sacó su disfraz y ayudó a plantar sus flores en su jardín. Y a esa era la única cosa que podía hacer para que podía casarse con ella."

O.S. (mid L2), LAS story score = 2, overall LAS score = 3

"Había una joven niña que se llama María Elena. Ella le gusta plantar plantas en su jardín todos los días. Y ella no pensó en los hombres o en casarse con un hombre pero sus ami . . . sus amigas quería que ella le gusta hombres. Una día uh, unos hombres le vinó y preguntó si ellos querían casarse con ella, pero ella dicía no. Una joven no fuiste, no se fue, y él se preguntó una pregunta a ella si él quería casarse con ella . . . si ella quería casarse con él. Después ella di, ella dijo no, pero después él vinó en una . . . con una máscara y se . . . él . . . la mascara era como una abuela. Y eh, ella, o él estaba hablando a ella, y, pero ella pensó que él era una abuelita. Y él estaba diciendo que los jov . . . los hombres son bien personas y ella necesitaba casarse con ellos. Y después ella se um, sa, sabía que la abuela no era . . . la abuela era él. Y um, ella estaba reiendo y después ella decía, 'Yo te voy a casarte con tú solo si te ayudas a plantar unas plantas.'"

T.A. (low L2), LAS story score = 2, overall LAS score = 1

"Primero una mujer estaba como, se estaba . . . hacer un jardín, *like*, . . . *caring for it* uh, jardinero. Y todos los hombres le querían y uno de los hombres se *guisó* en, como una vieja y se con*venció, or like convinced*, que *Vincent* que era el hombre que quería era que era desguido, or quisado. Dijo que él era muy guapo y, buen, *like* inteligente. Y ella dijo que tiene razón pero solo es un hombre. Pero um, entonces él se quitó su *guisa* y *they like fell in love.*"

C.D. (high L1), LAS story score = 5, overall LAS score = 5

"Se trata de una muchacha que se llamaba María Elena, y que, todo lo que daba placer era plantar plantas en su jardín. Y allí se olvidaba de todo. Y sus amigas pensaban que era rara porque no se interesaba en casarse ni tenía novio. Y le, la [sounds like "tucaban"] como le decían que ella, por qué no piensas en eso, nadie se va casar contigo. Y ella no le dijo que no le importaba por que su jardín la hacia feliz. Pero en verdad muchos querían pretenderla, um querían ser su novio y casarse. Pero a todos le dijo que no y eh, y ni uno volvió a insistir excepto por uno que se llamaba Vicente. Y parece que en verdad él sí la quiere. Y se disfrazó como una viejita cuando ella estaba en su jardín. Y le, le estaba diciendo que debería casarse con él por que era guapo, inteligente y le gustaba plantar cosas en el jardín, buen jardinero. Y ella le decía que sí era verdad pero solo era un hombre. Y él le dijo que um, las mujeres necesitan a los hombres como las plantas necesitan al sol. Y después se quitó la máscara y um. María Elena um, creo que pensó que era un acto muy cariñoso de su parte. Y al fin le dijo que sí, que se iba casar con él si le ayudaba con las plantas."

C.P. (mid L1), LAS story score = 4, overall LAS score = 4

"Había una vez una joven que se llamaba María Elena. María Elena le encantaba trabajar en su jardín. Cuando estaba en su jardín, ella estaba muy tranquila y se olvidaba de todo. Pero las amigas de María Elena le decían que se debería casar con alguien. Pero María Elena no le daba sentido. Entonces una vez, había un joven llamado Vicente que le gustaba María Elena. Pero María Elena no le dejaba casarse con ella. Entonces Vicente se disfrazó como una viejita y fue al jardín de María Elena. [pause] Cuando estaba como una viejita, le dijo a María Elena que él era muy guapo, inteligente y le gustaba hacer cosas en el jardín. Entonces María Elena se fijó que Vicente era lo que ella necesitaba. Después Vicente se sacó el disfr*ace* de la abuela y le dijo que, que le gustaba María mucho. Entonces María Elena se iba a casar con Vicente pero con una condición: que, le ayudaba en el jardín."

M.C. (low L1), LAS story score = 3, overall LAS score = 3

"María Elena le gustaba trabajar en su jardín. Y . . . se olvidaba de todas las otras cosas en su vida. Y, um, hombres querían casarse con ella. Y después um, . . . un hombre Vicente . . . se disfrazó como una vieja y después um, él estaba como *like, trying to get her to like her, or him, and then, um,* le estaba preguntando cosas. Le decía a ella por qué era bueno, porque sería un buen marido para ella, y las cosas en común que pueden tener *And then*, están plantando flores. Eso es todo."

Appendix 7.D
Written Story Narratives

Story prompt: *"Era una tarde soleada de junio y en el balcón de los Sánchez, dormía un gato tranquilamente. De repente, tres perros . . . "*

M.B. (high L2), written story score = 24/30

. . . atacáron al gato. El gato era muy sorprendido. Despúes los tres perros corrieron alrededor del gato y hizo que el gato era muy pareado [*mareado*]. Cayó del balcón y murió. Los Sánchez eran muy trístes y fueron afuera para correar alrededor delos tres perros. Despues los tres perros murieron y los dueños de los perros eran muy tristes. Fueron a correar alrededor de los Sánchzes, y murieron. Los dueños de los perros eran tán enojados, que comitieron suicidio. El fin.

O.S. (mid L2), written story score = 19/30

. . . estaba arancando de un gato porque ellos no se dara el comida y los jugetes al gato. Los perros estaban corriendo y corriendo pero el gato estaba persiguiendo a los perros. Unos minutos adelante los perros esta persiguiendo al gato y el gato se escodio en un arból. Despues los perros se fueron al casa. Cuando el gató brinco abajo un hombre se agarro y se rescate el gato.

T.A. (low L2), written story score = 16/30

...murieron. Despues el gato se subió un árbol y los tres perros muridos persiguieron. Como los perros estaban muertos los bomberos no vieron cuando sacaron el gato del arbol. Cuando se dan al gato al hombre que era el dueño de.

C.D. (high L1), written story score = 29/30

...vienen corriendo ladrando con furia. El pobre gatito salta del susto, ve que bienen a toda velocidad los perros hacia el. Asustado brinca sobre el balcon y despues por la cerda. Igual hacen losperros. El pobre gato hafligido se sube a un arbol, pasando a una niña. La niña sorprendida ve al gatito en la rama del arbol y tambien ve a los perros. Los olleron, un grito, era su amo y corrieron hacia el. La niña se subio al arbol y tomo al gatito, el pobre temblaba. El amo de los perros la vio y la ayudo ha bajarse. El gatito estaba a salvo.

C.P. (mid L1), written story score = 26/30

...isieron un pedo y se fueron. Era tan oleoso que el gato lo podia oler asta el encima del arbol donde estaba atrapado. Era noche y nadie salbo al gato por que a nadie le gusta a los gatos. Entonces el gato brinco y se cayo en el suelo. Murio imediatamente. Cuando murio, el gato se iso un Diablo porque el dios no le gusta a los gatos tampoco.

M.C. (low L1), written story score = 20/30

...comieron el gato pero despues estaban atrapados en el arbol y llamaron la policia para que tiren balazos para que los perros se caigan. Pero cuando trataron de disparrar a los perros no le dieron pero si pegaron a una vieja, un pajaro y una bomba, que causo una inundacion que causo que toda la gente se moviera al rio.

Notes

1. This scoring procedure differs slightly from that used in Allen *et al.* (1983) because it does not include the categories "additional explanatory information" or "concluding politeness marker." These categories were eliminated in our study because the students rarely produced them.
2. There were also six items targeting the conditional perfect ("Si Michael Jordan no hubiera jugado con los Bulls, ellos no *habrían ganado* tantos campeonatos"). However, the simple conditional is actually a permissible answer for such items,

because the apodosis can be interpreted in the present tense: "Si te hubieras portado bien [yesterday], tus papás te comprarían un PlayStation [today]." The simple conditional was in fact the most common verb form produced on two of the items, and less frequently on four other items. Since these items were not able to require the targeted verb form, the results are not reported.

3. The LAS-O story retelling scores are separated from the overall LAS-O scores because overall scores are potentially inflated by ten true/false listening comprehension items. The LAS-O story retellings by themselves provide a more accurate picture of oral proficiency than do the overall LAS-O scores.

4. However, it has been suggested that even English-speaking children in the United States may not be exposed to or expected to use different registers in English to signal respect or politeness (Diane Tedick, personal communication, 2005).

Chapter 8
Identity Investments in Eighth Grade

Chapter 6 presented a description of the Spanish use that took place during the students' eighth-grade Spanish language arts and social studies lessons, and Chapter 7 offered details about students' Spanish proficiency as examined through a number of measures. In this chapter, I attempt to explore *why* their Spanish use and proficiency looked the way it did, returning to Norton's (2000) concepts of investment and identity that were explored in Chapter 5. In other words, I seek to link students' classroom language use, investments in Spanish, and the ongoing production of their now adolescent identities.

As in the fifth-grade year of this study, I interviewed the four focal students and their parents, as well as all three eighth-grade teachers. I also examined seven months of classroom field notes and 21 classroom recordings for themes related to the use of Spanish and English at three levels: the school, the classroom, and in the lives of the individual students outside of school. In addition, I interviewed eight of the focal students' classmates, for a total of 12 eighth graders (23% of the graduating class). I interviewed these eight additional students to get a wider sense of language use attitudes among students at IAMS, and also as a context within which to further consider the decisions of the focal students, particularly since the focal students, like most adolescents, are often influenced by their classmates' behavior and expectations. Into the description of each focal student, I incorporate comments about them made by the other three focal students as well as by their eight classmates, among whom were several high academic achievers whom the others classified as "smart," some who got more average grades and were in the "cool" group, and a few who self-identified as "ghetto," which Ms. Castro described as "street" or "tough." I also present a separate section in which the eight non-focal students talk about issues related to language, identity, and their experiences at Inter-American. Once again, I sought threads that were common to all students, but each individual student had their own configuration of sometimes contradictory attitudes and linguistic behaviors, and each student was differently positioned by classmates.

In Chapter 5, four dimensions emerged as relevant to students' investments in Spanish: home language use and support for Spanish, student attitudes toward the dual immersion school and toward Spanish in general, the teacher's positioning of the student, and the student's position within her or his peer group. Similar lines of examination were explored during the eighth-grade year, with the exception of the eighth-grade teachers' positionings of the students. This consideration was only cursorily examined in eighth grade because I regularly observed the students with only one of their three eighth-grade teachers, Ms. Maas. Once again, I have attempted to highlight how and why each focal student created, responded to, and resisted opportunities to speak Spanish.

The Four Focal Students

All four focal students – Carolina, Melissa, Matt, and Otto – were still at Inter-American during their eighth-grade year. A handful of their fifth-grade classmates had moved or transferred to other schools. As would be expected, the eighth graders, now 13 or 14 years old, had undergone considerable physical and intellectual growth since they were 10 and 11 years old in fifth grade. Although Carolina was still relatively petite and of slight build, Otto was now taller than I was, Matt had a shadow of a mustache and a voice that sounded like that of a grown man, and Melissa had a tall, athletic frame. The students I had worked with in Ms. Torres's class were spread fairly evenly between the three eighth-grade classrooms, and although I had only returned to the school a handful of times between 2000 and 2003, they greeted me enthusiastically and facilitated my being accepted by their classmates who did not know me.

The four focal students had remained in basically the same social categories as they had been three years previously. Carolina was still quiet, slightly rebellious but under parental pressure to perform well in school, yet now very interested in boys and alternative music. Melissa was still studious and pursued her music lessons and theater, but was now on the basketball team. Matt was still very bright but underapplied, continued showing resistance to school, wore long, unruly hair, and stayed to himself and a skateboarding buddy. Otto was loud and outgoing, and still athletically talented. In the sections that follow, richer portraits of the four focal students will attempt to illustrate their investments in speaking Spanish and developing their proficiency in the language. I will also include greater detail about their Spanish proficiency test results, which were reported for the entire class in Chapter 7. Table 8.1 displays results for all four focal students on the global proficiency measures, while Table 8.2 presents their

Table 8.1 Global Spanish proficiency results of the four focal students

	L1		L2	
	Carolina	*Matt*	*Melissa*	*Otto*
Oral				
LAS-O, Total (*Max = 100*)	86.2 (mean = 85.5)	73.7 (mean = 85.5)	73.8 (mean = 64.9)	67.5 (mean = 64.9)
LAS-O, Story retelling (*Max = 5*)	4 (mean = 3.9)	3 (mean = 3.9)	3 (mean = 2.7)	3 (mean = 2.7)
FLOSEM (*Max = 6*)	4.5 (mean = 5.08)	4.2 (mean = 5.08)	4.2 (mean = 3.10)	2.6 (mean = 3.10)
Writing				
Global rating (*Max = 30*)	26 (mean = 24.9)	20 (mean = 24.9)	24 (mean = 17.5)	19 (mean = 17.5)
Reading				
Logramos vocabulary (National percentile rank)	29 (mean = 48.9)	46 (mean = 48.9)	60 (mean = 33.6)	8 (mean = 33.6)
Logramos reading comprehension (National percentile rank)	61 (mean = 66.7)	54 (mean = 66.7)	92 (mean = 58.1)	47 (mean = 58.1)
Sociolinguistic appropriateness				
Letter difference score (max = 6)	5 (mean = 3.10)	−1 (mean = 3.10)	1 (mean = 0.59)	−1 (mean = 0.59)
Oral difference score (max =12)	3 (mean = 4.8)	5 (mean = 4.8)	3 (mean = 2.94)	4 (mean = 2.94)
Multiple choice (max = 10)	6 (mean = 6.53)	4 (mean = 6.53)	8 (mean = 6.06)	4 (mean = 6.06)

Table 8.2 Grammatical accuracy results of the four focal students

	L1		L2	
	Carolina	*Matt*	*Melissa*	*Otto*
Subjunctive				
Present (max 6)	5 (mean = 4.39)	4 (mean = 4.39)	0 (mean = 0.31)	0 (mean = 0.31)
Past (max 6)	2 (mean = 3.16)	3 (mean = 3.16)	1 (mean = 0.5)	0 (mean = 0.5)
Conditional (max 6)	6 (mean = 5.00)	4 (mean = 5.00)	3 (mean = 1.19)	0 (mean = 1.19)
Gustar (max 8)	4 (mean = 2.9)	0 (mean = 2.9)	0 (mean = 0.0)	0 (mean = 0.0)
Infinitive in subject position (max 5)	3 (mean = 2.97)	2 (mean = 2.97)	2 (mean = 1.12)	1 (mean = 1.12)

grammatical results. I will elaborate on the scores for each focal student in the following sections.

Carolina

As during fifth grade, Carolina lived with her parents, her two sisters Natalie and Steffie, and her maternal grandparents. She claimed that she used only Spanish with her grandparents, because when her parents spoke to their daughters in Spanish, she and her older sister usually answered in English. Her mother confirmed that she and her husband had been "more lax" about Spanish use and had been using increasingly more English in the home. Whereas during fifth grade Carolina would regularly watch *novelas* (soap operas) in Spanish with her grandmother, her parents had established a new rule that the girls could not watch television from Monday through Thursday during the school year, in order that they would focus on homework. Thus, exposure to Spanish television with her grandmother had been practically eliminated. With her friends she used exclusively English, aside from her example of an occasional comment such as "El portero estaba muy malo" ('The goalie was bad') when discussing a soccer game.

Carolina's mother stated that her daughter's feelings about Spanish were less positive than before:

> I don't think she's comfortable with [Spanish]. I don't feel she dominates it, and it's a struggle to make her speak it. Especially when we're out, she doesn't want people to hear her speak Spanish. I find that she speaks it with more difficulty than Natalie and Steffie. Maybe because Natalie listens to bachata, merengue, but Carolina listens to hard rock, alternative. Although yesterday we were eating lunch in a Spanish restaurant and she asked for her food in Spanish.

Some interesting points about Carolina emerged through a comparison with her older sister, Natalie. I asked whether Carolina had expressed interest in having a *quinceaños* party. Her mother said that Carolina had refused, preferring to receive the money that such a party would have cost. In addition, her older sister Natalie "had to beg [Carolina] to be one of the *damas* [girls who wear special formal dresses and participate in a formal couple dance performance]" in her own *quinceaños* party, which the girls' mother stated that Carolina did not enjoy very much. Mrs. Padilla also noted that while Natalie was interested in Latin stars and listened to bachata and merengue music, Carolina preferred hard rock and alternative music in English and was more interested in sports. She said that after school and on the weekends, she rented movies and went shopping at the mall with friends, all of which she did in English.

The concerns that Carolina's mother expressed about her daughters' English in fifth grade continued. She claimed that both her daughters' English grammar was deficient because they "try to apply the same rules of Spanish grammar to English. English is such a difficult language. Spanish is simple, you see it, you say it, you spell it." This estimation of Spanish as "easy" meant that it could be acquired sufficiently in the home, whereas English required formal study. English is also what counts for admission to competitive high schools, a theme that arose repeatedly during our interview. Having already gone through the arduous procedure of applying to the city's top public magnet high schools for Natalie – schools which require high seventh-grade standardized test scores – Mrs. Padilla was frustrated with what she perceived as Inter-American's lack of focus on academics, particularly in the upper cycle (sixth through eighth grades). She noted that the college preparatory high school that Natalie attended, and to which Carolina had been accepted only after an appeal process, accepted an average of three or four students per year from IAMS, while they took up to 10 from other schools. "They haven't built into the curriculum things that challenge students. The focus is so much on the language, how can you provide an accelerated math or English literature program? How many of these kids are ready for freshman algebra?" For this and other issues at the school, primarily "the need for an administrative change, and ineffective upper-grade teachers who have been kept in order not to shake the boat," Mrs. Padilla decided to withdraw her youngest daughter, Steffie, from IAMS, despite Carolina's protests three years previously that Steffie should keep the "family tradition" by attending IAMS. Although Mrs. Padilla felt that IAMS had been "a positive experience for Carolina socially, because I felt comfortable knowing they other parents and letting her do things outside of school," she was not willing to risk her youngest daughter Steffie's academic opportunities by keeping her there.

The label that Carolina offered to describe herself was "Latina," which she defined as "your background is from South America or the Caribbean." When asked whether knowledge of Spanish was necessary for an identity as Latina, she replied that it was not, and added, "You don't need Spanish, it doesn't make you more Latina." She reflected on the importance of the language in her life by stating that if she were to suddenly lose the language, "it would be hard, I couldn't talk to my grandparents anymore. In Chicago they have so much, like, Spanish stuff, and I'd be sad because I wouldn't know about it." When asked whether her knowledge of the language made her feel proud, she mentioned only one incident at a summer camp in Wisconsin when people "asked her to talk Spanish."

She was also aware that IAMS wanted its students to be proud of their backgrounds and to develop Spanish. When I mentioned that some students graduate from IAMS but do not know Spanish, she said, "I think the school should enforce it. Because if that's their goal, they're not doing a good job at it." I asked what they could do differently, and she said that instead of 50% Spanish, they should offer some classes entirely in Spanish, "because if you start doing 50% and then you have to do 25% once you get older, you're losing it right there. But I understand they are trying to prepare you for high school, which is going to be all in English." She did say that knowing Spanish will be a big advantage when she is an adult entering the workforce.

From Table 8.1, we can see that Carolina's Spanish proficiency, when compared with that of her classmates, placed her at the level of Mid L1. Her FLOSEM (informal oral Spanish) score was 4.5, which was slightly below the mean of 5.08 attained by her L1 classmates. On the LAS-O (a more formal measure of oral Spanish), she scored slightly above the L1 average. Her oral story text appears below.

"Había una vez una joven que se llamaba María Elena. María Elena le encantaba trabajar en su jardín. Cuando estaba en su jardín, ella estaba muy tranquila y se olvidaba de todo. Pero las amigas de María Elena le decían que se debería casar con alguien. Pero María Elena no le daba sentido. Entonces una vez, había un joven llamado Vicente que le gustaba María Elena. Pero María Elena no le dejaba casarse con ella. Entonces Vicente se disfrazó como una viejita y fue al jardín de María Elena. Cuando estaba como una viejita, le dijo a María Elena que él era muy guapo, inteligente y le gustaba hacer cosas en el jardín. Entonces María Elena se fijó que Vicente era lo que ella necesitaba. Después Vicente se sacó el disfrace de la abuela y le dijo que, que le gustaba María mucho. Entonces María Elena se iba a casar con Vicente pero con una condición: que, le ayudaba en el jardín."

Her narrative is discursively coherent, it contains a variety of appropriate lexical items, and it contains few grammatical errors, notably the lack of the personal pronoun "a," which is supposed to accompany objects in sentences like "A Maria Elena le encantaba trabajar en su jardin."

Carolina's Spanish writing, too, was rated as slightly above the L1 mean. Her story text appears below, along with the story prompt.

Era una tarde soleada de junio, y en el patio de los Sánchez dormía un gato tranquilamente. De repente, tres perros...

... isieron un pedo y se fueron. Era tan oleoso que el gato lo podia oler asta el encima del arbol donde estaba atrapado. Era noche y nadie salbo al gato por que a nadie le gusta a los gatos. Entonces el gato brinco y se cayo en el suelo. Murio imediatamente. Cuando murio, el gato se iso un Diablo porque el dios no le gusta a los gatos tampoco.

Aside from several spelling errors that were fairly common among her classmates ("isieron," "asta") and a lack of diacritic marks, her writing was perfectly comprehensible and able to convey humor. However, her scores on the *Logramos* test of Spanish reading and vocabulary recognition were below the L1 mean, particularly the vocabulary recognition task, where she scored almost 20 percentage points below the L1 average. Upon finishing the *Logramos* test, several students complained about how difficult it had been. I noticed a correlation between *Logramos* scores and overall academic achievement, which may explain why Melissa – an L2 Spanish speaker but a very good student – outscored both Carolina and Matt.

Carolina's grammatical accuracy was the highest of all four focal students, scoring above the L1 mean on four of the five elicited forms. Although she scored below the mean on the past subjunctive task, she had in fact produced the present subjunctive on two of the sentences designed to elicit the past subjunctive (for example, "El año pasado, un amigo me pidió que no *diga* sus secretos."), indicating the robustness of the subjunctive mood in her grammar. Given that the subjunctive is a fairly early acquired form, it is likely that Carolina's almost exclusive use of Spanish at home when she was young contributed to her well-developed modal system. Her non-target-like production included four faulty *gustar* translations (such as "Gloria le gusta Emilio") and the use of the Spanish gerund in subject position ("Fumando es malo por su salud").

Carolina's sociolinguistic performance was higher than average for the letter of request, in which she consistently used the "usted" form and several conditional verbs ("Usted no debería tener que pagar" and "Yo sería muy feliz"). In fact, her letter of request showed one of the highest difference scores (which indicates sensitivity to register) in the entire class; most students only evidenced substantial difference scores on the oral task. She scored lower than the L1 average on the oral role play, but this was primarily due to her family's dialect variety: she used *usted* in the directive to the dog, her younger sibling, and her friend (but inexplicably used *tú* with the police officer). Therefore, her overall sociolinguistic performance can be said to be in tandem with her higher-than-average grammatical performance.

In spite of having comparably high levels of Spanish proficiency, Carolinas' participation during her eighth grade Spanish class, like that of her classmates, was minimal and almost always in English. I often observed her writing up her current events summary while her classmates were presenting their summaries. She claimed that math was her most important class, followed by social studies and Spanish, and that English was last because "it's boring" and "the spelling kills me," although she said she worked the hardest in English class.[1] She claimed that she would study Spanish and French in high school because her Spanish was "kind of rusty. I want to get better at it." She also said that her future children would know Spanish because she would "put them in a Spanish environment, like a Spanish day care. Also, by having determination to talk to them in Spanish, especially when they are two or three, because that's when their brain soaks it up." Through these two responses, Carolina does express connection to and investment in knowing Spanish and keeping it alive in her present and future. Her lack of participation in Spanish classes simply adhered to the norm of her peers.

Examination of Carolina's position within her school peer group revealed that she was generally well liked. Her classmates, ranging from "smart" students to "cool" students and "ghetto"-identified students, reported that she was "nice," "funny," and "cool." One student said that she was "average, in between everything. Not hyper, kind of calm, but sometimes she makes jokes or she can laugh." One "ghetto"-identified girl said, "She's cool, even though I don't talk to her that much". Another girl said that she went specifically to Carolina for help with Spanish "because she knows her Spanish really well." A different student listed Carolina among those whom she would pick for a Spanish competition team. When asked what she thought her classmates would say about her, I was surprised when Carolina replied "aggressive" and "mean." Ms. Gingiss, the eighth-grade English teacher, said that Carolina would be a leader of her class if she were not so quiet, and Ms. Castro, the math and science teacher, stated that Carolina was a "sweet young lady" but that her self-confidence about her academic abilities was lower than it should be. She also noted that Carolina and Otto (unlike Melissa, Matt, and other students) refused to take Spanish versions of the textbook when, at the beginning of a new quarter of study, her group was asked to do so.

In summary, Carolina seemed content with her identity as an English-dominant Latina. She was well liked by her peers and teachers and received a certain amount of recognition for knowing Spanish well, which was corroborated by formal measures of her Spanish proficiency. She admitted that her Spanish was "rusty" and that she wanted to improve it, and was confident that her future children would learn it. However, she clearly experienced pressure from her parents to perform well academically and in English, which may explain her refusal to use Spanish versions of the math and science textbooks. Although she played soccer and spoke some Spanish with her grandparents daily, she did not affiliate with many Latino cultural practices such as a *quinceaños* party or music.

Melissa

Melissa and her younger brother, also a student at IAMS, lived with their parents. Their home language was still English, but the children occasionally spoke Spanish when doing homework or when they did not want their mother to understand something. The family occasionally watched Spanish-language movies subtitled in Spanish, and Melissa and her brother would comment when something was translated poorly. The family had not returned to Mexico since their trip in 1999, but Melissa spoke occasionally on the phone with a friend named Margaret who lived there. In addition, Mrs. Butler often heard her daughter talking on the phone in Spanish with the parents of her friends at school, and Melissa occasionally implored her mother to learn Spanish so that her mother could talk with her friends' mothers, particularly those who were very strict. This way, a better relationship could develop between the parents, and Melissa could then see those friends more often.

When I asked her what ethnic label she used for herself, she said that she "didn't call herself anything" although other people called her white. On forms that requested this information, she would check "Other" and fill in "Human Race," until her mother requested that she stop doing so. When I asked whether knowing Spanish was part of the identity of being "white," she replied,

> "Well, it is a part of *my* identity, because I've grown up since kindergarten with Spanish. It's become a part of me, I guess you could say, even though I wasn't born with it and it wasn't part of my identity for the first four years of my life."

Yet when I asked how her life would be affected if she suddenly lost her ability to communicate in Spanish, she said only that she would have trouble at school and reading public signs in Spanish. I probed further by asking whether it would affect her friendship with Margaret and her reading habits – at the time, she was reading a book in Spanish – and she said that it would. It is not clear why she did not think of these repercussions herself. Her response to this question surprised me in that it seemed to underestimate the role of Spanish in her life, since a few minutes previously she claimed it as an important part of her identity. She did engage in more literary activities in English than in Spanish, including communicating with 11 pen pals, reading several books per week, and even publishing an article that she wrote about a friend in an English-language teen magazine called *New Moon*.

Melissa's attitudes toward Spanish were still positive, as they had been in fifth grade. When I asked whether her knowledge of Spanish made her feel proud, she repeated the same idea she had mentioned when she was in fifth grade: she enjoys knowing what strangers around her are saying, for example on the train, "and they think they're speaking in a secret code." She also felt good that she could assist her brother with his Spanish homework, but added that she did not like when her parents "show off" her and her brother's Spanish abilities to their coworkers. I asked Mrs. Butler whether Melissa, now only a year away from turning 15, still wanted a *quinceaños* party. She replied that Melissa "was backing off a bit because she feels maybe it's not right, a white kid having this kind of party. Her friends Cynthia and Lily are having these parties... how would they feel about it? It's a respect level. She hasn't worked it all out yet."

Melissa was accepted by all of the highly competitive high schools to which she had applied, and decided to attend a college preparatory school – the same one that Carolina would be attending – because it was a smaller school, and because her next-door-neighbor would also be attending. Her mother said that given her "eclectic" group of friends, it was hard on Melissa that some of her friends did not get accepted by the same school. Mrs. Butler, like Carolina's mom, felt that one of IAMS's biggest weaknesses was that it did not prepare all students equally for competing at the next level: "No matter how they justify their different focus, it's not fair. I have an advantage, because we started educating ourselves on what we needed to do. The first quarter of seventh grade is very important for getting into high school. [IAMS needs] highly qualified people teaching math and reading in all the grades. A language focus has to be *in addition to* the basic requirements." However, she did add that "now that I'm working at one of the worst schools in the city, Inter-American looks like heaven." Melissa said that she would teach Spanish to her future children: "I probably wouldn't be able to teach them everything, but I'd try to get them into a school that speaks Spanish, like I did, 'cause I'd want them to have what I had." She also exhibited awareness of the mission of the school by emphasizing that "lots of schools have Spanish class, but we get taught in Spanish. That's two totally different things." She did want to continue studying Spanish in high school

Melissa had several of the same preferences for English as her class-mates. She said she would vote for science being taught in English, "be-cause a lot of people know English, it's what more people communicate in. And last quarter I had a Spanish science book and it was really hard to understand." In addition, her musical preferences for U2, opera, and mu-sicals did not include any Spanish-language artists or genres. She used far less Spanish in class than she had in fifth grade, and no longer insisted on Spanish use with her peers. When I asked her why the students did not use more Spanish during Spanish class, she said it was because "we're lazy, we don't want to make the effort. English just sort of comes first. We're just used to it," a response very similar to those given by her classmates. I also asked whether her Spanish was as good as she would like it to be, to which she replied, "Well that's not really [the school's] fault. They're trying as hard as they can to make it good for us. They hire good teachers and get us all these books."

I found it intriguing that Melissa claimed that her most important class during eighth grade was math because it represented "real life skills, that will help me more in my future. I've never been bad at English or reading, so it's not as important to me, because I feel I have a natural thing for read-ing and writing." This suggests that the school subject most "important" to her was that which was the most challenging. This comment is also dishar-monious with her statement that in the future she wanted to be a film critic, a profession requiring more writing skills than math. She may have inter-nalized Ms. Castro's messages, as had most of her classmates, that math was the most important subject the eighth grade class was studying.

Melissa's Spanish proficiency, as reported in Table 8.1, placed her at the level of High L2. Her FLOSEM score was 4.2, which was exactly what Matt scored, only 0.8 below what Carolina scored, and over a full point higher than the L2 mean of 3.1. This suggests that Melissa was one of the most proficient L2 students in her class, and, like other High L2 students, was on some measures more proficient than Low L1 students. Her LAS-O story text appears below:

> "La jardinera. Había una vez una jardinera que se llamaba María Elena. Ella le gustaba plantar y jardinar en su jardín. Y, pero eso es, era todo lo que his, hice. Um, sus amigas dicieron por qué, por qué no tienes novio y por qué nada más eh um... trabajas con tus plantas en vez de tener una vida con un hombre. Y ella dicía que, que no quería tener un novio y . . . Pero muchos hombres querían casarse con ella pero um ella dice, dijo a ellos no, porque uh, no eran interesados en lo que ella gustaba. Pero había un hombre que se llamaba Vicente que, uh, que

amaba mucho a ella. Y una, un día, uh, se vino disfrazado en, como una abuelita a su jardín. Y ella creía que estaba hablando con algo totalmente diferente. Y dis, dije a María Elena que debes casarse con Vicente porque él es muy guapo y fuerte y le gusta jardinar. *Is that a word?* Y ella dijo sí, él es todos esas cosas pero solamente es un hombre. Y la abuelita dijo sí, es un hombre, pero um. . . quiere casarse con ti. Y ella dije en, oh, y después él ah uh, . . . sacó su disfraz y ayudó a plantar sus flores en su jardín. Y a esa era la única cosa que podía hacer para que podía casarse con ella."

Melissa's story retelling, although it has some conjugation errors ("dicía," "dicieron," "con ti," "ella dije"), is one of the longest narratives produced in the class. It includes a number of details from the original story and the meaning is very clear. Her Spanish writing was also rated slightly above the L2 mean. Her story text appears below. Similarly to Carolina's story, Melissa's story expresses some humor.

Era una tarde soleada de junio, y en el patio de los Sánchez dormía un gato tranquilamente. De repente, tres perros. . .

. . . atacáron al gato. El gato era muy sorprendido. Despúes los tres perros corrieron alrededor del gato y hizo que el gato era muy pareado [*mareado*]. Cayó del balcón y murió. Los Sánchez eran muy trístes y fueron afuera para correar alrededor delos tres perros. Despues los tres perros murieron y los dueños de los perros eran muy tristes. Fueron a correar alrededor de los Sánchzes, y murieron. Los dueños de los perros eran tán enojados, que comitieron suicidio. El fin.

Although she spelled correctly many words that both L1 and L2 students misspelled ("hizo") and used more diacritic marks than many of her classmates, she had several vocabulary difficulties such as "pareado" (instead of "mareado") and "comitieron suicidio."

On the *Logramos* test, Melissa scored at the 60thpercentile on the vocabulary recognition task, outscoring 35 of her classmates, including 20 L1 students, 1 Recent Arrival student, and 14 of the other 16 students who, liker herself, were Spanish L2. She scored at the 92nd percentile in reading comprehension, outscoring an even greater number of her classmates: 27 of the L1 students, 3 of the Recent Arrival students, and 14 of the L2 students, for a total of 44 classmates. As mentioned previously, students found the *Logramos* vocabulary test extremely difficult, and there was a correlation between *Logramos* scores and overall academic achievement.

Melissa's scores on the grammatical items were equal to or slightly higher than the average of her L2 peers on all forms except the present subjunctive, where she did not produce a single token. That is, overall, she was rather inaccurate grammatically, with no correct *gustar* translations and three instances of the Spanish gerund in subject position (such as "Mary era arestado por tomando algo que no pertenecia a ella."). She did, however, produce three correct tokens for the conditional prompts.

Her sociolinguistic scores were slightly above the L2 mean on the oral and written measures, and were actually greater than the L1 mean on the multiple-choice measure. I also noticed an awareness of formality in Spanish one day when Melissa greeted me. She said "Hi," to which I replied, "¿Cómo estás?" She said, "Muy bien, ¿y tú?... oh... ¿Y usted?" This self-correction showed that Melissa had some control over the appropriate use of formal pronouns and verb forms. The reason her letter of request score was not higher, I believe, was that she did not complete the assigned task of convincing a landlord to let her family's dog live in their apartment. Upon reading this prompt, she got visibly upset and told me she would rather not complete the letter. So I asked her instead to imagine that the school wanted to require uniforms and to write a letter to the Board of Education convincing them to reject the proposal. In this letter, she appealed to a general principle of diversity, which I believe resulted in less personalized attempts of persuasion.

Although Melissa no longer insisted on Spanish use with her peers as she had during fifth grade, she still experienced a degree of marginalization from her peers; her mother said that she called herself a "geek." Of the 11 students I asked about her, approximately half of them mentioned that she was very sensitive, took things too seriously, or that she was "too proper and polite, like the way we act around adults." I also found it interesting that, at a class Halloween party in the cafeteria, Melissa was the only student wearing a Halloween costume. Ms. Castro noted that Melissa was very hard on herself academically, and that her perfectionism and her preference not to tolerate the behavior of disruptive students alienated some of her classmates, but that she was perfectly integrated within her group of like-minded friends. Her answer to my question about what she thought the other students would say about her reveals this split: "If they're my friends, I think they'll say that I'm smart, that I could be a good friend, I give good advice. And they can trust me. And that I can be funny, a little bit. And if it's not my friend, I think they'll say, Oh she's a little smart girl who doesn't let anybody copy off of her, and very quiet I guess." Melissa stated that she wanted her teachers to think that she was "smart, mature, and respectful, because I know how it feels to be made fun of, for people to be disrespectful to me, and I wouldn't want other people to feel like that."

In general, however, in eighth grade Melissa acted like and was accepted by her peers. The other half of the students I asked about her mentioned that she was very nice and helpful, that she got along with a lot of people and played good basketball, that she was determined and dedicated to her schoolwork. I often observed her chatting off task with classmates about basketball practices and other topics. As described in Chapter 7, many students did not complete their work for Spanish class. Although Melissa did turn in all work for Ms. Maas, there were signs that she was letting herself be a bit more lax. I never observed her writing her current events article while others presented, the way I did other students including Carolina, Matt, and Otto, but I did observe her presentations being underprepared in Spanish: "Mi artículo es un... ¿cómo se dice review? Una reseña de *Our Town*. [...] How do you say version? [...] They don't fit the roles well. No es realística." This lack of preparation made her look much more like her peers than she did in fifth grade.

There were other indications that Melissa was less stressed about schoolwork than in the first year of my study. This was revealed in her comments about Ms. Gingiss, the English teacher: "I'm sick of her. She thinks of me as all worried about school, that I don't think about anything else. But I'm not all school." Yet she also stated that she wanted Ms. Maas and Ms. Castro to think she was a responsible student, "that I keep promises. If I take home work that I didn't finish in class, I'll bring it back the next day completed." It is also true that competitive high schools focused on student performance in seventh grade and the very beginning of eighth grade, so by the time of my observations and interviews, Melissa may have been allowing herself to relax on schoolwork.

To conclude, Melissa was still academically oriented, but she no longer used Spanish in contrast to classmates' English. It seemed that her participation on the school basketball team, as well as her no longer insisting on Spanish use, facilitated her acceptance by a greater number of her classmates. Spanish still played a role in her life, and she was still one of the most proficient L2 students in the graduating class, but I saw no signs of the frustration about speaking Spanish that Ms. Torres had described in fifth grade.

Matt

Matt lived at home with his Salvadoran mother, his European American stepfather, and his younger sister. He said that at home he spoke English with everyone except his mother, with whom he estimated that he used Spanish 60% of the time. His mother, however, claimed that although she used 100% Spanish with Matt, he almost always answered in English. His maternal grandmother and great-grandparents lived in the same building, and Matt stayed with them – and spoke only Spanish – each day after school.

Mrs. Castillo had similar comments about Inter-American as did Carolina's mother. She said that only half of the Hispanic children "salen bien" (end up doing well); the other half, in her opinion, have trouble with English and general preparation for high school. She said that her husband, who was "not in favor of bilingual education," noticed that their daughter, now in second grade at the school, did not have solid grade-level writing skills in English, and that he also corrected Mike's English quite often. Since the family had been considering moving to a suburb, Mrs. Castillo was convinced that her daughter would require tutoring in English to catch up to her new classmates. However, if they did not move, Mrs. Castillo was not worried about her children's English because they would "continue perfecting their English in high school and in college." In general, she felt that Inter-American was a good school, particularly because its small size allowed frequent communication, and that she was very happy that Matt had learned to read and write Spanish there.

Mrs. Castillo noted that eighth grade was a particularly difficult year for Matt on several levels. He resisted doing schoolwork to the point that she feared he would not graduate. He got Ds and Fs in English reading and in social studies, and when she would ask, he regularly told her that the teacher had not assigned any English homework. At one point, she considered sending him to Mexico or to a local boarding school. Finally, the English teacher informed her that if Matt did not begin doing better work, he would have to attend summer school in order to graduate. He eventually did put in enough effort to graduate without attending summer school, and Ms. Castro, the math and science teacher, told his mother that had he done the quality of work throughout the year that he produced during the last month of classes, he would have had excellent grades.

Mrs. Castillo disliked Matt's friends during eighth grade. He had gotten interested in skateboarding and let his hair grow long: "Parecía oso. Y la ropa rara. Los de skateboard creo que no se bañan, es el signature, y tenía que seguirle" ("He looked like a bear. And the strange clothing. Skateboarders, I think they don't bathe, that's their signature, and he had to follow that"). On one occasion Matt told her that he was spending the night with one of his friends, but when he was not there when she called the house, she ended up calling all of his friends and eventually picking him up very late at night. I spoke with her again once Matt had finished his first year of high school, and by then he had a new group of friends, no longer skateboarded, and was at home by 4:00 pm each day after school.

However, the rebelliousness he had begun to demonstrate in fifth grade had reached worrisome proportions for his mother during eighth grade.

The label Matt used for himself was "Hispanic." Interestingly, Mrs. Castillo said that Matt had begun identifying as Mexican because of his Mexican father, who had died when Matt was a child. She would remind him that he was also half Salvadoran, but Matt more frequently claimed Mexican ancestry. His mother speculated that this was because of a need to identify with his father. It may also have been due to the large Mexican population in Chicago and the likelihood that he had contact with Mexican-origin peers. Like Carolina, Matt claimed that one does not have to know Spanish in order to be Hispanic. He admitted to feeling proud when classmates in a workgroup asked him for help with Spanish, or when people stopped him on the street to ask him for directions in Spanish. His mother corroborated that Matt did use Spanish in stores, unlike other young Hispanics she had observed who resisted Spanish to such a degree that they would not use it even with people who clearly struggled to express themselves in English. She said that for a young person attending school in the United States and speaking only English with his friends, she thought his Spanish was quite good.

Matt was aware of the mission of the school to "get us to appreciate Spanish, like having the advantage." He cited a talk that an administrator had given to the class only a week before our interview. The class had to stay in during recess because of rain, so the Assistant Principal "told us, like, the whole story about two moms that didn't like how their kids were treated because they talked Spanish. And so they started it, like, in the basement of a church, and moved up from there." He acknowledged that if he suddenly lost his Spanish, his life would change radically because he used it at home and at school. Then he clarified: "Well, I don't really use it a lot at school." When I asked him to elaborate, he said simply, like most of the other students, "We're just used to speaking English." He also noted that knowing Spanish was very important to his mother, "because I come from Spanish descent." Matt spoke only English with his friends, but said that they occasionally used Spanish insults and swearwords with one another, such as calling each other "puto" (faggot). The musical groups that he liked were all alternative rock bands that sang in English.

When I asked him whether he was going to study a foreign language in high school, he said that he was going to study French during his freshman year of high school and "save Spanish for my sophomore year" because freshman Spanish would "probably be too easy" for him. He said his future children would have to know Spanish "because I'll take them to my mom's house. I won't use it as much as I do now, but I think I'll use it sometimes."

From Table 8.1, we can see that Matt's Spanish proficiency placed him in the Low L1 range. His FLOSEM score was a 4.2 out of 6. His LAS-O story retelling appears below.

"María Elena le gustaba trabajar en su jardín. Y... se olvidaba de todas las otras cosas en su vida. Y, um, hombres querían casarse con ella. Y después um,... un hombre Vicente... se disfrazó como una vieja y después um, él estaba como *like, trying to get her to like her, or him, and then, um,* le estaba preguntando cosas. Le decía a ella por qué era bueno, porque sería un buen marido para ella, y las cosas en común que pueden tener *And then,* están plantando flores. Eso es todo."

This story retelling received a 3 out of 5 from the LAS raters. Although there are no glaring errors (a few required prepositions and definite articles are missing), there are two switches to English and the narrative is relatively short.

Matt invested a bit more effort into his writing sample:

Era una tarde soleada de junio y en el balcón de los Sánchez, dormía un gato tranquilamente. De repente, tres perros...
...comieron el gato pero despues estaban atrapados en el arbol y llamaron la policia para que tiren balazos para que los perros se caigan. Pero cuando trataron de disparrar a los perros no le dieron pero si pegaron a una vieja, un pajaro y una bomba, que causo una inundacion que causo que toda la gente se moviera al rio.

This writing sample exhibits creativity and humor, in addition to required subjunctive uses *(tiren, se caigan, se moviera)*, gender and number agreement, and some advanced vocabulary *(atrapados, balazos, disparar, inundación)*. It received only a 20 out of 30 by the raters, though, owing to the lack of development of the story line, the use of simple constructions, and its relatively short length. His scores on the *Logramos* test of Spanish reading and vocabulary were very close to the means of the L1 students in the class. And, along with most of the L1 students in the class, he was outperformed on the *Logramos* test by Melissa and a few other L2 students who were high academic achievers.

Matt's grammatical accuracy was either at or slightly below the L1 mean on all measures. As mentioned previously when discussing Carolina's performance, the subjunctive is required relatively early in Spanish L1 development, which may explain why even relatively low proficiency L1 students like Matt still outperformed high proficiency L2 students like Melissa on these measures. He produced both the subjunctive and the conditional in approximately half of the required contexts, but did not translate correctly any sentences with *gustar*, omitting the required impersonal "a" in seven out of eight sentences and lacking number agreement with "le(s)" and/or with "gusta(n)" in half of the items. He incorrectly used the Spanish gerund in three out of five contexts (such as "Mary fue arrestada por robando").

His sociolinguistic scores were uneven. On the oral directives he scored slightly above the L1 mean, in fact the highest of all four focal students. But on the multiple choice measure he was two points below the mean, and on the letter of request he actually had a negative difference score, meaning that his formal letter was actually rated as less formal than his informal letter. One senses that he was purposely trying to be irreverent (and therefore informal) on the formal letter task, stating that his dog was small and that he planned on throwing it out on the street when it grew bigger and began barking loudly.

As was the case in fifth grade, Matt demonstrated overall resistance to school activities, but showed occasional signs of paying attention and following the lesson. In many instances of the recorded corpus, Matt shouted out answers or interjections relevant to what the teacher was discussing, indicating that he was at least minimally tuned in to the lesson. Sometimes his interjections were meant to be contrary, like the day that Ms. Maas asked the group whether they had understood a story and he immediately shouted out "No!" I often saw him writing his current events report while his classmates gave their presentations, which was very common. However, unlike the other three focal students, I never saw him actually present a current events summary.

In general, the students I asked to describe Matt said that he was "funny," and several added that he was a "skateboarder," an investment that clearly got him recognition. Two students mentioned that he was "smart," although one added that he was also lazy. One student added that he often helped her with her Spanish and her math work. Otto mentioned that Matt was always listening to music on his MP3 player. Ms. Gingiss, the English teacher, noted that Matt was very popular with the girls, as Ms. Torres had begun to notice in fifth grade. Ms. Castro said that Matt worked only when pushed to work: "Academically he's sharp but lazy, lazy, lazy. But that's a boy thing. He has great potential. I failed him one quarter and gave him extra work the following quarter."

In summary, despite the fact that he used Spanish regularly with his grandparents at home, Matt was one of the less proficient L1 Spanish students in the class. His investments in music, skateboarding, and girls did not create any pressing need for Spanish. His mother was satisfied with his level of oral Spanish and was happy that he used it with her parents and with Spanish-dominant strangers; she was also grateful that he had learned to read and write Spanish at Inter-American. The rebelliousness he was beginning to exhibit in fifth grade had escalated to the point of almost failing eighth grade, and his appearance and behavior with friends were causing far more concern at home than was his Spanish development.

Otto

Otto lived at home with his mom, Mrs. Setton, and his older sister and younger brother. He had regular contact with his father, who lived on the south side of the city. His family spoke English, although his father was fluent in French. Otto said that "practically every other day" in his neighborhood, he would need to use Spanish on the street or in a store with people who did not know English. He also recalled that during a soccer tournament the summer before eighth grade, he and some of his friends used Spanish with a team from Mexico. Other than occasional instances such as these, he did not hear or speak Spanish outside of school. He said that his future kids would know Spanish only if he sent them to a bilingual school.

The label he used to identify himself was "African American," an identity that he stated did not require knowing Spanish. He said that if he lost his Spanish, "it would be hard to understand what some people say to me, 'cause there's a lot of Mexicans and Latinos around where I live." When I asked him whether his knowledge of Spanish ever made him look good or feel proud, he said that he often noticed that "strangers, like white people" were often surprised that he knew Spanish: "One time I was with José and he was saying some things in Spanish. A lady just came up off the street and said 'Oh, you understand him?'" He was the only student I interviewed who did not indicate any musical interests or preferences.

As in fifth grade, Otto often shouted out answers relevant to the lesson in progress, usually in English but occasionally in Spanish. For example, one day in November, Ms. Maas asked the class whether it was landowners or non-landowners who had promoted the Industrial Revolution, and when Otto shouted out "Con propiedad" (landowners), he was the only student to answer her question. On several occasions, he tried to say something in Spanish, but when he was repeatedly interrupted, he gave up and made his comment in English, most likely because he could be more forceful in English. In Chapter 6, I mentioned how Otto would tell Ms. Maas that he was going to read his current events article in English first, followed by Spanish, but did not follow through on the promise of a Spanish reading. I once saw him hand in a current events summary with "Otto's artículo" written across the top. This struck me as a humorous attempt to incorporate Spanish into an English text, although in fact he may have thought this was an acceptable Spanish construction. His Spanish still evidenced basic subject-verb agreement problems such as "yo puede" and "nosotros fueron" (although after writing this particular phrase, he asked me, "It's *fuimos*, right?").

His understanding of the mission of the school came through when he explained to me that the music teacher recently told his class that an IAMS graduate had returned for a visit. The former student was now a well-paid lawyer in New York and used Spanish often, "and that's what they want for us." According to Otto, his father had initially been resistant to the idea of him learning Spanish, preferring that he learn French instead. However, Mr. Setton regularly saw the need for Spanish at his job as a math teacher at a school with a large Mexican population, so he eventually saw the benefits of his son studying Spanish. Otto claimed that it "wasn't really that important" to his mother that he learn Spanish, which was the impression I got during the fifth-grade and eighth-grade interviews with her. She did say that the school was very good, but that it was difficult for her because she did not know Spanish or have many resources to help her children with the language. The tutor volunteers at her church, who helped Otto with his schoolwork, did not know Spanish: "Sometimes I have to run downstairs and ask the janitor to help me." Otto said he called his classmates Jesús, Melissa, or Ángel for help with Spanish homework. Another parent, who was impressed with the way that Otto's younger brother spoke Spanish, asked Mrs. Setton about local public schools, and she recommended IAMS very highly. She said that her oldest daughter, an IAMS graduate, was reaping benefits from her Spanish knowledge at her relatively prestigious high school.

Otto said that his math and science classes were most important, and that he would not read anything in Spanish "unless someone can explain it to me." When I asked him why he and his classmates did not use more Spanish during Ms. Maas's class, he replied, "They don't like Spanish anymore. Most of them." While this may certainly have been true for many of his classmates, this struck me as a very clear personal explanation: Otto did not like Spanish anymore. Given his struggles to express himself in Spanish and to read and understand texts in Spanish, as well as the lack of support for Spanish in his home, it is likely that he was simply tired of the effort. He said he was going to study French in high school. His father had taken him to Paris the previous summer, and he was returning there a few months after our eighth-grade interview to attend a World Cup soccer tournament for kids. His mother told me that Otto was going to live with his father during high school in order to attend a school on the city's south side, and that his father's household was primarily French-speaking. Otto often bragged about his father and showed excitement that he was going to live with him. This strong connection with his father, combined with the trips to Paris and the fact that he was about to move into his father's French-speaking home, offer a strong argument that Otto felt a greater investment in learning French than in continuing to develop his Spanish.

Otto's Spanish proficiency, relative to that of his classmates, placed him in the Low L2 category. According to Table 1, his LAS-O scores were slightly above the L2 mean for his class. His LAS-O story retelling appears below.

> "Había una joven niña que se llama María Elena. Ella le gusta plantar plantas en su jardín todos los días. Y ella no pensó en los hombres o en casarse con un hombre pero sus ami... sus amigas quería que ella le gusta hombres. Una día uh, unos hombres le vinó y preguntó si ellos querían casarse con ella, pero ella dicía no. Una joven no fuiste... no se fue, y él se preguntó una pregunta a ella si él quería casarse con ella... si ella quería casarse con él. Después ella di, ella dijo no, pero después él vinó en una... con una máscara y se... él... la mascara era como una abuela. Y eh, ella, o él estaba hablando a ella, y, pero ella pensó que él era una abuelita. Y él estaba diciendo que los jov... los hombres son bien personas y ella necesitaba casarse con ellos. Y después ella se um, sa, sabía que la abuela no era... la abuela era él. Y um, ella estaba reiendo y después ella decía, 'Yo te voy a casarte con tú solo si te ayudas a plantar unas plantas'."

Otto's story retelling indicates that he understood most of the details within the original story, but that he had trouble reproducing them accurately. He evidences some agreement problems ("sus amigas quería"), one of which he self-corrected ("Una joven no fuiste... no se fue"). He also overuses the reflexive pronoun "se."

His written story narrative was also rated slightly above the L1 mean. His text appears below.

> *Era una tarde soleada de junio y en el balcón de los Sánchez, dormía un gato tranquilamente. De repente, tres perros...*
>
> ...estaba arancando de un gato porque ellos no se dara el comida y los jugetes al gato. Los perros estaban corriendo y corriendo pero el gato estaba persiguiendo a los perros. Unos minutos adelante los perros esta persiguiendo al gato y el gato se escodio en un arból. Despues los perros se fueron al casa. Cuando el gató brinco abajo un hombre se agarro y se rescate el gato.

Although there is one vocabulary selection that is difficult to understand ("Estaba aracando de un gato"), in general Otto gets his point across despite agreement problems ("Los perros esta persiguiendo al gato" and "al casa") and overuse of "se."

However, Otto's FLOSEM rating was below the class' L2 mean, indicating that he lacked general fluency. In fact, he was named by one of the 12 students I interviewed as a classmate who did not know Spanish very well. His *Logramos* reading and writing scores were also very low. He scored at the 8th percentile on the vocabulary section, which was the lowest score in the class. He did a bit better on the reading comprehension section, at the 47th percentile, which was higher than the reading comprehension scores of eight of his classmates (four L1 and four L2 students). He also failed to produce a single use of the subjunctive, although this placed him only very slightly below the L2 mean on the subjunctive measures.

Otto's grammatical accuracy was the lowest of all four focal students and, in fact, was one of the lowest in the entire eighth-grade class. He scored zero on all of the measures, except for one correct translation of an English gerund in subject position. But he did understand the tasks and produced appropriate responses for every single prompt, albeit linguistically inaccurate. His sociolinguistic scores, like Matt's, were uneven. He scored above the L2 mean on the oral directives – and one point higher than Melissa – but scored two points below the mean on the multiple choice measure, and also evidenced a negative difference score on the letter of request. However, unlike Matt's letter of request, in which his attempt to be humorous and irreverent led to no use of tempering verbs or requests, Otto did make an earnest attempt to politely appeal to an authority figure. It was his lack of linguistic control, for example "Por favor deja que yo si puede tener perros," that led to his low difference score.

Otto had a reputation as a sports buff. When he presented current events articles, they were almost always about sports events and would go something like this: "Mi artículo es de un equipo de NFL. Ellos estaban en un, um, como dice, un *serie* de juegos perdidos y necesitaban ganar. Ellos ganó a los Cleveland Browns." Many people also felt that he had an aggressive personality, as he did in fifth grade. Several of his classmates said that he was always making jokes about other people, that he was "funny sometimes, but he gets annoying" and that he was loud, talkative, and outgoing. The English teacher said that Otto was "very verbal, I have trouble with him because he's always talking. He is not malicious – he always says he's sorry – but he doesn't focus or concentrate. He could be a leader, but he lets others do it." Ms. Castro said that Otto "needed to learn how to be tactful. He was extremely abrasive and thought the world revolved around Otto.

And he struggled in math, but he knew it. Early on he knew he couldn't get away with things just from his talk. He was used to that, but I didn't play that." She also noted that both he and Carolina refused to take Spanish textbooks when she would request that the students switch from one language to the other.

Otto said that he thought his classmates would describe him as funny, and that he sings a lot in class. He wanted his teachers to think that he did his work and was involved in classroom activities. When he grew up, he wanted to be a lawyer, a sport agent, or an athlete, all professions for which he seemed particularly well suited. He felt that knowledge of Spanish would help him as a lawyer, and perhaps also as a sports agent, depending on the sport he represented.

In general, Otto felt no need to improve his Spanish, and sometimes complained that it was not necessary because he did not plan on continuing studying it in high school. In fifth grade, he felt more pressure to use Spanish in order to have his participation accepted, but in eighth-grade Spanish language classes, where little if any Spanish was required from students, he used only very minimal amounts of Spanish in class.

Other Students

In order to round out my understandings of students' language use during eighth grade, I interviewed eight students in addition to the four focal students. They were selected from a pool of students who fulfilled the consent requirements. There were three boys and five girls, and a total of six L1 students and two L2 students. Three were high academic achievers whom the others classified as "smart," some who got more average grades and were in the "cool" group, and a few who self-identified as "ghetto," which Ms. Castro described as "street" or "tough." These eight students, combined with the four focal students, formed almost 30% of the eighth-grade class.

I asked these students about the same topics that I asked the four focal students, which included questions about home language use, the labels they used to identify themselves, favorite music groups, best friends, and language use during Spanish classes. The two points that I feel are most relevant and illuminating for the purposes at hand are students' explanations for their language use, and their observations about classmates who had very high and very low Spanish proficiency.

Unfortunately, students' explanations for not using more Spanish during Spanish lessons were not very revealing, along the lines of "It's just more natural to speak English. More people contribute if we're having a conversation in English." Another said, "It's an English speaking country, everything you do here is in English, not Spanish, so we just carry that into the schools, it's part of the culture." When I asked students whether they would want science to be taught 100% in Spanish, not surprisingly, most said no.

I then asked students who they would want on their team for a fictitious Spanish competition, as well as whether any of their classmates did not know very much Spanish. I was seeking to understand whether one's Spanish proficiency, good or bad, brought any social recognition among this group of students. Students were quickly able to name students in the category of those with strong Spanish proficiency. A total of nine students were named, including the five Recent Arrival students and four students with medium to high Spanish proficiency. Melissa was the only L2 student mentioned, and she was named three times. Carolina was named only once. Neither Matt nor Otto was named in this category. Interestingly, of the nine students cited as having high levels of Spanish proficiency, there was only one boy, who was the only male Recent Arrival student. It may be an interesting area for future study to determine whether girls develop and retain higher levels of heritage language proficiency than do boys.

When I asked whether there were some students who did not know Spanish well, three students would not name anyone. Melissa added, "I'm not really like that," suggesting that she did not wish to judge her classmates based on this characteristic. But then she added, "Maybe they don't pay attention. Maybe they don't care, they don't think it's important. If they've been here since preschool, then I think it might be more of the student's fault for not putting in effort. But if you care about it and you're trying to learn it, then you will. If you don't want to learn... it's like they shut it out." The other nine students I interviewed did name at least one student who did not know Spanish well, and two names came up repeatedly: Kyle (7 times) and Lisa (4 times), both African-American and both identified to receive Special Education services. Another six students were named once each, including Otto, although the student who named him clarified: "He understands it, but he doesn't like it." And Otto said simply of Kyle, "He probably didn't care about Spanish." Although these nine students were able to name peers with weak Spanish proficiency, they were reluctant to lay any blame on them.

I also asked why it might be the case that some L2 students learned Spanish very well, while others did not. One girl seemed to believe that Spanish proficiency was tied to overall academic effort: "I once asked Margaret why her Spanish is so good, and she's white and her parents are Jewish. She said that they only let her watch TV on weekends, and that she was more focused on her work than on TV." Another student chalked it up in part to race: "[The students who don't know Spanish] are black, they don't have Spanish in their lives and in their house." When I followed up by naming two white students, one (Melissa) with very high Spanish proficiency and another with very low Spanish proficiency, the student replied, "I don't know, their parents make them. Melissa's mom is a teacher." Other students listed a combination of factors including home support, academically oriented activities such as visiting museums, and effort:

> "Kyle's parents don't push him that much. It's not that he can't be smart, he just doesn't try. I also guess his parents didn't take him to museums and stuff."

> "Ariel's parents aren't involved with the school, and don't take him to cultural stuff, whereas Melissa's mom is really involved with the school and Melissa goes to the Mexican Fine Arts Museum."

> "They pay more attention in class, maybe their friends speak Spanish... maybe something outside of school."

> "Melissa and Teo [both Spanish L2] actually want to learn it, put more effort into it. Kyle or Lisa, I guess they think they're never going to have to use it."

This group of IAMS students did not assign a great deal of importance to learning Spanish. While most were aware of which classmates had high levels of Spanish proficiency, there were no peer-based negative repercussions to not having learned the language well. Given the strong pull of adolescent peer groups, the fact that Spanish held little social value severely limited students' desire to invest in it. And, unlike in Ms. Torres' fifth-grade classroom, during this eighth-grade year there was no pressure from teachers to perform in Spanish, leaving virtually no need for students to publicly invest in identities as Spanish-speakers.

Conclusions

Forming and performing social and linguistic identities is at the heart of the development and maintenance of any language. It is generally agreed that when people feel that their languages and cultures are valued, they will be more likely to claim themselves speakers of the language and members of the cultural group. On the contrary, when a language is stigmatized and the cultural inheritance is ridiculed, people will be less willing to be identified with it, whether they are heritage speakers or L2 learners.

IAMS attempts to provide students, for nine continuous years and beginning at a very young age, the opportunity to develop strong Spanish proficiency and build a healthy identity as Spanish speakers, with which they can negotiate group membership within both Spanish- and English-speaking groups. Although students' Spanish is clearly not as strong as their English upon graduating from IAMS, school cofounder Adela Coronado-Greeley stated, "The seed has been planted" for students' continued development and appreciation of the language. Although we would have to follow up on these students in high school and beyond to find solid evidence in support of this claim, the data presented in this chapter do suggest that the majority students at IAMS develop positive attitudes toward Spanish, in spite of the fact that they strongly resist using it in the classroom. Given the tendency for adolescents to focus exclusively on themselves and their peers while opposing the suggestions of parents, teachers, and other adults, this snapshot of 14-year-olds' investments in Spanish, a language that was dispreferred among peers and pushed only by school authorities and occasionally their families, was remarkably positive.

Carolina, Matt, Melissa, and Otto exhibited in eighth grade the same basic personality traits as they had in fifth grade. However, the absence of any eighth-grade classroom-based pressure to perform in Spanish virtually eliminated the investments that had led to their Spanish use in fifth grade – for Carolina to gain the floor and display engagement during teacher-fronted lessons, for Matt to stay out of trouble, for Melissa to fulfill her sense of academic obligation, and for Otto to have his otherwise problematic participation accepted. Under such circumstances, Norton's (2000) framework of investment which stresses that language learning is a complex social practice that engages the identities of language learners is less applicable. That is, this eighth-grade environment appeared more like a typical foreign language classroom, in which students produce very little of the target language and all important communication takes place in English, than like an immersion classroom where students regularly communicate through the medium of the immersion language and experience opportunities to engage their social identities through that language.

Note

1. The question I asked all 12 of the eighth-grade students I interviewed was, "Which of your three classes is most important to you?" Judging by their responses, they equated the "importance" of a class with how much they enjoyed it.

Chapter 9
Conclusions

Inter-American Magnet School, during its 30-year history, has provided a remarkable educational experience to Chicago public school youth. It can be considered a highly successful school in numerous ways, four of which merit repetition here. First, children study an innovative "Curriculum of the Americas" that teaches them interactively and across content areas about the many different peoples who form part of the American continent. Although I majored in Spanish in college, I did not learn about the Taíno indigenous people that inhabited Puerto Rico until graduate school. Yet Inter-American students study this group in depth during their entire second-grade year, learning native words for Taíno housing, musical instruments, and other cultural practices. They focus on the Aztecs, Mayans, and Incas during subsequent years at the school. Even a student like Leslie, an African-American girl who was receiving Special Education services, who had received pullout Spanish as a Second Language (SSL) during all of her years at IAMS, and who was unable to perform the most basic Spanish tasks, correctly identified the Cuban poet José Martí when his name appeared on a language arts worksheet in eighth grade.

Second, the school's social justice committee strives to provide students with experiences that encourage reflection on issues of race and class. One IAMS parent told me about her son's experiences in college:

His worldview was definitely influenced, he got it all day long for years at [IAMS]. The ability to understand the complexities of how people are alike and different at the same time. At a certain point he felt like a victim of the diversity here, but that didn't scar him. He got the big picture. He doesn't get confused about issues of privilege. It's second nature to him to understand racial and cultural issues, the way we're divided and united. It's normal to him to be in a group of people who are all different from each other. He gets fed up with people in [small college town] who have only been around their own kind.

Third, students at IAMS perform well academically. According to the state-mandated school report card (http://statereportcards.cps.k12.il.us).

In both 2003 and 2004, IAMS students' overall performance on state standardized tests was higher than that of students in the subregion, in the district, and in the state of Illinois. Students are also assessed using an alternative report card that documents their growth in a number of areas using portfolios and other developmental rubrics.

Finally, IAMS students develop respectable levels of Spanish proficiency and investment in the language. Chapter 7 provided a detailed description of graduates' performance on a variety of Spanish language tasks, tests of reading and writing ability, and sociolinguistic awareness. Even a student like T.A., whose problematic oral and written narratives were displayed in Appendices 7.C and 7.D, would often volunteer to read Spanish aloud in class and did so with targetlike pronunciation. Common sense dictates that heritage speakers and second language Spanish learners alike develop stronger levels of Spanish than they would in elementary schools where only English is used. With few exceptions, IAMS students also develop positive attitudes toward Spanish, even though getting them to actually speak Spanish is often a challenge. The school provides an affirmative environment for heritage speakers who, in mainstream schools, may feel little incentive to invest in identities as Latinos and as Spanish speakers – perhaps even preferring to downplay their backgrounds entirely – as well as for students like Melissa, who, although not Latino, received encouragement and recognition for her Spanish abilities at IAMS.

This being said, this study has shown that graduates of IAMS do not achieve the school's stated goals of balanced bilingualism. That is, their Spanish proficiency was clearly less developed than their English proficiency, and getting them to speak Spanish in class was a substantial challenge. Given the dominance of English at all levels of U.S. society, it is hardly surprising that students' English systems would be stronger. In fact, the goal of "balanced bilingualism" is likely unattainable in a dual language context in the United States. But is it possible for Inter-American students to develop stronger levels of Spanish proficiency than those reported here? If so, how? Although at the outset of this study, I stated that this would not be a pedagogically oriented book, my conversations with IAMS teachers, parents, and administrators, as well as with other immersion researchers, have led to the formulation of a few recommendations on what IAMS in particular, and dual language programs in general, might consider to strengthen the minority language component of their programs. Some of these suggestions focus on schoolwide practices, while others involve classroom-based lessons aimed at developing greater accuracy and range of expression in Spanish.

School-Level Practices

Policies and activities to promote Spanish

One teacher, commenting on the fact that there were several school-wide competitions carried out in English but none in Spanish, described campaigns that had taken place in the past at Inter-American to build the status of Spanish. One such effort was a week-long fair that included carnival games that older students made for younger students, guests from a local Spanish-language radio station who spoke in Spanish about how important the language was, and Spanish contests involving giving speeches, spelling bees, and writing. This seemed to me an excellent way to involve the entire school in Spanish-language activities and reward students who put effort into expressing themselves in Spanish. Unfortunately, there were no such schoolwide activities during the two years I spent at the school or, to my knowledge, between 2004 and the publication of this book.

In addition to schoolwide academic Spanish-focused activities, immersion schools might explore ways to incorporate high expectations of Spanish proficiency into the grading system. Inter-American is unique among Chicago Public Schools in that it administers a standardized Spanish reading test to all students, while most schools give such tests to only limited English proficient (LEP) students who are deemed unprepared to take mandated standardized English tests. Although Spanish-dominant and English-dominant students alike are required to take the standardized Spanish test, this test has no bearing on students' records. Nor did I see evidence that results on this measure were used for any pedagogical purpose. It is already difficult enough for teachers to assist their students in mastering grade-level content in English. I am not advocating additional pressure from standardized tests, but rather reiterating what was noted in Chapter 6: it was very clear to students that there was no required minimal level of Spanish proficiency (or effort) to pass from grade to grade, or to graduate from the school. Although there is a section on the school's report card where teachers assign a grade for students' Spanish development, many teachers I consulted told me that parents rarely showed concern about this grade. One teacher pointed out that even her English-monolingual colleagues at Inter-American were not held responsible for learning Spanish.

The IAMS community, therefore, may wish to consider ideas for holding all school members accountable for some baseline level of Spanish proficiency, and developing effective systems to support those who need additional help. Such a system would look much different than the SSL classes described in Chapter 3. They would be taught by a second language acquisition professional and would be developed in close harmony with an SSL committee, which would include main classroom teachers, so that content and linguistic structures would be integrated in ways that would support the students on several levels. They would also be closely monitored and evaluated for effectiveness. To the extent possible, SSL students' parents would also be called upon to assist in their children's Spanish development in ways that could be suggested by the SSL committee.

Even more difficult than raising standards for students' academic use of Spanish is to encourage their social use of Spanish and investments in identities as Spanish speakers. As noted by Elías-Olivares _et al._ (1985: 4) in research on sociolinguistic communities, only after we understand the linguistic habits of its speakers can we begin to formulate a program of language planning that can be implemented successfully. Dual immersion is arguably a form of linguistic planning (Freeman 1998). This study revealed that in fifth grade, students used very little Spanish for off-task social purposes, and that in eighth grade they used none at all. Tarone and Swain (1995) mentioned that educators might content themselves with students' academic performance in the minority language and resign themselves to the fact that social use of that language is not a feasible school goal.

Although increasing the proportion of Spanish-dominant students (to be addressed in the next section) may be a way to bolster the amount of social Spanish use at Inter-American during the early grades, other ideas were suggested by several teachers. One of them was to create a sequence of four schoolwide, extracurricular activities per year like games, movies, and songs that students could talk about. The school cofounder Janet Nolan described a similar project that had been discussed in the past: teachers planned to produce a book of children's games in Spanish that was to be used in classrooms, on the playground, and in physical education classes. In order to gather material, they asked teachers about the games they used to play in their home countries. However, Janet did not know if the book was ever completed.

The Inter-American community, therefore, was conscious of the need to actively and consistently promote the Spanish language, and had produced many good ideas for doing so. However, many of these ideas had either ceased being promoted or were not completed. Among the six teachers and administrators I interviewed at the end of 2003, I noted enthusiasm and a desire to improve on this level from four of them, and a more resigned and negative attitude from two of them. On the basis of two years of observations and informal conversations, I found that the positive responses were more representative of the school community in general. What appears to be necessary is a focused drive to make improvements, the willingness to decide on a group plan, and the support necessary to carry the group's ideas out to fruition over the long term. Despite the difficulties in carrying out new ideas, one teacher noted, "We're lucky because teachers come here with a purpose. We constantly get new blood, and there are enough of us oldies but goodies who never say die. We're easy to reinspire."

One final idea about increasing Spanish use among dual immersion students involves program structure. Chapter 4 of this study showed that, when speaking with their fifth-grade teacher, the four focal students spoke Spanish 82% of the time. Similarly, in a one-way immersion classroom, Broner (2000) found 98% Spanish use with school adults (however, only 15% of that corpus included an adult as an interlocutor, while in this study, almost half of all student turns were directed to the teacher). Greater expectations for IAMS students to use 100% Spanish with their teachers during Spanish lessons – and for teachers themselves to use 100% Spanish during these lessons – would support the school's goals of language development. The dual immersion schools profiled by Perez (2004) maintained a strict separation of languages for instruction. Perhaps IAMS would benefit from such a "one-teacher, one-language" approach, or some other kind of stricter separation of languages.

I would like to briefly return to the issue of students' investments (Norton 2000) in speaking Spanish. It is probably not realistic to hope for an immersion school to create such investments. Caldas (2006), noticing that none of the students at his daughters' French immersion school actually spoke French with each other, "began to soberly assess the limits of a school language immersion program, especially when it came up against adolescence in America." (Caldas 2006: 6). The author concluded that societal immersion with friends – that is, being entirely cut off from English and among same-age peers – was the key factor to developing his children's French fluency, adding that "Even if tremendous effort is exerted to preserve a minority language, if that language is not cherished by the adolescent's peer group, he or she will likely not speak the language" (Caldas 2006: 163). Even less, I would argue, can we expect adolescents to use a minority language in schools. But Caldas does give credit to the French immersion school that his daughters attended for strengthening their French writing and grammar. I feel that IAMS provides the same advantage in Spanish to children in Chicago. On a positive note, Caldas' (2006) children had grown to appreciate their bilingualism as young adults, which may also be true of IAMS graduates.

Admission of students based on language background

During the school years 1999–2000 and 2002–2003, Inter-American's lottery admission policy consisted of selecting applicants on the basis of racial/ethnic category – which usually averaged 70% Latino, 20% white, and 10% black – and split evenly by gender. Several teachers and administrators confirmed to me that the school was not permitted to select students on the basis of language background. This means that, although the majority of students admitted each year were Latino, there was no way to ensure that a given portion of them were Spanish dominant, or even Spanish speaking. One way to measure the proportion of Spanish-dominant children enrolled at the school is through their classification as Limited English Proficient (LEP), a category that every school is required to report. In 2004, 30% of Inter-American's student population was classified as LEP. Assuming that this 30% of LEP students came from the 70% Latino population, this means that the Spanish proficiency of the other 40% of Latinos is unknown.

Raising the proportion of Spanish-dominant students (who are sometimes but not always LEP) admitted each year would likely support the school's mission to encourage Spanish use. Although a student who was admitted in preschool or kindergarten as LEP very often becomes English dominant by third grade, increasing the number of Spanish-dominant[1] students will likely promote greater student Spanish use, particularly in the earlier grades. Beginning in the school year 2005–2006, the school gained the right to select students from the lottery based on language dominance in an effort spearheaded by the teachers' social justice committee.

Another aspect of school policy involving students' language proficiency is the admittance of older students. Many dual immersion schools do not admit monolingual English-speaking students past a certain grade level, the rationale being that they would not be able to complete the required grade-level work in the non-English language. For example, in the two San Antonio schools profiled by Perez (2004), English-dominant children were not admitted after first grade. IAMS' official policy was not to admit English-dominant children after third grade, but I saw this guideline violated repeatedly. Dual immersion schools might examine admission policies more closely and decide whether adhering to them provides more advantages in supporting their language mission than any advantages to be gained by overlooking them.

Strengthening upper cycle and creating articulation with high schools

Chapters 6, 7, and 8 described some of the ways in which the 2002–2003 eighth-grade Spanish classes suffered from an acute lack of trained personnel and school support. Dual immersion schools that extend beyond elementary school (which typically runs through fifth or sixth grade) need to consider ways to balance the academic rigor required in the middle school grades along with the school's language mission. The Spanish component of IAMS's upper cycle was, to my eyes, one of the most challenging areas for the school to address, given adolescent resistance to using Spanish as well as the academic load of the curriculum and the students' impending transition to all-English high schools. Strengthening the upper cycle would require a concerted effort by teachers and administrators, as well as appropriate professional development experiences for the teachers, including exposure to tenets of heritage language development, sociolinguistics, and other issues related to teaching Spanish to heritage speakers (Potowski 2005); second language acquisition and language arts, which will be revisited in the section on classroom activity types; and standard teacher professional development issues, such as classroom management and curriculum development.

The issue of articulation with local high schools was another concern among several parents and teachers I interviewed. Inter-American's language mission was swimming against the tide; its vision of the importance of Spanish was not shared by other schools in the community, and the Spanish skills of many of its graduates stagnated once they were in high school. Many of them, especially non-Latino students, were placed in beginning Spanish classes in high school, either because they were not tested properly or because there were no other courses available. Parents of students with high levels of Spanish proficiency, no matter what their ethnic background, should be given the option to enroll their children in Spanish for Native Speakers courses at schools where these programs are offered. Such courses are tailored to suit the strengths and challenges of heritage speakers and most likely are more appropriate for many dual immersion graduates, even when they are not ethnically heritage speakers. These courses often prepare students to take Advanced Placement courses by tenth or eleventh grade, and the culminating Advanced Placement exams, one in Spanish language and one in Spanish literature, grant college credit. If dual immersion schools can work with local high schools and school boards, making clear the importance of Spanish in students' academic careers both during the elementary and the high school years, there could be a resultant strengthening of the Spanish component in the upper cycle of the elementary school years in dual immersion programs.

Classroom Activity Types

In addition to seeking to increase overall Spanish use at the school, there was concern among several IAMS educators about increasing students' grammatical accuracy. The school's curriculum was unit based, focusing on different themes, but less on grammar. As one teacher explained,

> Once, we all sat down and analyzed how many minutes of Spanish students were really getting at each grade level. We found surprises. It's a constant topic of conversation, we're always worrying about it. Then, through a grant, we spent time in the summer working on projects that carried over from year to year, that integrated Spanish grammar into our units. But there are always so many interruptions. And you need to get momentum. We would do a few lessons, the whole faculty would be involved, we'd look at the scope and sequence, but it was frustrating because you need to spend massive amounts of time. Grammar has been a pressing issue that comes up periodically among teachers and parents.

This speaks to the ongoing struggle of immersion educators to create content-based language instruction that maximizes both content and language learning. Tedick et al. (2004) studied the beliefs of a group of immersion educators about how to integrate language and content. The authors identified five themes that revealed underlying teacher beliefs about these topics, and proposed implications for classroom practice. The first three themes are related to the issue of the "primacy of content": many teachers felt that there simply was not enough time to integrate language focus into content instruction, often accompanied by the belief that their primary accountability was for content only, or that language was already being attended to through the attention to content. This suggests that these immersion teachers did not focus on language in any systematic way. The authors proposed that teachers need to become more "language aware and informed" by understanding educational linguistics and by being able to teach Spanish structure.

However, educational linguistics and the teaching of Spanish – both its grammatical structures as well as developing students' overall communicative competence – do not form part of most elementary school teaching degree programs. Indeed, as explored in Chapter 2, the teaching of foreign languages in elementary schools is relatively rare, taking place in approximately just one third of U.S. elementary schools. In the state of Illinois, an endorsement in foreign languages consists of 24 hours of university coursework. Technically, up to 12 of those hours could consist of beginner courses in which the teacher candidate was herself learning the foreign language, followed by only 12 hours (4 classes) of intermediate coursework. There is no requirement for elementary school foreign language teachers to undergo any professional preparation in language acquisition or second language teaching methodologies. Rarer still are immersion programs, which should require far more professional preparation, particularly dual immersion programs for which teachers need training in heritage language development; yet no such preservice professional development is required to become certified to teach in either one-way or two-way immersion. Inter-American does have a solid professional development structure in collaboration with a local university, whose teacher candidates carry out their student teaching at IAMS and receive coursework tailored to the needs of immersion educators. However, not all IAMS teachers come through this program, nor do such programs exist at many other immersion schools around the country. Immersion schools, therefore, may choose to seek out the assistance of local universities in this regard, with the understanding that the partnership should ideally operate as a two-way exchange of knowledge and experience.

Beyond focusing on students' Spanish grammar, the development of their overall communicative competence should be a primary goal. Communicative competence (Canale & Swain, 1980; Hymes, 1971) addresses the idea that speakers of a language need more than grammatical competence in order to be able communicate effectively in it. They also need to know how language is used by members of a speech community to accomplish their purposes. Communicative competence is generally understood to encompass four areas: (1) grammatical competence, including words and rules; (2) sociolinguistic competence, such as what is appropriate to say in a given situation; (3) discursive competence, including things like cohesion and coherence within text; and (4) strategic competence, including the appropriate use of strategies to communicate effectively. My study examined several aspects of students' grammatical, sociolinguistic, and discursive competence and found that there was room for improvement in all of them.

Two sources for standards-based Spanish language arts curricula have been published since the completion of my study at Inter-American and may be of use to dual immersion educators in bolstering the Spanish language component of their programs. One is the WIDA Spanish Language Arts Standards (2006), which is intended to provide a framework for instruction and assessment for Spanish language arts instruction across grades K through 12. The other is the K-8 Spanish for Heritage Speakers curriculum developed by the Chicago Public Schools' Office of Language and Cultural Education (forthcoming). This curriculum, aligned with the WIDA Spanish Language Arts Standards as well as other sets of standards at both the national and state of Illinois levels, is composed of learning scenarios that guide classroom teachers in activities designed to fit within a 30- to 50-minute framework several times a week.

The fourth theme identified by Tedick *et al.* (2004) concerned immersion teachers' language use expectations. Some teachers believed that students had a right to speak, and to understand teachers' messages, in either language. The authors suggested that, instead, teachers should be consistent in communicating to students their language use expectations, that they adhere to a clear and sustained separation of the two languages, and that they design tasks that require a final product in the target language. These suggestions are appropriate for IAMS as well.

The authors identified a fifth and final theme that they called "overreliance on input." It included the belief expressed by many immersion teachers that students needed only to listen and have grammar points explained to them in order to learn the language. In response, the authors suggested that teachers elicit more talk from students and that they themselves talk less; to structure an environment including resources such as grammar posters where students can find language information without teacher assistance; to position students as active coparticipants of classroom interaction; and to design tasks that require target language use. Of equal importance to the suggestion that students be expected to speak more Spanish is to attend to the type of feedback they receive on their output, a point addressed by Lyster (2001) and others. Much more research is needed on immersion teacher talk and on the feedback immersion students receive on their linguistic production in order to maximize language learning in these environments.

The structure of classroom groupwork also merits attention. Fortune (2004) analyzed which activity types and participant structures led to the greatest quantity and quality of Spanish use among fifth-grade immersion students. The two activity types that led to the highest quantity of Spanish use were student presentations (68% Spanish) and open-ended question and answer sessions (65% Spanish). My findings at Inter-American were very similar. However, Fortune found that student-led whole class work and groupwork were the two participant structures resulting in the greatest quantity of Spanish use (52% and 45%, respectively). However, at IAMS I found that groupwork led to larger amounts of *English* than Spanish use. Groupwork is believed to foster collaborative knowledge construction, and when it comes to language learning, ESL research has shown that students who engage in groupwork with native speakers produce language of greater complexity (Liu, 1994). But at Inter-American and, very likely, in many immersion contexts in which students are supposed to speak a minority language with one another, groupwork results in high levels of English use. I do not advocate abandoning groupwork in favor of exclusively teacher-fronted lessons in the name of reducing the amount of

English used in the classroom, but some adjustments to groupwork activity might assist in promoting students' Spanish use. For example, requiring that the resulting product of groupwork activity be in Spanish, as well as monitoring students' language use with an effective reward and sanction system, might bolster their groupwork Spanish use.

Another avenue worth considering to improve students' grammatical accuracy in Spanish is to incorporate specially designed lessons containing a focus on form. For example, Harley (1989) found that fifth-grade French immersion students who received eight weeks' worth of contextualized, age-appropriate, and interesting lessons focusing on the difference between the preterite and the imperfect outperformed a control group on immediate posttest measures (although not on a delayed posttest given three months after instruction had ended). The author suggested that such lessons could be adapted to even younger groups of immersion students, such as third or fourth graders, particularly since their L2 development has been shown to slow down in these grades and the fact that it may become more difficult to overcome grammatically inaccurate communicative strategies as students get older. Since Harley (1989) does an excellent job describing the materials that were used in her study, interested readers are directed to the original study both as an example of the structure of such lessons, as well as notes of caution in the training of teachers in their implementation. Such activities that are contextually based yet also focus on linguistic accuracy have great potential to bolster minority language proficiency among immersion students.

The Important Role of Dual Immersion in Heritage Language Maintenance and Foreign Language Learning

I would like to conclude by emphasizing the important role of Inter-American, and of dual immersion schools generally, in foreign language education and heritage language maintenance. Such schools swim against the hegemonic tide in the United States, which since its colonial days has considered the English language a primary factor in uniting its citizens. American English was thought to both reflect and constitute the democratic nature of the country, such that its acquisition and use was a litmus test of citizenship. Lacking a common culture or common history, English became the essential part of "real" Americanism (Baron, 1990). In schools and in public life, more than just proficiency in English, monolingualism in English was linked to democracy, national unity, and allegiance to the country. Even those immigrants who learned English but kept their mother tongue were suspect, while elite English speakers who learned another language

were not. A case in point is Benjamin Franklin, who was adamantly opposed to the practices of Germans who settled in the American colonies
but maintained their language, while he himself developed such high-level
French skills that he engaged in political discussions with France's elite.

Dual immersion schools embrace the idea that not only should children
of immigrants maintain their home language, but that children from monolingual homes should learn another language. In this way, these schools
support a much broader view of global citizenship that marks the current and future direction of the world. Given the growth of the Hispanic
population in the United States, both in sheer numbers and as an international economic market; the tremendous increase in dual immersion
around the country to at least 315 documented programs in 2005; and
national movements for heritage language maintenance, there may come
a day when dual immersion schools are part of the mainstream national
educational mission. Indeed, United States dual immersion educators and
supporters should continue their efforts, eventually meeting and exceed-
ing the 2000 proposal made by the United States Secretary of Education to
increase the number of dual immersion schools to 1000.

However, for such schools to be successful, they require several levels
of support. One IAMS teacher lamented that the school was "surviving
instead of thriving," citing among other factors recent local pressure to
eliminate magnet school funding. Magnet school initiatives are being dis-
mantled in many cities with high numbers of minority group students, the
argument being that such schools do not produce the intended result of desegregation. Combined with this pressure are overall financial restrictions
in the Chicago Public School district, which led to the cut in school busing
described in Chapter 3. To achieve its goals of academic, social, and linguistic development, a school like IAMS requires substantial commitment and
finances for materials, professional development, adequate physical facil-
ities, and busing of students from areas with large Hispanic populations,
among other considerations. School districts with large numbers of minority language speakers in states like New Jersey, where foreign language
study is mandatory in the elementary schools, may eventually develop
the infrastructure necessary to support the development and expansion
of dual immersion programs. Educators and parents living in states without a foreign language requirement in the elementary schools may find
their efforts well spent in working to have such a requirement created.
Even more insidious are the problems posed by the federal No Child Left
Behind act passed in 2002, which promotes a heavy focus on standardized testing in areas like English and math at the expense of homegrown
curricula, multilingual development, and alternative assessment.

In addition to securing much needed external support, educators must also continue to work within our profession to propose solutions to the vexing issue of minority language maintenance. An internationally known leader in Spanish heritage language education issues, Guadalupe Valdes (2005: 16) has noted that if practitioners believe that they can contribute in some small way to language maintenance, they must address the following questions, which to date remain largely unanswered: What levels of linguistic development correlate with students' desire to maintain Spanish? What kinds of interactions with other Spanish speakers in school promote an increased interest in continuing to participate in such interactions? What kinds of readings promote an understanding of students' linguistic circumstances and a concomitant awareness of the efforts involved in maintaining the language? Which classroom activities contribute to students' positive attitudes about themselves and their Spanish? We must also increase the amount of research documenting the linguistic results of language maintenance initiatives such as dual immersion. In addition to the linguistic portrait provided by the present study, Montrul & Potowski (forthcoming) show that Inter-American heritage speakers in first, third, and fifth grade evidence greater accuracy on Spanish gender and number tasks than has been shown among heritage speakers in previous studies. That is, it constitutes evidence that dual immersion contributes to language maintenance by either arresting attrition or promoting more complete Spanish acquisition (it has not yet been determined whether one or both phenomenon, attrition or incomplete acquisition, are at work) as compared to students in all-English programs.

Valdés (2005: 39), citing an important observation by Joshua Fishman, who long ago emphasized that the only true language maintenance lies with intergenerational transmission from parents to children, also notes that schools often fail to teach heritage languages successfully because they cannot reproduce an environment even remotely close to the total sociocultural and interpersonal reality that is required for post-adolescent language maintenance. Her cautions against the effectiveness of dual language programs (Valdés 1997) were discussed in chapter 2. It is beyond the scope of this book to address language policy issues in the wider United States society that would lead to the creation of the circumstances necessary to support complete and lasting intergenerational transmission of Spanish. Although most children spend only 180 days per year in school, they are there for eight hours per day, which represents approximately half of the time they are awake. I believe it is a worthwhile effort to continuously seek ways of maximizing the language maintenance possibilities that children receive during that time.

Inter-American teachers, administrators, and parents alike repeatedly mentioned the tradition of collaboration between them. Teachers who had previously worked elsewhere commented how rare it was to find that type of partnership. The sense of mission they have as a school, the kind of teachers they attract, and their strength and resilience in keeping their vision alive are a source of inspiration to me as a researcher, as a heritage language educator, and as a parent raising bilingual children. I agree with the sentiments of the fourth grade teacher who told me, when considering the difficulty of integrating content and language, "We don't have to exchange the language mission for the pedagogical mission. I wouldn't have my kids go anywhere else."

Note

1. The school's use of the terms "Spanish dominant" and "English dominant" constitutes a point of interest. Although a person's language dominance usually varies by topic, context, and mode of communication, the word "dominant" implies that the person knows more and can express herself more extensively in most contexts in that language (Baker 1996: 25). However, at IAMS, the term "Spanish dominant" was used for students who spoke *some* Spanish in the home, but the student could in fact be English dominant in the sense of the word just described. It may be that, as in many public schools, the use of labels like "LEP" or "Spanish dominant" are important for funding considerations. It may also be a convenient way to refer to students' home language, or a way to bolster the impression of Spanish "dominance" in the school. In any case, what I am suggesting is admitting a greater proportion of students who are truly dominant in Spanish.

Epilogue

There have been several major changes at Inter-American since the 2002–2003 school year when this study concluded. This brief epilogue tells just a portion of the story, and, as with any controversy, there are several sides to it. My own interpretations and inclinations, based on my experiences in the school and my personal beliefs about how it should be run, will likely color the presentation.

The principal of Inter-American for over 20 years, Mrs. Harding, retired in June 2005. The process of identifying and selecting a new principal was highly controversial, reflecting ideological divisions that were becoming more acute among the school's stakeholders. One example of these ideological divisions became apparent in response to the United States' attack of Iraq in 2003. Some teachers had engaged students in anti-war discussions and the creation of anti-war signs for the classroom, acting within their view of the social justice goals of the school. However, other teachers and some parents were opposed to the expression of such political ideologies in the classroom. In addition, power struggles among various stakeholders about the possibility of relocating the school to a different building – which will be described in greater detail – caused further divisions. These power struggles dominated the principal selection process, and the principal who was finally selected by the Local School Council was not the choice indicated by a majority of parents attending the public forum.

The new principal began in August 2005. I found her to be well informed about the theory behind dual immersion education, and she stated that she was dedicated to the continued success of the school. She showed some interest in the professional development of her staff, as well as in research such as this study. Although some teachers were happy with her having been selected as principal, others found the work environment increasingly difficult. Many of them complained that their professional experience was not being valued, and that the collaborative and child-friendly atmosphere of the school had been lost. When the new principal began having health problems, an interim principal was hired. An already tumultuous situation became unbearable for some of the teachers when two of their highly respected colleagues were fired without notice. A large group of teachers left Inter-American in fall 2006, and several parents that I know transferred their children to other schools because they became uncomfortable with the "constant battles" and the loss of vision and leadership in the school. At this writing, the 2006–2007 school year had not yet started and approximately 15 teacher vacancies were being filled.

Another important change is that, during summer 2006, Inter-American was finally relocated out of the deteriorating building in which it had been operating since 1983. Le Moyne school, located about two miles north of Inter-American, had been experiencing declining enrollment, and the Chicago Public Schools Board decided that Le Moyne was to absorb Inter-American's dual immersion program as a strand within the building. However, Le Moyne had a large special education program, and as a result of this decision, many students were switched to other programs, causing some Le Moyne parents to file a lawsuit against the school district. Ironically, as was narrated in Chapter 3, Inter-American had been a school-within-a school at LeMoyne from 1980–1983 with one principal for both schools. It was moved to the Robert Morris school in 1983 in order for them to "have their own school" and had to absorb over 200 students and some teachers in K through 8 at Robert Morris. Now, the reverse is happening as Inter-American is being moved back to LeMoyne, with much controversy surrounding the move.

Many in the Inter-American community opposed the move as well, in part because of the hardship it presented to the Le Moyne special education program, but principally because of the demographics of the area in which Le Moyne was located. As described in Chapter 3, Inter-American was already struggling with the effects of the demographic changes in Lakeview, and was constantly looking for ways to attract Spanish dominant students. With continued cuts to student bussing – bussing for preschool was discontinued in 2002, causing great hardship to working parents who then had to transport their children to a half-day preschool – many saw it as a death wish to commit to a new home in the predominately white Le Moyne area. Many teachers and parents, including Janet Nolan, co-founder of Inter-American and now a grandmother of a student there, vociferously opposed the move to Le Moyne. Some teachers confided that they felt they had fallen out of favor with the administration who did not support the move.

These two changes, in leadership and in location, will profoundly affect the nature of Inter-American. Community buy-in into the principles of dual language seems to have taken a back seat to other issues. In a sense, the school portrayed in this book no longer exists. Since its founding in 1975, Inter-American fostered an environment that addressed the three principles of language revitalization proposed by Hernández-Chávez (1993): (1) it infused the ethnic language and culture with a positive image and value through its incorporation into a public school curriculum; (2) abundant native language interactions took place in an attempt to maximize the acquisition of Spanish; and (3) there was active involvement of parents and other segments of the community. The new configuration of Inter-American, including the loss of a core group of experienced dual immersion teachers and dedicated parents as well as the relocation to a neighborhood with few Spanish-speaking children, will undoubtedly affect the future of the school. It remains to be seen to what extent Inter-American, with its commitment to providing quality dual immersion to Hispanic children, its Curriculum of the Americas, and its roots in social justice, can continue to swim against the hegemonic United States tide.

References

Adiv, E. (1980) An analysis of second language performance in two types of immersion programs. Unpublished doctoral dissertation, McGill University.

Allen, P., Swain, M., Harley, B. and Cummins, J. (1990) Aspects of classroom treatment: Toward a more comprehensive view of second language education. In B. Harley, P. Allen, J. Cummins and M. Swain (eds) *The Development of Second Language Proficiency* (pp. 57–81). Cambridge: Cambridge University Press.

Artigal, J. (1997) The Catalan immersion program. In R. Johnson and M. Swain (eds) *Immersion: International Perspectives* (pp. 133–50). Cambridge: Cambridge University Press.

Arzamendi, J. and Genesee, F. (1997) Reflections on immersion education in the Basque Country. In R. Johnson and M. Swain (eds) *Immersion: International Perspectives* (pp. 151–66). Cambridge: Cambridge University Press.

Bardovi-Harlig, K. (2000) *Tense and Aspect in Second Language Acquisition: Form, Meaning, and Use*. Malden, MA: Blackwell.

Bardovi-Harlig, K. (2001) Evaluating the empirical evidence: Grounds for instruction in pragmatics? In K. Rose and G. Kasper (eds) *Pragmatics and Language Teaching*. Cambridge: Cambridge University Press.

Bardovi-Harlig, K. and Bergström, A. (1996) The acquisition of tense and aspect in SLA and FLL: A study of learner narratives in English (SL) and French (FL). *Canadian Modern Language Review* 52, 308–30.

Barfield, S. and Rhodes, N. (1993) Review of the eighth year of the partial immersion program at Key Elementary School, Arlington, VA. Washington, DC: Center for Applied Linguistics.

Baron, D. (1990) *The English-Only Question: An Official Language for Americans?* New Haven, CT: Yale University Press.

Beckerman, Z. (2005) Complex contexts and ideologies: Bilingual education in conflict-ridden areas. *Journal of Language, Identity and Education* 4 (1), 1–20.

Björklund, S. (1997) Immersion in Finland in the 1990s: A state of development and expansion. In R. Johnson and M. Swain (eds) *Immersion: International Perspectives* (85–101). Cambridge: Cambridge University Press.

Blake, R. (1983) Mood selection among Spanish-speaking children, ages 4 to 12. *Bilingual Review/La Revista Bilingüe* 10, 21–32.

Blanco-Iglesias, S., Broner, J. and Tarone, E. (1995) Observations of language use in Spanish immersion classroom interactions. In L. Eubank, L. Selinker and M. Sharwood Smith (eds) *The Current State of Interlanguage* (pp. 241–54). Philadelphia: John Benjamin.

Boyd, P. (1975) The development of grammar categories in Spanish by Anglo children learning a second language. *TESOL Quarterly* 9 (2), 125–35.

Branaman, L., Rhodes, N. and Rennie, J. (1998) A national survey of K-12 foreign language education. *ERIC Review, K-12 Foreign Language Education*

6 (1). On WWW at http://www.accesseric.org/resources/ericreview/vol6no1/ survey.html. Accessed March 19, 2002.

Broner, M. (2000) Impact of interlocutor and task on first and second language use in a Spanish immersion program. Unpublished doctoral dissertation, University of Minnesota, Minneapolis.

Caldas, S. (2006) *Raising Bilingual-Biliterate Children in Monolingual Cultures*. Clevedon: Multilingual Matters.

Campbell, R. (1984) The immersion education approach to foreign language teaching. In *Studies on Immersion Education: A Collection for United States Educators* (pp. 114–43). Sacramento: California State Department of Education.

Canale, M. and Swain, M. (1980). Theoretical bases of communicative approaches to second language teaching and testing. *Applied Linguistics* 1, 1–47.

Carranza, I. (1995) Multilevel analysis of two-way immersion discourse. In J. Alatis, C. Straehle, B. Gallenberger and M. Ronkin (eds) *Georgetown University Round Table on Languages and Linguistics* (169–87). Washington, DC: Georgetown University Press.

Carrigo, D. (2000) Just how much English are they using? Teacher and student language distribution patterns, between Spanish and English, in upper-grade, two-way immersion Spanish classes. Unpublished doctoral dissertation, Harvard University, Cambridge, MA.

Cazabon, M., Nicoladis, E. and Lambert W. (1998) *Becoming Bilingual in the Amigos Two-Way Immersion Program*. Washington, DC: Center for Applied Linguistics.

Cazden, C. (1988) *Classroom Discourse: The Language of Teaching and Learning*. Portsmouth: Heinemann.

Center for Applied Linguistics (2005) Directory of two-way bilingual immersion programs in the U.S. On WWW at http://www.cal.org/twi/directory. Accessed March 6, 2006.

Center for Applied Linguistics (2003) Immersion program directory. On WWW at www.cal.org/resources/immersion/ImmersionSearch.jsp. Accessed March 8, 2006.

Chesterfield, R., Chesterfield, K.B., Hayes-Latimer, K. and Chávez, R. (1983) The influence of teachers and peers on second language acquisition in bilingual preschool programs. *TESOL Quarterly* 17 (3), 401–19.

Chicago Public Schools, Office of Language and Cultural Education. (Forthcoming). K-8 curriculum for heritage speakers.

Christian, D. (1996) Two-way immersion education: Students learning through two languages. *Modern Language Journal* 80, 66–76.

Christian, D., Montone, C., Lindholm, K. and Carranza, I. (1997) Profiles in two-way immersion education. McHenry, IL: Delta Systems and Center for Applied Linguistics.

Christian, D. and Whitcher, A. (1995) *Directory of Two-Way Bilingual Programs in the U.S.* (rev. edn) Santa Cruz, CA, and Washington, DC: National Center for Research on Cultural Diversity and Second Language Learning.

Cohen, A. (1975) *A Sociolinguistic Approach to Bilingual Education: Experiments in the American Southwest*. Rowley, MA: Newbury.

Cohen, A. (1976) The case for partial or total immersion education. In A. Simoes, Jr. (ed.) *The Bilingual Child* (pp. 65–89). New York: Academic Press.

Cohen, A. and Lebach, S. (1974) A language experiment in California: Student, teacher, parent and community reactions after three years. *Working Papers in Teaching English as a Second Language*, 8, 171–95.

Cohen, A. and Swain, M. (1976) Bilingual education: The "immersion" model' in the North American context. *TESOL Quarterly* 31 (1), 113–34.

Colombi, C. and Alarcon, F. (eds) (1997) *La enseñanza del español a hispanohablantes: Praxis y teoría*. New York: Houghton Mifflin.

Comrie, B. (1976) *Aspect*. Cambridge: Cambridge University Press.

Crawford, J. (1995) *Bilingual Education: History, Politics, Theory and Practice* (3rd edn). Los Angeles: Bilingual Educational Services.

de Courcy, M. (2002) *Learners' Experiences of Immersion Education: Case Studies of French and Chinese*. Clevedon, UK: Multilingual Matters.

Delgado-Larocco, E. (1998) Classroom processes in a two-way immersion kindergarten classroom. Unpublished doctoral dissertation, University of California, Davis.

Dillard, J.L. (1975) *Toward a Social History of American English*. Contributions to the Sociology of Language 39. New York: Random House.

Donato, R. (1994) Collective scaffolding in second language learning. In J. Lantolf and G. Appel (eds) *Vygotskian Approaches to Second Language Research*. Norwood, NJ: Ablex.

Duff, P. (1995) An ethnography of communication in immersion classrooms in Hungary. *TESOL Quarterly* 29 (3), 505–37.

Duff, P. (1997) Immersion in Hungary: An EFL experiment. In R. Johnson and M. Swain (eds) *Immersion: International Perspectives* (pp. 44–62). Cambridge: Cambridge University Press.

Edelsky, C. and Hudelson, S. (1982) The acquisition (?) of Spanish as a second language. In F. Barkin, E. Brandt A. and J. Ornstein-Galicia (eds) *Bilingualism and Language Contact* (pp. 203–27). New York: Teacher's College Press.

Elías-Olivares, L., Leone, E. A., Cisneros, R. and Gutiérrez, J. (eds) (1985) *Spanish Language Use and Public Life in the USA*. Berlin: Mouton Publishers.

Ellis, R. (1994) *The Study of Second Language Acquisition*. Oxford: Oxford University Press.

Fasold, R. (1984) *The Sociolinguistics of Society*. New York: Blackwell.

Feenstra, H.J. (1969) Parents and teacher attitudes: Their role in second-language acquisition. *Canadian Modern Language Review* 26, 5–13.

Félix-Brasdefer, F. (In progress). Exploring the grammatical performance of dual immersion students at the end of fifth grade.

Ferguson, C. (1972) Diglossia. In P.P. Giglioli (ed.) *Language and Social Context* (pp. 232–52). Harmondsworth: Penguin.

Feuerverger, G. (2001) *Oasis of Dreams: Teaching and Learning Peace in a Jewish-Palestinian Village in Israel*. New York: RoutledgeFalmer.

Flores, W. (2001) *Características de la buena escritura en espanol* [*Traits of Effective Spanish Writing*]. Portland, OR: Northwest Regional Educational Laboratory.

Fortune, T. (2000) Immersion teaching strategies observation checklist. *ACIE Newsletter* 4 (1).

Fortune, T. (2001) Understanding immersion students' oral language use as a mediator of social interaction in the classroom. Unpublished doctoral dissertation, The University of Minnesota, Minneapolis.

Fortune, T. (2005) Immersion student language use across program contexts: Internal and external influences. Presentation at the 14th World Congress of Applied Linguistics.

Freeman, D. (1998) *Bilingual Education and Social Change*. Clevedon: Multilingual Matters.

Gal, S. (1979) *Language Shift, Social Determinants of Linguistic Change in Bilingual Austria*. New York: Academic Press.

Genesee, F. (1978) A longitudinal evaluation of an early immersion school program. *Canadian Journal of Education* 3, 31–50.

Genesee, F. (1983) Bilingual education of majority language children: The immersion experiments in review. *Applied Psycholinguistics* 4, 1–46.

Genesee, F. (1985) Second language learning through immersion: A review of U.S. programs. *Review of Educational Research* 55, 541–61.

Genesee, F. (1987) *Learning through Two Languages: Studies of Immersion and Bilingual Education*. Cambridge, MA: Newbury House.

Genesee, F. (1991) Second language learning in school settings: Lessons from immersion. In A. Reynolds (ed.) *Bilingualism, Multculturalism, and Second Language Learning: The McGill Conference in Honor of Wallace E. Lambert* (pp. 183–201). Hillsdale, NJ: Lawrence Erlbaum.

Grosjean, F. (1998) Studying bilinguals: Methodological and conceptual issues. *Bilingualism: Language and Cognition* 1, 131–49.

Hadi-Tabassum, S. (2006) *Language, Space and Power: A Critical Look at Bilingual Education*. Clevedon: Multilingual Matters.

Harley, B. (1984) How good is their French? *Language and Society* 10, 55–60.

Harley, B. (1989) Functional grammar in French immersion: A classroom experiment. *Applied Linguistics* 10 (3), 331–59.

Harley, B., Cummins, J., Swain, M. and Allen, P. (1990) The nature of language proficiency. In B. Harley, P. Allen, J. Cummins and M. Swain (eds) *The Development of Second Language Proficiency* (pp. 7–25). Cambridge: Cambridge University Press.

Harley, B. and Swain, M. (1977) An analysis of verb form and function in the speech of French immersion pupils. *Working Papers on Bilingualism* 14, 31–40.

Harley, B. and Swain, M. (1984) The interlanguage of immersion students and its implications for second language teaching. In A. Davies, C. Criper and P. Howatts (eds) *Interlanguage* (pp. 291–311). Edinburgh: Edinburgh University Press.

Hasbún, L. (1995) The role of lexical aspect in the acquisition of tense and grammatical aspect in Spanish as a foreign language. Doctoral dissertation, Indiana University, Bloomington.

Hatch, E. (1992) *Discourse and Language Education*. Cambridge: Cambridge University Press.

Heitzman, S. (1994) Language use in full immersion classrooms: Public and private speech. ERIC document ED 372–622.

Holobow, N., Genesee, F., Lambert, W., Met, M. and Gastright, J. (1991) The effectiveness of a foreign language immersion program for children from different ethnic and social class backgrounds: Report 2. *Applied Psycholinguistics*, 12, 179–198.

Hornberger, N. (1991) Extending enrichment bilingual education: Revisiting typologies and redirecting policy. In O. García (ed.) *Bilingual Education: Focusschrift in Honor of Joshua A. Fishman on the Occasion of his 65th Birthday* (Vol. 1) (pp. 215–34). Philadelphia: John Benjamins.

Hornberger, N. (1989) *Haku Yachaywasiman: la educación bilingüe y el futuro del quechua en Puno*. Lima-Puno: Programa de educación bilingüe de Puno.

Hymes, D.H. (1971). *On Communicative Competence*. Philadelphia: University of Pennsylvania Press.

Illinois State Board of Education (2002) Illinois School report card. On WWW at http://www.isbe.state.il.us/research/htmls/report_card.htm. Accessed March 7, 2006.

Jackson, P. and Costa, C. (1974) The inequality of educational opportunity in the Southwest: An observational study of ethnically mixed classrooms. *American Educational Research Journal* 11, 219–29.

Johnson, R.K. (1997) The Hong Kong education system: Late immersion under stress. In R. Johnson and M. Swain (eds) *Immersion: International Perspectives* (pp. 171–89). Cambridge: Cambridge University Press.

Kasper, G. and Dahl, M. (1991) Research methods in interlanguage pragmatics. *Studies in Second Language Acquisition* 13, 215–47.

Kasper, G. and Rose, K. (2002) *Pragmatic Development in a Second Language*. Oxford: Blackwell.

Kirk Senesac, B. (2002) Two-way bilingual immersion: A portrait of quality schooling. *Bilingual Research Journal*, 26 (1), 85–101.

Kirk, J.M. (2000) *Corpora Galore, Analyses and Techniques in Describing English*. Rodopi: Amsterdam-Atlanta, GA.

Koike, D. (1989) Pragmatic competence and adult L2 acquisition: Speech acts and L2 Acquisition. *Modern Language Journal* 73 (3), 279–89.

Krashen, S. (1981) *Second Language Acquisition and Second Language Learning*. Oxford: Pergamon Press.

Krashen, S. (1982) *Principles and Practice in Second Language Acquisition*. New York: Pergamon Press.

Labov, W. (1972) The linguistic consequences of being a lame. In *Language in the Inner City* (pp. 255–92). Philadelphia: University of Pennsylvania Press.

Lambert, W. (1984) An overview of issues in immersion education. *Studies on Immersion Education: A Collection for United States Educators* (pp. 8–29). Sacramento, CA: California State Department of Education.

Lambert, W. and Tucker, G. (1972) *The Bilingual Education of Children: The St. Lambert Experiment*. Rowley, MA: Newbury House.

Lavandera, B. (1984) *Variación y significado*. Buenos Aires: Hachette.

Levinson, S. (1983) *Pragmatics*. Cambridge: Cambridge University Press.

Lim Swee English, A., Gan, L. and Sharpe, P. (1997) Immersion in Singapore preschools. In R. Johnson and M. Swain (eds) *Immersion: International Perspectives* (pp. 190–209). Cambridge: Cambridge University Press.

Lindholm, K. (1987) *Directory of Bilingual Immersion Programs: Two-Way Bilingual Education for Language Minority and Majority Students*. Los Angeles: University of California at Los Angeles, Center for Language Education and Research.

Lindholm, K. and Aclan, Z. (1991) Bilingual proficiency as a bridge to academic achievement: Results from bilingual/immersion programs. *Journal of Education* 173 (2), 99–113.

Lindholm-Leary, K. (2000) *Biliteracy for a Global Society: An Idea Book on Dual Language Education*. Washington, DC: National Clearinghouse for Bilingual Education.

Lindholm-Leary, K. (2001) *Dual Language Education*. Clevedon: Multilingual Matters.

Liu, G. (1994) Interaction and SLA: A case study. Unpublished manuscript, Deakin University, Melbourne, Australia.

Loban (1976) *Language Development: Kindergarten through Grade 12.* Urbana, IL: NCTE.

London Times Educational Supplement (2003) Turning teaching upside down (May 16, 2003). On WWW at http://www.tes.co.uk/search/story/?story_id=379442. Accessed March 8, 2006.

Long, M. (1981) Input, interaction and second language acquisition. *Annals of the New York Academy of Sciences* 379, 259–78.

Lyster, R. (1998) Form in immersion classroom discourse: In or out of focus? *Canadian Journal of Applied Linguistics* 20, 1–2.

Lyster, R. (2001) Negotiation of form, recases, and explicit correction in relation to error types and learner repair in immersion classrooms. *Language Learning* 51 (1), 265–301.

Marckwardt, M.H. (1980) *American English.* Revised by J.L. Dillard. New York: Oxford University Press.

McCollum, P. (1994) Language use in two-way bilingual programs. *IDRA Newsletter* 21 (2), 1, 9–11.

McKay, S.L. and Wong, S.C. (1996) Multiple discourses, multiple identities: Investment and agency in second-language learning among Chinese adolescent immigrant students. *Harvard Educational Review* 66 (3), 577–608.

Mejia, A.M. (ed.) *Bilingual Education in South America.* Clevedon, UK: Multilingual Matters.

Met, M. and Lorenz, E. (1997) Lessons from U.S. immersion programs: Two decades of experience. In R.K. Johnson and M. Swain (eds) *Immersion Education: International Perspectives* (pp. 243–64). Cambridge: Cambridge University Press.

Montrul, S. (2002) Incomplete acquisition and attrition of Spanish tense/aspect distinctions in adult bilinguals. *Bilingualism: Language and Cognition* 5 (1), 39–68.

Montrul and Potowski (under review). Command of gender agreement in school-age Spanish-English bilingual children.

Myers-Scotton, C. (1993) *Dueling Languages: Grammatical Structure in Codeswitching.* Oxford: Clarendon.

Northwest Regional Educational Laboratory (2002) Las características de la buena escritura (versión corta). On WWW at www.nwrel.org/assessment/pdfRubrics/spanishrubric.pdf.

Norton, B. (2000) *Identity and Language Learning: Gender, Ethnicity and Educational Change.* Essex, UK: Pearson Education.

Nuttall, C. and Langhan, D. (1997) The Molteno Project: A case study of immersion for English-medium instruction in South Africa. In R. Johnson and M. Swain (eds) *Immersion: International Perspectives* (pp. 210–37). Cambridge: Cambridge University Press.

Ó Riagáin, P. (1988) Bilingualism in Ireland 1973–1983: An overview of national sociolinguistic surveys. *International Journal of the Sociology of Language* 70, 29–51.

Ortega, L. (2003) Syntactic complexity and L2 proficiency. *Applied Linguistics* 24 (4), 492–518.

Parker, J.E., Heitzman, S.M., Fjerstad, A.M., Babbs, L.M. and Cohen, A.D. (1995) Exploring the role of foreign language in immersion education. In F.R. Eckman, D. Highland, P.W. Lee, J. Milcham and R.R. Weber (eds) *Second Language Acquisition Theory and Pedagogy* (pp. 235–53). Mahwah, NJ: Lawrence Erlbaum.

Pérez, B. (2004) *Becoming Bilterate: A Study of Two-Way Bilingual Immersion Education.* Mahwah, NJ: Lawrence Erlbaum.

Plann, S. (1979) Morphological problems in the acquisition of Spanish in an immersion classroom. In R. Andersen (ed.) *The Acquisition and Use of Spanish and English as First and Second Languages* (pp. 119–32). Washington, DC: TESOL.

Potowski, K. (2004) Student Spanish use and investment in a dual immersion classroom: Implications for second language acquisition and heritage language maintenance. *Modern Language Journal* 88 (1), 75–101.

Potowski, K. (2005) *Fundamentos en la enseñanza del español a hispanohablantes en los Estados Unidos.* Madrid: Arco.

Romaine, S. (1995) *Bilingualism* (2nd edn). Oxford, UK: Basil Blackwell.

Salaberry, R. (2000) *The Development of Past Tense Morphology in L2 Spanish.* Philadelphia: John Benjamins.

Schumann, J. (1978) The acculturation model for second-language acquisition. In R.C. Gringas (ed.) *Second Language Acquisition and Foreign Language Teaching* (pp. 27–50). Washington, DC: Center for Applied Linguistics.

Shirai, Y. and Andersen, R. (1995) The acquisition of tense-aspect morphology: A prototype account. *Language* 71 (4), 743–62.

Silva Corvalán, Carmen (2003) Linguistic consequences of reduced input in bilingual first language acquisition. In S. Montrul and F. Ordóñez (eds) *Linguistic Theory and Language Development in Hispanic Languages.* Sommerville, MA: Cascadilla Press.

Silva Corvalán, C. (1994) *Language Contact and Change: Spanish in Los Angeles.* Oxford: Clarendon.

Slaughter, H. (1997) indigenous language immersion in Hawai'i: A case study of Kula Kaiapuni Hawai'i, and effort to save the indigenous language of Hawai'i. In R. K. Johnson and M. Swain (eds) *Immersion Education: International Perspectives* (pp. 105–129). Cambridge: Cambridge University Press.

Snow, M.A., Padilla, A. and Campbell, R. (1988). Patterns of second language retention of graduates of a Spanish immersion program. *Applied Linguistics* 9, 182–97.

Soltero, S.W. (2004) *Dual Language: Teaching and Learning in Two Languages.* Boston: Pearson Education.

Spezzini, S. (2005) English immersion in Paraguay: Individual and sociocultural dimensions of language learning and use. In A.M. Mejia (ed.) *Bilingual Education in South America* (pp. 79–98). Clevedon, UK: Multilingual Matters.

Swain, M. (1981) Linguistic environment as a factor in the acquisition of target language skills. In R. Andersen (ed.) *Second Language Acquisition and Use under Different Circumstances* (pp. 104–22). Rowley, MA: Newbury House.

Swain, M. (1985) Communicative competence: Some roles for comprehensible input and comprehensible output in its development. In S. Goss and C. Madden (eds) *Input in Second Language Acquisition* (pp. 235–56). Rowley, MA: Newbury House.

Swain, M. and Carroll, S. (1987) The immersion observation study. In B. Harley, P. Allen, J. Cummins and M. Swain (eds) *The Development of Bilingual Proficiency: Final Report* (Vol. 2) (pp. 190–263). Toronto: Modern Language Center, O.I.S.E.

Swain, M. and Johnson, R.K. (1997) Immersion education: A category within bilingual education. In R.K. Johnson and M. Swain (eds) *Immersion Education: International Perspectives* (pp. 1–16). Cambridge: Cambridge University Press.

Swain, M. and Lapkin, S. (1982) *Evaluating Bilingual Education: A Canadian Case Study.* Clevedon: Multilingual Matters.

Swain, M. and Lapkin, S. (1990) Aspects of the sociolinguistic performance of early and late French immersion students. In R. Scarcella and S. Krashen (eds)

Developing Communicative Competence in a Second Language (pp. 41–54). New York: Newbury House.

Swain, M. and Lapkin, S. (1998) Interaction and second language learning: Two adolescent French immersion students working together. *Modern Language Journal* 82 (3), 320–37.

Tardiff, C. (1994) Classroom teacher talk in early immersion. *Canadian Modern Language Review* 50 (3), 466–81.

Tarone, E. and Swain, M. (1995) A sociolinguistic perspective on second language use in immersion classrooms. *Modern Language Journal* 79, 166–78.

Tedick, D. and Fortune, T. (2004) Immersion student output: Exploring 5th graders oral language use practices. Paper presented at at the annual meeting of the American Association of Applied Linguistics, Portland, OR (May 1).

Tedick, D., Walker, C. and Fortune, T. (2004) The complexity of integrating language and content in immersion teaching. Paper presented at at the annual meeting of the American Association of Applied Linguistics, Portland, OR (May 4).

Thomas, W. and Coller, V. (1997) *School Effectiveness for Language Minority Students.* Washington, DC: National Clearinghouse for Bilingual Education.

Toohey, K. (2000) *Learning English at School: Identity, Social Relations and Classroom Practice.* Clevedon, UK: Multilingual Matters.

Tucker, R. and Lambert, W. (1973) Sociocultural aspects of language study. In J. Oller and J. Richards (eds) *Focus on the learner.* Rowley, MA: Newbury House.

United States Department of Education (2000) Remarks as prepared for delivery by U.S. Secretary of Education Richard W. Riley: "Excelencia Para Todos- Excellence for All. The Progress of Hispanic Education and the Challenges of a New Century." On WWW at http://www.ed.gov /Speeches/ 03-2000/000315.html.

Urow, C. and Sontag, J. (2001) Creating community – Un mundo entero: The Inter-American experience. In J. Burton (series ed.), D. Christian and F. Genesee (volume eds) *Case Studies in TESOL Practice Series. Bilingual education* (pp. 11–25). Alexandria, VA: Teachers of English to Speakers of Other Languages.

Valdés, G. (1997) Dual-language immersion programs: A cautionary note concerning the education of language-minority students. *Harvard Educational Review* 67 (3), 391–429.

Valdés, G. (2005) Making connections: Second language acquisition research and heritage language teaching. In R. Salaberry and B. Lafford (eds) *Spanish Second Language Acquisition: State of the Art of Application.* Washington, DC: Georgetown University Press.

Willett, J. (1995) Becoming first graders in an L2: An ethnographic study of L2 socialization. *TESOL Quarterly* 29, 473–503.

World-Class Instructional Design and Assessment (WIDA) (2006) *Spanish Language Arts Standards.* Madison, WI: State of Wisconsin.

Wright, R. (1996) A study of the acquisition of verbs of motion by grade 4/5 early French immersion students. *Canadian Modern Language Review* 53 (1), 257–80.

Zucker, C. (1995) The role of ESL in a dual language program. *Bilingual Research Journal* 19 (3–4), 513–23.

① include p.156 &
155

0   0   interlocutor
    0

# of turns/student
of ~~total~~ turns
of corrections/ turns/student
# of c/t/s + interlocutors
# of c/t/s +i + response +/−
           (accept) (reject)

1 HL-S
2 HL-E   Dom
a Span. Dom
b Eng. Dom

           2a (none)
1a
1b   2b

口3